Greening the City

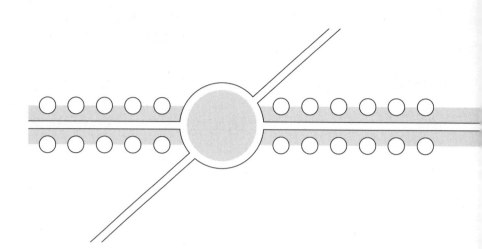

Greening the City

Urban Landscapes in the Twentieth Century

Edited by Dorothee Brantz
and Sonja Dümpelmann

University of Virginia Press | Charlottesville and London

University of Virginia Press
© 2011 by the Rector and Visitors of the University of Virginia
Printed in the United States of America on acid-free paper

First published 2011

9 8 7 6 5 4 3 2 1

LIBRARY OF CONGRESS CATALOGING-IN-PUBLICATION DATA

Greening the city : urban landscapes in the twentieth century / edited by Dorothee Brantz and
Dümpelmann, Sonja.
     p.   cm.
   Includes bibliographical references and index.
   ISBN 978-0-8139-3114-2 (cloth : alk. paper) — ISBN 978-0-8139-3138-8 (e-book)
   1. Urban ecology (Sociology) 2. Social ecology. 3. City planning. 4. Garden cities.
5. Public spaces. 6. Sustainable living. 7. Sustainable architecture. I. Brantz, Dorothee.
II. Dümpelmann, Sonja.
   HT241.G744 2011
   307.76—dc22

                                                                    2010047177

Contents

Acknowledgments

This book originated at a conference at the German Historical Institute (GHI) in Washington, D.C. We would like to thank Christof Mauch, the former GHI director, for co-chairing and providing the opportunity for this conference in the first place. We are grateful to the staff of the GHI, especially Bärbel Thomas and Christa Brown, for their most capable help in organizing the conference. We are also thankful to our co-convener Jennifer Price. Most of all, we owe a big thanks to all of the conference participants, whose contributions enriched the discussions tremendously. Unfortunately, we could not integrate all of their essays in this volume. This book took a long time to produce, and in the process we incurred many debts. Our editor at the University of Virginia Press, Boyd Zenner, was most generous with her time and expertise. Mark Mones, Angie Hogan, Susan Murray, and Martin White provided crucial assistance with all of the aspects that transformed these essays into a book. We are very thankful to all of them.

Greening the City

Introduction

Dorothee Brantz and Sonja Dümpelmann

"A City! It is the grip of man upon nature. It is a human operation directed against nature, a human organism both for protection and for work. It is a creation."[1] This quotation poignantly expresses a principal paradigm of modernity—that human creation stands in stark contrast to nature. The city, primarily understood as a man-made built environment, stands as a material embodiment of this contrast. But this quotation also inadvertently illustrates a deep-seated ambiguity in the relationship between cities and nature because its author, Le Corbusier, also happened to be one of the twentieth century's leading proponents of the integration of vast green spaces into urban areas.

This ambiguity might be the result of a disjunction between the conceptualization of cities and nature, on the one hand, and the actual planning and design practices within urban living environments, on the other. While social theorists have often regarded the city as a space where, as Henry Lefebvre put it, "nature is emptied out" and replaced by the social production of urban space, urban reformers, activists, and inhabitants have long pleaded for the preservation or reintegration of natural elements into the urban landscape. Many scholars—particularly environmental and landscape historians, urban ecologists, landscape architects, and planners—have focused on the role of natural factors and features in the development of cities.

Considering the place of nature in the city raises numerous questions, not the least about the meaning of nature. This is, of course, a complex philosophical issue that cannot be adequately addressed here.[2] What can be noted, however, is that concepts of nature always have to be viewed in relation to the cultural context in which they arose. Consequently, conceptions of urban nature in particular can be understood only in reference to the geohistorical specificities in which they operate. Interestingly, though, ideas of nature and the city were, for the most part—and especially in the modern period—viewed as contrasting rather than entwined.

Starting in the sixteenth century, cities were increasingly viewed in contrast to the countryside.[3] This distinction between the urban and the rural was premised on the fact that urban populations were no longer self-sufficient and that cities were regarded as built environments and thus man-made spaces of cultural, economic, and social production. Cities have usually been viewed as a physical manifestation of humanity's separation from and control over nature. The association of the urban with a distinct way of life goes back to antiquity, but it came into common usage following the Industrial Revolution. Interestingly, though, as cities grew and became industrialized, calls for the integration of natural elements also intensified.

The livability of cities has always been closely tied to natural factors such as the presence of water, climatic conditions, and topography; but the rise of large industrial cities during the past two centuries heightened awareness of urban pollution and its negative effects on low-income residents in particular. As a result, urban reformers increasingly demanded the amelioration of the urban environment and the incorporation of green spaces for the health and well-being of city dwellers. Many reformers compared cities to organisms, and green spaces to the much-needed "lungs" of that urban organism.

European rulers and municipal authorities made isolated attempts to create urban green spaces in the early modern era, but it was not until the nineteenth century that local and national governments set out to bring about the large-scale greening of cities. Efforts to bring nature into the city became much more extensive and elaborate in the twentieth century as new patterns of production and consumption, of work and leisure prompted a reevaluation of the function and makeup of the urban environment. Professionals in the newly emerging fields of public hygiene, landscape architecture, and urban planning worked to integrate public green spaces and to improve environmental conditions in cities.

Ever since the breaching of town walls in the early nineteenth century, parks, squares, gardens, and tree-lined streets have been gradually integrated into European and North American cities. Even earlier, however, European autocratic rulers and colonists in North America had become aware of the need to include green open space in the form of tree-lined streets, squares, parks, commons, and gardens in the urban fabric for reasons of aesthetics and public health. For example, many town walls on the European continent were planted with trees in the sixteenth century, and during the seventeenth century, many towns in Europe either introduced a variety of tree-lined promenades and public walks or attempted to realize the idea of *rus in urbe* with garden squares, as was the case in many British towns. In the New World, the city plans for Philadelphia and Savannah drawn up for William Penn and James Oglethorpe in 1683 and 1733, respectively, included open squares to be used as markets, pastureland, and for other communal purposes. With increasing industrialization and urbanization in the nineteenth century, developers and industrialists began to assess these green spaces in terms of their potential to generate profits, but utopian socialists, and social and public-health reformers continued to regard them as necessary components of a "healthy" city fabric and community. The park movement in the United States that was later supported by the ideas of Progressive Era social reform led to the inclusion of parks and parkways into comprehensive city plans. In his lecture "Public Parks and the Enlargement of Towns," delivered to the American Social Science Association at Boston's Lowell Institute in 1870, the landscape architect Frederick Law Olmsted Jr. asked "for trees to remain as permanent furniture of the city."[4] Olmsted's colleague Horace William Shaler Cleveland, who, like Olmsted, promoted the picturesque and pastoral aesthetic in his writings and works, argued for the adaptation of new city plans along the western frontier to the site conditions, by incorporating existing natural features. In his 1873 book *Landscape Architecture as Applied to the Wants of the West,* Cleveland asked: "How can any naturally attractive features, such as a river, a lake or a mountain, near or distant, be made to minister to the beautiful or picturesque character of the place, by adapting the arrangement to the development of their most attractive aspects?"[5]

In Europe, new public urban parks were created throughout the second half of the nineteenth century, complementing the first truly public urban parks opened in Munich in 1792, in Magdeburg in 1823, and in the British town of Derby in 1840. Many of the best-known early-nineteenth-century landscape gardeners, such as Friedrich Ludwig von Sckell, Peter Joseph Lenné, his student Gustav Meyer, and Joseph Paxton, had begun their careers working on the private gardens of aristocrats but eventually turned their attention to the design of public grounds. Although usually commissioned by enlightened kings and princes, these parks were intended to educate the public and provide amenities that would improve public welfare.

These developments provided the basis for an increased awareness of open space issues in the cities of twentieth-century Europe and North

America. The city planning schemes developed during the City Beautiful movement in American cities included municipal and metropolitan park systems that structured, ordered, confined, but also connected cities to their rural environs. It was no coincidence, then, that members of the first generation of professional landscape architects often were also pioneers of city planning. Probably the two most famous among them were Frederick Law Olmsted Jr. and John Nolen, who later also became instrumental in the founding of the American City Planning Institute in 1917. Garden and landscape architecture itself had emerged as a professional discipline in the last decades of the nineteenth century. While landscape architecture and city planning were necessarily linked to specific locations, they always also had strong transnational dimensions, which became visible, among other things, in the garden city movement. Originating with Ebenezer Howard in England, the movement influenced continental European developments like Hellerau near Dresden, La Garbatella in Rome, and Drancy outside of Paris. It moved across the Atlantic to inspire the new garden suburbs Forest Hills Gardens, Sunnyside Gardens, and Radburn, among others, and even influenced the Greenbelt Towns created as part of President Franklin Roosevelt's New Deal during the 1930s. The garden city idea provided a model for the balanced relationship between city and countryside in an increasingly urbanized world. While using "nature" to confine the city, natural elements in the form of gardens and parks were also used to infiltrate the city and to provide spaces for social interaction.

Besides playing an important role in Howard's garden city concept, green open space was instrumental in the urban utopias of Frank Lloyd Wright and Le Corbusier. In the late 1920s, Frank Lloyd Wright conceived his utopian Broadacre City, where "the country itself" would "come alive as a truly great city."[6] In contrast to Howard's garden city, which was confined by extensive greenbelts including forests, agricultural land, and allotments, Wright's Broadacre City eliminated the boundary between the urban and natural world altogether. It was initially designed to cover 100 square miles, but Wright thought it might eventually spread to cover the entire continent. In line with Wright's vision of a new agrarian future, family homesteads, factories, schools, churches, and other necessary institutions were to be decentralized and evenly distributed across the land. Like Howard, Wright believed that the green and "natural" environment could enhance social harmony. Underscoring Wright's anti-urban bias, the houses of Broadacre City appeared to grow out of the fields; they were disguised as part of nature.[7]

Although Wright's ideas were visionary, utopian, and lacking any pragmatic instructions for implementation, they corresponded to the spirit of the time not the least because they depended on the automobile.

In Europe, Le Corbusier's urban utopia of the 1920s also attempted to reconcile man, nature, and the machine. Unlike Wright's Broadacre City, Le Corbusier's visionary Ville Contemporaine (Contemporary City) consisted of skyscrapers and highways within extensive parklands with trees, grass, sports fields, and winding paths. The city was not disguised as nature; it was surrounded by it. Contemporary City's buildings and streets were supposed to occupy only 15 percent of the land, leaving the rest open for green spaces and forested areas.[8]

Although no city attempted as radical a reconstruction of its urban landscape as Le Corbusier envisioned, the increasing density of inner cities, new building technologies and functionalist architecture, and the construction of high-rise buildings and skyscrapers in American cities like Chicago and New York prompted the search for new surfaces for open and green space. Roof gardens gained popularity, for example, and were used as play spaces and both private and public gardens. Natural elements in the form of vegetable plots and public urban parks continued to be considered a tool to educate, to provide moral uplift, and, in the United States, to "naturalize" immigrants and their children. On a smaller scale than parks, vacant-lot cultivation, school gardens, and other civic garden campaigns that began in the 1890s provided the basis for several national urban garden campaigns until the end of World War II. During the world wars, these early urban garden movements that brought natural elements into the cities turned into or merged with initiatives that promoted war and victory gardens. With slogans such as "Every Garden a Munition Plant," the U.S. National War Garden Commission urged the establishment of such gardens toward the end of World War I. More urban garden programs were implemented in the postwar period and all these early initiatives provided forerunners for the community garden movement of the 1970s and 1980s. In Europe, allotment gardens have an even longer history. The first were established in England in the early eighteenth century. Only in the twentieth century, however, did allotment gardens become a category in the land-use plans of many cities. As a result of the postwar food shortages, the City of Berlin, where working-class citizens had fought for their gardens since the last decades of the nineteenth century, began to provide areas for allotment gardening on peripheral sites, for example, along railway embankments and adjacent to parks. Interwar modernist housing developments, such as Praunheim and Römerstadt in Frankfurt, included garden plots, thereby adding distinct green open spaces to the urban landscape.

City planning schemes drawn up during and shortly after World War II often aimed at decentralization. Architects across the political spectrum believed that neighborhood units and "residential cells" dispersed in the countryside would provide better protection against air raids. These concepts continuously influenced postwar planning and European reconstruction, as did the modernist building schemes. In the postwar period, decentralized city plans with vast open green spaces that catered to the growing population of private automobile owners came to embody democratic planning in the United States and Europe alike. While cities were working out open space ratios and establishing numbers that determined how much "nature" urbanites needed, the actual quality and the design of "nature" remained a more contentious issue. Designers such as the American landscape architect Lawrence Halprin constructed roaring waterfalls and planting beds above inner-city freeways, thus covering one man-made environment with another that was considered more social and "natural." The counterculture and environmental movements of the 1960s and 1970s strengthened positions that questioned notions of man-made environments more generally. In the United States, many followers of the counterculture movement opposed weed ordinances that still determine much of the aesthetics of green open areas in cities, and, as in Europe, many homeowners and landscape architects condemned non-native species in garden design.

Reflecting rising concerns for the environment and the depletion of natural resources, a 1964 article by the landscape planner Ian McHarg entitled "The Place of Nature in the City of Man," argued that all city planning should be based on a thorough analysis of the natural processes and on "an ecological model of the metropolis,"[9] an idea that was taken up by, among others, his student Anne W. Spirn. In the 1980s, Spirn conceptualized the city as an urban ecosystem, as part of nature—a "granite garden"— that could be designed on the basis of cultural and natural processes.[10] In Europe, the Dutch artist Louis Le Roy promoted public open space whose design would be left to nature, including humans. Le Roy's intention was to engage the public and let local communities create their own landscapes over time using recycled materials. If the public did not see any need for an adorned or designed space, it would simply be left fallow. The relationship between humans and nonhuman nature was looked at from a slightly different angle by the American artist Alan Sonfist. His explicit wish to memorialize and make visible the natural history of urban sites found expression in his *Time Landscape* in New York City. In 1965, Sonfist planned to plant a miniature forest on a lot in Greenwich Village that re-created the vegetation on this site during Manhattan's colonization. Carried out in 1977, Sonfist's idea seems to reverberate in the Mannahatta Project. Run by Eric Sanderson and the Wildlife Conservation Society during this last decade, the project aimed at illustrating the ecology, early history, and geography of Manhattan Island when it was first discovered by Dutch and English sailors at the beginning of the seventeenth century and to educate the public about Manhattan's natural history.[11]

While the growing concern for the environment in the 1980s led many private garden owners to design biotopes that would—as many liked to believe—provide endangered species with a safe haven in the urban environment, urban ecologists brought similar concerns to the attention of city, regional, and national governments. In the 1990s, finally, officials, designers, and the public began to reconsider the cultural and historical implications of "nature" in the city. Besides citizen participation and environmental concerns, the social, cultural, and natural history of open space began to generate designs and shape the urban environment. At the end of the 1990s, the progress that had been made in the environmental sciences and in ecology on the one hand, and an increasing awareness of the social and cultural constructions that underlie our understanding of "nature" in the city on the other hand, led to the conception of "landscape urbanism" by a group of landscape architects spearheaded by Charles Waldheim. Landscape in its broadest sense, encompassing plants, animals, parks, gardens, sidewalks, roads, freeways, and the processes that shape it, is here understood as the agent in urban design.[12] In this concept, that sought to transcend the clichéd opposition of the man-made city and nonhuman nature, natural factors became part of the city.

The contributions in this volume deal with some of the issues mentioned above. The essays are based on selected papers that were presented at the conference entitled "The Place of Nature in the City in Twentieth-Century Europe and North America" held at the German Historical Institute, Washington, D.C. One of the overarching aims of this conference was to investigate how the use of natural elements changed over the course of the twentieth century as many industrial cities were transformed into postindustrial landscapes. The conference's transatlantic focus also led to the question of how cultural and national peculiarities influenced the place of nature in specific cities in Europe and North America.

This volume brings together essays from scholars in a number of fields, including urban and environmental history, landscape architecture, architecture, planning history, urban ecology, and anthropology. Indeed, the volume offers a wide array of not only topics, but also methodologies and approaches to the theme of "nature in the city." Not surprisingly then, the definition of "nature" in the urban context varies in the contributions compiled here. "Nature" is variously defined as a social, cultural, and political construct. Individual plant species, green open spaces including parks, sports grounds, and nature preserves, and, more generally, countercultural ecotopias and the public urban realm are all presented as forms of "nature" by the authors in this volume. Thus, the aim of this book is not so much to present a coherent definition of "nature" or a coherent line of argumentation in this regard, but rather to provide examples of recent approaches in various fields of scholarship that deal with the relationship between the built and natural environment.

The essays in this book look at the space in between, space that has often been described as urban "nature" because it was considered open space that seemed more malleable than built form constructed out of stone. What has throughout history been described as "nature," in these essays appears as a socially, culturally, and politically constructed landscape. In this sense, the essays reveal what Dianne Harris in 1999 delineated as the "postmodernization of landscape."[13] Nature in its constructed form and space has in recent historiography increasingly appeared as an "active," or "critical," agent in the formation of culture. It is in this vein that the authors in this book reveal the importance that different concepts of nature have had for city politics, planning, and design. "Nature" in this volume is no longer the container, foil, setting, or scenery for social, cultural, and political developments. Instead, it is portrayed as an active force that influences and affects these developments.

We believe that the interconnectedness of the "natural" and urban environment, of the "natural" and built world, calls for scholarship that bridges a variety of disciplines like urban, and environmental, landscape, architectural, and planning history. While the environmental historian Martin Melosi in 1993 pointed toward the opportunities that lie in urban history for environmental historians and vice versa,[14] the theoreticians and historians from the design professions, especially landscape architecture, have in the last decades noted the fruitful sources that the various strands of the "new cultural history," urban and environmental history, and cultural geography provide for the theoretical and historical grounding of their applied disciplines. Thus, the increased focus of historians on the diverse types of urban infrastructures beginning in the 1980s almost seems to reverberate in the growing literature in the field of landscape architecture that, since the late 1990s, has begun to conceptualize landscape—a term that referred to the aesthetic visual dimensions of the land from the sixteenth to the eighteenth century—as urban, or suburban, infrastructure.[15]

The book is divided into four parts that illustrate the variety of approaches to greening the city. The essays in part 1, "Constructing Green Urban Spaces," provide insights into the influence of politics and international exchange on the establishment of green urban spaces and park systems. The texts comprising part 2, entitled "Nature and Urban Identity," show "nature" as contested ground and how it was used to forge urban and regional identities. In part 3, "The Function of Nature in the City," the authors discuss the social construction of nature and its aesthetics and function for public health. Part 4, entitled "Ecology and the Urban Environment," assembles essays that critically address selected aspects of the history of urban ecology and the urban environmental movement. Despite their differentiation and placement under these subheadings, most essays overlap in more aspects than one and could also be categorized in more ways than one. It appears that "nature" has not only provided an "active binder" for city and community building throughout the twentieth century, but, figuratively speaking, also provides a matrix for scholarship from a variety of disciplines. What this shows is that the studies of "the place of nature in the city" are "forms of indiscipline," to borrow from W. J. T. Mitchell's elaborations on the place of visual culture studies within a variety of disciplines.[16] As the essays in this volume exemplify, a number of disciplines have come to explore their edges and in doing so have explored the relationships between the natural and built environment.

The attempt to use landscape and the understanding of natural processes in the design of cities, of course, goes back centuries if not thousands of years. However, the concerted effort to draw up master and land-use plans on the basis of natural features and processes is more recent. On the basis of nineteenth-century models and experiences, many cities in Europe and North America tried to incorporate entire park systems into their planning frameworks. Two examples of this development are discussed by Sonia Hirt and Alfonso Valenzuela Aguilera in their contributions to this volume. They examine the incorporation of green spaces into large-scale urban planning schemes in twentieth-century Bulgaria and Mexico, respectively. Sonia Hirt compares and contrasts the three master plans for rebuilding greater Sofia throughout the twentieth century. She explores how diverse political regimes sought to inscribe Sofia's urban landscape with their specific ideological visions regarding the use of green spaces in the city, oscillating between plans that favored single-family homes with individual gardens during the 1930s, a polycentric system of multifamily homes with collective green areas during the socialist period, and the current reliance on a mixture of public and private green spaces. Valenzuela Aguilera explains how the physical transformation of Mexico City in the early decades of the twentieth century was inspired by European models like Ebenezer Howard's garden city and Jean Claude Nicolas Forestier's park systems. Analyzing the work of urban planners like Miguel Angel de Quevedo, Carlos Contreras, and José Luis Cuevas Pietrasanta, Valenzuela Aguilera examines the challenges that arose from adapting European ideas to the specific environmental, hygienic, and infrastructural circumstances of Mexico City.

The ideological implications of open space and its design are at the center of Gary McDonogh's and Stefanie Hennecke's essays on Barcelona and Berlin. Together with a third text by Lawrence Culver, these essays offer specific case studies that illustrate the political and social construction of nature in urban environments. McDonogh analyzes how the Mediterranean landscape influenced different visions of how green spaces could be integrated into the city and how such green spaces were, in turn, used to boost and reenliven Barcelona's role as the Catalan capital. Looking at a range of examples, including Antoni Gaudí's designs and the planning for the 1992 Olympics and the 2004 Universal Forum of Cultures, McDonogh argues that Barcelona's green spaces became an embodiment of different forms of nationalism.

Like McDonogh, Hennecke examines the parallels between ideological beliefs concerning nature and their implementation in urban and open space planning at the beginning and the end of the twentieth century. Focusing on the example of Berlin's Schiller Park, she shows how the 1907 design of this public urban park was supposed to re-create a specific form of "German nature" where humans played a part but were not considered the primary protagonists. Hennecke undertakes a detailed study of the genesis and reception of Schiller Park throughout the twentieth century to reveal that the park design reflected the holistic worldview of its reactionary modernist creator, Friedrich Bauer, and that, despite its progressive design, it had little to do with progressive social views.

In his article "Race, Recreation, and the Conflict between Public and Private Nature in Twentieth-Century Los Angeles," Lawrence Culver examines how Los Angeles's natural and recreational spaces became increasingly privatized in the course of the twentieth century. Culver demonstrates that this privatization, which was closely linked to the growing suburbanization of the Greater Los Angeles area, where green spaces were increasingly locked away in the private gardens of single-family homes, underscored the racial and class segregation that persists in Southern California.

The contributions by Clark, Jokela, and Saarikivi; and Domhardt not only emphasize the social construction of nature in the city throughout the twentieth century, but also explore its functional and aesthetic value for the public realm. In their comparative essay, Peter Clark, Salla Jokela, and Jarmo Saarikivi trace the development of urban sports grounds and their social construction as "nature" in Helsinki and London. Focusing especially on the example of golf clubs, they show that these sports grounds, contrary to a long-standing popular perception, have contributed to a new type of biodiversity in these cities. The provision of sports areas in urban master plans of the postwar period was also one of the topics in the theoretical deliberations and planning schemes put forth by the eighth Congrès International d'Architecture Moderne (CIAM). In her essay on green and public space in the CIAM debates of 1942–52, Konstanze Domhardt discusses the role that CIAM attributed to green open space in post–World War II city planning. She shows how green open space was understood as a means to confine the city and guide its future development, while at the same time creating new public urban realms that served as a social binding agent and hence a "civic landscape."

Zachary Falck shifts the focus to the specific use of plants within the urban fabric in his essay entitled "Property Rights, Popular Ecology, and Problems with Wild Plants in Twentieth-Century American Cities." Falck explores how weeds and vacant lots added an unusual dimension to concerns about urban landscapes, in part because people often disagreed about which plants should be considered weeds. Drawing on examples from St. Louis, Lincoln, and Chicago, Falck examines the outcome of legal disputes over the use of urban space, the presence of vacant lots, and the eradication of unwanted plants.

Jeffrey Sanders examines Seattle's "Urban Homesteads," a grassroots effort that sought to reconnect human habitats with the natural world within the urban fabric in response to the oil crisis and the growing environmental awareness of the early 1970s. Describing several examples of countercultural housing and community garden projects, Sanders explores how these ecotopian attempts to turn Seattle into a more sustainable urban environment linked private housing initiatives to the quest for larger ecological and political transformations.

While such private initiatives were prevalent in Seattle, institutional initiatives and scientific research projects led to a heightened environmental consciousness in Berlin, as Jens Lachmund explains in the essay concluding this volume. Focusing on biological expertise and wildlife preservation in Berlin, Lachmund shows how the development of urban ecology, bolstered by West Berlin's strong environmental and countercultural movements, served as a basis for the establishment of contemporary urban ecological models that equate the city to a biotope for humans, animals, and plants. Lachmund argues that the comparatively early emergence and the outstanding role of urban ecology in West Berlin were partly caused by the city's physical isolation due to the Berlin Wall.

Overall, these essays shed light on the diverse uses and interpretations of urban green spaces throughout the twentieth century. They demonstrate that the relationship between cities and nature carried variable meanings depending on political circumstances, scientific knowledge, and sociocultural representations. The use of urban green spaces functions as a historical manifestation of how social values were translated into physical space, which, in turn, often expressed racial and class divisions. Moreover, the integration of natural elements in the urban environment was shaped by a broad range of architectural, legal, and political institutions as well as different social movements, all of which injected their own particular understanding of the relationship between urban nature and culture. These understandings were often contested and driven by conflicts over the public and private use of urban space. As a result, urban green spaces often became politicized and even instrumentalized by different interest groups and political regimes. In that sense, the history of twentieth-century cities attests to the social and cultural construction of urban nature but also to the way natural elements have affected the human social and cultural world on both sides of the Atlantic.

Notes

1. Le Corbusier, *The City of To-Morrow and Its Planning* (1929; New York, 1987), xxi.
2. Peter Coates, *Nature: Western Attitudes since Ancient Times* (Berkeley, 1998); R. G. Collingwood, *The Idea of Nature* (London, 1945); Alfred North Whitehead, *The Concept of Nature* (New York, 1920).
3. Raymond Williams, *Keywords*, rev. ed. (New York, 1983), 219–24.
4. Frederick Law Olmsted Jr., "Public Parks and the Enlargement of Towns," speech delivered

to the American Social Science Association at Boston's Lowell Institute, 1870 (Cambridge, Mass., 1870), 16.

5. Horace William Shaler Cleveland, *Landscape Architecture as Applied to the Wants of the West* (Chicago, 1873), 34.

6. Wright in Baker Brownell and Frank Lloyd Wright, *Architecture and Modern Life* (New York, 1938), 309.

7. Robert Fishman, *Urban Utopias in the Twentieth Century* (Cambridge and London, 1991), 91–160.

8. Ibid., 163–263.

9. Ian L. McHarg, "The Place of Nature in the City of Man," *Annals of the American Academy of Political and Social Science* 352 (March 1964): 1–12.

10. Anne Whiston Spirn, *The Granite Garden: Urban Nature and Human Design* (New York, 1984).

11. Eric W. Sanderson, *Mannahatta: A Natural History of New York City* (New York, 2009).

12. See, for example, Charles Waldheim, "Landscape as Urbanism"; and Grahame Shane, "The Emergence of Landscape Urbanism," both in *The Landscape Urbanism Reader,* ed. Charles Waldheim (New York, 2006), 35–53; 55–67.

13. Dianne Harris, "The Postmodernization of Landscape," *Journal of the Society of Architectural Historians* 58, no. 3 (1999): 434–43.

14. Martin Melosi, "The Place of the City in Environmental History," *Environmental History Review* 17, no. 1 (1993): 1–23.

15. See, for example, Waldheim, ed., *Landscape Urbanism Reader*; Mohsen Mostafavi and Ciro Najle, eds., *Landscape Urbanism: A Manual for the Machinic Landscape* (London, 2003); and Georgia Daskalakis, Charles Waldheim, Jason Young, eds., *Stalking Detroit* (Barcelona, 2001).

16. W. J. T. Mitchell, "Interdisciplinarity and Visual Culture," *Art Bulletin* 77, no. 4 (1995): 540–44.

Part I

Constructing Green Urban Spaces

Integrating City and Nature

Urban Planning Debates in Sofia, Bulgaria

Sonia Hirt

Modern city planning emerged as a profession to amend the deplorable conditions of the nineteenth-century Western city, appropriately labeled "the city of dreadful night."[1] Conceived over a relatively short period of time as the unavoidable offspring of the Industrial Revolution, this city offered its inhabitants not only the promise of employment, but also crowding, dirt, smoke, noise, and darkness at nightmarish levels that were unknown to the inhabitants of preindustrial settlements, whether urban or rural.

Of course, humans and all their artifacts, including cities—no matter how dreadful they may have been at certain historic periods—have always been part of nature. Yet, as industrial cities plunged into a state of misery, they came to be seen as the stark opposite of the "lost paradise" of pastoral rural life and the grim antipode of nature itself.[2] The city became defined by its lack of nature—lack of open green spaces, lack of clean air, lack of light—lack of all aspects of nature that humans believed necessary for their health and happiness. The story of modern city planning has thus in many ways been the story of trying to bring these desirable aspects of nature back into the city.

Almost all city planning movements, which achieved international significance during the nineteenth and the twentieth centuries, can be read as replays of the debate on the city-nature union. Since Western nations dominated the world in the nineteenth and twentieth centuries, and since Western cities were the first to experience a "lack of nature," all influential planning ideas of how to remodel the city originated in the West (mostly Europe and the United States). From there, they were quickly diffused across the globe.[3] Small Balkan states emerging from the centuries-long Ottoman occupation were among the most enthusiastic importers of such transformative ideas.[4] Among these states, Bulgaria has not been an exception.

Since independence in 1878, the country has consistently struggled to escape its ostensibly backward past and define itself as a "modern" "European" nation.[5] To that end, Bulgaria has been remarkably eager to adopt Western planning ideas[6]—a trend that has intensified with the nation's recent entry into the European Union.

This essay traces planning debates about how to shape the Bulgarian capital of Sofia. The story of Sofia is significant in that it demonstrates the resilience of the planning dilemma of how to integrate city and nature. It also illustrates the tensions that arise when local plans addressing this dilemma are based on foreign models. The foreign theories developed as responses to the specific urban circumstances that prevailed in the countries where the theories originated (mostly in Western Europe). But Sofia's conditions were different and often represented a stage of growth that Western cities had passed. To address this issue, Sofia's plans relied on Western rhetorical postulates but often endowed them with alternative, local meanings. The foreign theories then acquired a vernacular flavor that sometimes ran contrary to their original intent. Sofia's story is thus one of renegotiating and domesticating Western postulates of the city-nature reunion—a story that exhibits the multiplicity of meanings with which these postulates can be endowed.

To present the history of Sofia, this essay uses a combination of primary and secondary sources. These include the series of Sofia's comprehensive plans; scholarly, archival, and media accounts of Sofia's planning; and related published interviews, protocols from meetings, and publications by the chief participants in the master-planning processes. To tell the story of postcommunist planning, the research also relies on several drafts of the new comprehensive plan, *Sofia 2020,* and on two dozen interviews with planners involved in its writing, conducted in person by the author.

The essay is divided into several sections. The theoretical section reviews the evolution of planning ideas concerning the relationship between city and nature. It is followed by an account of the debates on Sofia's form presented in three periods: the pre–World War II period (1879–1939), the communist period (1945–89), and the contemporary period (1990–2005). The conclusion discusses stability and change in the planning notions of city and nature, and the interplay between foreign ideas and their local interpretations.

City and Nature, City and Region: An Overview of International Planning Ideas

The relationship between the industrial city and nature was conflicted from the start. On one side, the city embodied the core promise of the Industrial

Revolution and Western modernity: to free humanity from crippling dependence on nature's whims.[7] The city, in this view, was the supreme achievement of civilization. Nature, in contrast, was crude, hostile, and savage; it had to be tamed for human benefit.[8]

Yet, perhaps paradoxically, many urban observers perceived the severing of the city-nature link as the root of urban misery.[9] Cities were, in their view, the rotted scenes of "unwholesome excitements and tensions,"[10] no less than "blasphemy against nature."[11] Nature, in contrast, was pristine, sacred, and inspiring. Reconnecting city to nature promised many benefits such as restored beauty, more sunlight and cleaner air, better protection from climate extremes, improved sanitation, and enhanced public health. Ostensibly, it also provided an opportunity for the moral education of the urban masses.[12] This "dual-scripting" of city and nature—each category being simultaneously good and evil—has permeated debates on urban form since the nineteenth century.[13] The contradiction was resolved by attempting to engineer a city-nature union that kept only the desirable aspects of each category—a notion perhaps best articulated by Ebenezer Howard as the "marriage of town and country."[14] This reunion became one of the few unchanging themes and goals of city planning. And while there have been many ideas about how to achieve it, the final goal has remained remarkably stable.

Despite the rich variety of planning ideas and often contradictory proposals for how to attain this union, most fall into two broad categories—the first sought means to allow nature in the city (for example, by infusing large parks into the urban fabric), while the second promoted strategies to disperse the city amid nature (for example, by reducing urban densities and distributing populations across the countryside). The latter model inherently mandated not only a reconsideration of the city-nature link, but also a substantial rethinking of the relationship between the city and its region. The first influential modern planning movement, loosely entitled the "monumental city movement," as practiced by Eugene Haussmann in Paris and the American "City Beautiful" planners, followed the first model by inserting islands of carefully landscaped nature for public enjoyment into the densely built fabric. The planners created large parks intended to function as the "lungs" of the city.[15]

The replacement of the monumental city efforts with avant-garde movements caused a small setback in the planned attempts to unite city and nature. Architects with utopian ideas like Tony Garnier, for example, drew inspiration not from nature but from machines. But even they surrounded their urban utopias with greenbelts.[16] And, when avant-garde evolved into mainstream modernism, the city-nature union moved back to center stage.

Consistent with earlier planning ideas, modernism's champion, Le Corbusier, saw the human-nature relationship as a heroic battle: "Man undermines and hacks Nature. He opposes himself to her; he fights with her; he digs himself in. A childish but magnificent effort!"[17] Yet his Radiant City was an effort to unite nature and city once again.[18] Instead of piercing the built fabric with individual parks, however, Le Corbusier sought to concentrate the population in massive "towers in the park," thus reserving 95 percent of urban land for green space. In this manner, he transformed the whole city into a park[19] and transgressed the city-nature polarity that he had earlier defined.

If the monumental and the modernist planners aimed to reform the city from the inside, Ebenezer Howard fathered a more radical approach. Rather than confining his proposals to the urban borders, he looked beyond them. Of course, the bourgeoisie had sought to escape the city and settle in pastoral suburbia for many decades before 1898, when Howard published *Garden Cities of Tomorrow*.[20] Howard, however, conceived a complete reformist program of urban decentralization by building onto the incipient suburban movement. He envisioned the reunion of city and nature—or town and country, as he phrased it—in pastoral garden cities surrounded by greenbelts. The idea was inherently embedded in the radical rethinking not only of the relationship between city and nature, but also between city and region. As settlements dispersed, the central city and its new neighbors were to form a coherent regional system, a mutually beneficial alliance in which each part would perform well-defined functions. And although the city was to retain its supremacy, the region would become clearly polycentric.

Such regional and decentralizing visions rose to further prominence on both sides of the North Atlantic through the works of such influential thinkers as the American urbanist Lewis Mumford[21] and the Scottish biologist Patrick Geddes.[22] Because of its potential to ensure healthier living conditions and a "more equitable distribution of land values," the idea was soon widely perceived as a core goal of planning in the United States and western Europe.[23] Soviet architects also made a distinctive contribution. Among them, the school appropriately labeled as the "de-urbanists" promoted the "greening" of Russia—the abolition of cities and the dispersal of populations into the country. Perhaps the most famous of the Soviet schemes was that of Nikolai Milyutin, who proposed the construction of linear forms surrounded and separated by greenbelts.[24]

The American architect Frank Lloyd Wright, famous for his professed deep love of nature, took the dispersal idea to new heights. He welcomed the "disappearance" of all cities larger than a county seat as unsuitable for the "Machine Age" and unfit for the free American spirit. He proposed a radical dispersal scheme called Broadacre City, where each household would own at least one acre, and all industry would be spread throughout vast green territories and linked by highways. This, in his view, would be the only city that could rebuild the fractured link between people and nature.[25]

These early-twentieth-century utopias were taken increasingly seriously throughout the following decades. Although some of their radical elements were removed, the idea of greening the city center in a Corbusian fashion and dispersing populations in the country was adopted as official policy in many Western countries. The mere fact that midcentury plans were looking at Greater London, Greater Stockholm, or Greater Copenhagen illustrates the shift to regional thinking.[26] The core idea of such plans was to promote the controlled spread of populations in satellite towns separated by greenbelts. In so doing, the plans aimed to achieve a polycentric system of settlements all of which, because of the elongated form of the "fingers," would remain close to nature. And while in Europe the greenbelts ensured the relative compactness of new settlements, in the United States the uncontrolled spread of low-density suburbs produced a system that came closer to Frank Lloyd Wright's amorphous Broadacre City.[27]

In the 1960s, Jane Jacobs astutely pointed out what united most "green" (or "De-centrist," as she called them) visions. Whether they were driven by "love" of nature or sought to develop equitable regions, they promoted the dispersal of human activity across "large territories, dovetailing into natural resources."[28] In so doing, however, these visions promoted the consumption of ever-larger pieces of nature and helped create the problems we today associate with urban sprawl.[29]

This type of "green" regionalism was a response to specific conditions: crowded but wealthy cities versus green but poor periphery. It was also premised on the belief that nature's riches, including land, are limitless and exist solely for human benefit.[30] But the massive spread of suburbia caused a gradual role reversal: the city became less crowded but poorer; the periphery more sprawling and richer. It also became apparent that urban dispersal had unforeseen social, economic, and environmental costs. Simultaneously, an alternative view of nature as having an intrinsic value beyond the benefits it yields to humans increasingly challenged earlier anthropocentric notions.[31] Planners became interested in designing human settlements in harmony with nature rather than taming nature for human use.[32]

In reaction to the dispersed nature of today's regional landscapes and the problems of environmental damage, traffic congestion, and social inequities between city and suburbs, the most influential current Western planning movements advocate the reurbanization of central cities. In this sense, they represent a 180-degree reversal of the earlier planning agendas for urban decentralization.[33] Compact urban forms comprise a key component of the new regionalism, smart growth, and new urbanism movements.[34] They promise many benefits in efficiency (for example, compact forms utilize existing infrastructure to its full potential), ecological protection (for example, compact forms require less car use and thus reduce pollution), and social equity (for example, compact forms have the potential to foster greater social integration). The sustainable development concept, which is the broadest paradigm that aspires to provide guidance for human development,[35] clearly favors compact urban forms and advocates the preservation of open spaces instead of their unlimited exploitation for human needs.[36] Programmatic policy documents at national and international levels also broadly sustain this view.[37] Planning in Sofia evolved under the clear influence of all the foreign ideas described above. Yet, local judgment also reflected local conditions, sometimes resulting in interpretations that took the original meaning of the ideas in quite peculiar new directions.

Sofia and Its Planning, 1879–1939

Sofia was elected as the Bulgarian capital in March 1879, after the country gained independence from the Ottoman Empire. Unlike other European capitals that have been permanent seats of power throughout medieval history, Sofia was a town of little importance through the five hundred years of Ottoman rule. Thus, despite the city's ancient history, most of its fabric has been built since the late nineteenth century, following dominant Western, and later Soviet, planning doctrines.[38] The first generation of Sofia's planners were foreign-born architects or engineers; the second, Bulgarian architects educated in western Europe, most notably Germany, Italy, and France. All were familiar with the sources of mainstream European urbanism.[39] Predictably, then, early proposals for reshaping Sofia aimed at erasing the Ottoman heritage, and emulated, in modest form, the main Western urban planning ideas of the time—the Parisian boulevards and the Viennese Ring Road.[40]

Over the next sixty years, Sofia grew exponentially in population and size. In 1879, its territory was only 1.16 square miles (3 square kilometers).[41] By 1939, it had expanded to 16 square miles (42 square kilometers) through the annexation of fifty-three adjacent villages.[42] Its population rose from 18,000 to 400,000, making Sofia the fastest-growing Balkan capital.[43] The economic profile of the city also changed. From 1904 to 1921, the number of factories quadrupled.[44] By the early 1930s, industry employed a third of the city's population, and Sofia was established as the nation's unrivaled industrial center, with 50 percent of the Bulgarian industrial workforce. Natural growth and the influx of rural migrants seeking industrial jobs in the city—trends typical for all large European cities at the time—partially caused this phenomenon. In Sofia's case, fast growth was further facilitated by the entry of refugees expelled from territories lost in the Balkan Wars.[45] These dramatic changes made Sofia appear to be a city whose phenomenal growth was comparable to that of North American and Bavarian industrial cities in the mid- to late nineteenth century.[46]

With fast expansion and industrialization came predictable problems reminiscent of those that had overwhelmed nineteenth-century Western cities. Sofia became crowded and polluted.[47] And although there were many plans to reshape its street system,[48] none addressed the urban problems comprehensively. Under these conditions, foreign ideas for uniting the city and nature attracted increasingly favorable attention among the local urban planners. The views of Ebenezer Howard and Frank Lloyd Wright, in particular, gained prominence through the work of two architects, Trendafil Trendafilov and Georgi Nenov, who published an account of garden cities in 1912 and 1924.[49] A few years later, Sofia's chief architect, Todor Goranov, praised urban dispersal as the correct "system adopted by all new English and German cities."[50]

Sofia's first master plan, *Building Greater Sofia*, was prepared between 1934 and 1937. The plan was put together under the leadership of the German Nazi-backed architect Adolph Muesmann. His rather suspicious victory in the international competition was probably the result of Bulgaria's political alliance with Germany.[51] The plan came at the height of the garden cities' popularity, and it predictably reflected the fundamental elements of that movement.[52] The plan's basic premise was the transformation of Sofia into a conglomerate of garden cities.[53] As Chief Architect Goranov noted,[54] Greater Sofia was to acquire a "star-shaped form," in which the urban areas, extending like fingers from the center, would be separated from each other by greenbelts serving as the "lungs of the city." The "lungs" offered many benefits: beauty, health, improved sanitation, and even protection against gas attacks. At the same time, congestion in the center was to be alleviated by dispersing some of the city-center functions in the new self-contained garden districts. Greater Sofia was thus to attain a distinct polycentric form.

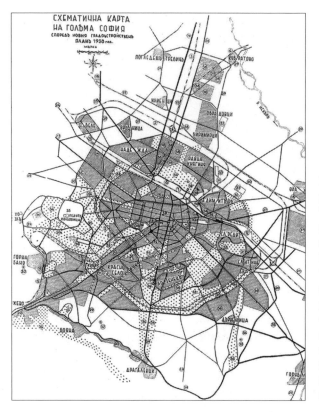

Part of Muesmann's
plan of Greater Sofia.
The dotted areas are
green spaces, which
clearly separate the ur-
banized zones (i.e., the
"garden districts"). Some
greenbelts were pro-
posed in built-out areas,
which had to be cleared
according to the plan.
(Sofia State Archives and
the National Library of
St. Cyril and Methodius,
Sofia)

The building block of Greater Sofia was to be the quaint single-family
house with a private green yard that stood in stark contrast to the apartment
blocks that defined Sofia's central districts. This house was seen as both offering a healthy living environment and providing a means of connecting
people with "nature" and "our roots."[55] This idea was also supported by the
Nazis, who asserted that pastoral single-family living fostered nationalist
sentiment and a national identity.[56]

Not only did the plan reflect the ideals of the international garden city
movement; it was also the result of specific local conditions. Although Sofia
had begun to experience the typical problems of Western industrial centers,
it had not yet reached their stage of development and faced some unique
issues. The bourgeoisie still lived in the center, and upscale suburbanization
had not yet begun. In fact, the outskirts were occupied by low-income workers and war refugees. Their quarters were built without planning wherever
land was cheapest, and they often lacked all infrastructure.[57] The authorities
considered the city to be too dispersed already and doubted funds could ever

be found to service its periphery. Thus the plan's paradoxical objective was to decentralize some commercial and civic functions, while at the same time decreasing the urbanized area.[58]

The outcome was a plan to concentrate growth in selected built-out areas, while "clearing" all development in other outlying districts and transforming them into greenbelts. The "clearance" idea caused a heated public controversy. Desperate citizens protested at city hall that their neighborhoods would be "converted into mighty forests, as if Sofia's future lay in raising wildlife."[59] This controversy, along with fears of the impending war, was one of the most important reasons why few concrete steps were taken to implement Muesmann's plan.[60] Ultimately, however, the plan did prove influential. For the first time in Sofia's history, it proposed an integrated system of parks—a system of "green wedges" that started in the mountains and penetrated into the urban fabric." The scheme was preserved and enhanced in subsequent master plans, and several of Sofia's finest parks today, such as West Park and South Park, trace their origins to Muesmann's sketches.[61]

Planning Communist Sofia, 1945–1989

After the communist victory in 1945, Muesmann's plan was criticized as fascist and discarded. A new plan, under the lead of Lyuben Tonev, was adopted in 1945.[62] Sofia had experienced substantial wartime damage.[63] Because of the daunting reconstruction tasks and the limited resources, the plan's goal was fairly modest. Sofia was to stay within its existing borders of 16 square miles (42 square kilometers). Dispersal of any type was no longer on the agenda; Tonev had already condemned the dispersal idea when Muesmann proposed it.[64] The plan's new focus was on reconstruction.

But despite the rhetorical shift, Muesmann's ideas for a green and polycentric city were carried forward.[65] Like Muesmann, Tonev sought to relocate downtown functions in neighborhood nodes. He also retained the idea of radial greenbelts that ran from the mountains toward the center separating the urban districts without clearing any of the low-income areas.[66] There was, however, a basic difference in organizing the green open space. Muesmann had intended single-family homes with private yards, an idea that Tonev deemed contrary to communist ideals. He in fact believed that "it is the [private] yard that makes the bourgeois."[67] The building block of Sofia was thus to be a group of mid-rise apartment buildings surrounding a shared green open space.

After the mid-1950s, the construction of large factories in the city's outskirts attracted thousands of workers from the provinces. The 1945 plan fore-saw a population growth of up to 800,000 in 1975, but by 1955, the popu-lation had already reached 600,000. In 1956, therefore, the Council of Ministers required a new plan. Two teams were selected to develop alterna-tive plans, one led by Lyubomir Neikov, and one by Vassil Siromahov. They presented competing visions. Neikov's team kept close to Tonev's ideas. It sought to keep Sofia in its borders, to promote infill development, and to create new public parks. Siromahov's team, in contrast, sought territorial growth. Its main idea was to incorporate large tracts of farms into the city and construct massive new housing districts.[68] Neikov's plan was deemed more realistic and thus adopted.[69]

In the meantime, industrialized building methods had been imported from the USSR. The opportunities presented by economy of scale were quickly appreciated. In 1963, an update of the 1961 plan was adopted that was, in essence, the rejected Siromahov plan. Following the Soviet lead in building mass-produced housing,[70] the plan's update proposed several large new housing districts to be built along the city edge. For the next twenty-five years, Sofia embarked on a road of spatial expansion. More than 200,000 new dwelling units were erected, which today house around two-thirds of the city's population.

The new housing projects carried on the idea of polycentricity. According to the plan, they were meant to function as self-contained districts with their own civic and retail nodes, providing a full range of services. But the dwell-ings were built first, and other uses lagged behind (for example, the Mladost District, home of 100,000 people, never had a single cinema or swimming pool). The housing design followed ideas of Le Corbusier, who had become the most respected foreign architect. The housing slabs stood like sculptures amid vast common green areas that, however, were never properly main-tained. To the credit of the communist authorities, Sofia acquired an im-pressive series of large parks (for example, South, West, and North parks). Some of them had been proposed first by Muesmann or Neikov; others were planned in the 1960s or 1970s.[71]

Post-Communist Plans, 1989–2005

The year 1989 brought radical changes to Bulgaria and its capital city. The 1990s were a period of economic crisis and dwindling incomes. The indus-trialized economy crashed; inflation ranged from 40 to 80 percent per year; and the GDP fell by a third.[72] Although economic conditions in Sofia were always better than in the rest of Bulgaria, the poverty rate in 1997 reached 37 percent.[73] Economic recovery started in 1998.[74] By then, most of the state assets and enterprises, including the massive home-building companies that erected the mass-produced housing projects, were broken apart and privatized.[75] The state largely withdrew from building housing. As of 2000, 90 percent of all new dwellings were privately built.[76] Simultaneously, land that had been nationalized by the communist regime in 1947–48 became eligible for sale and/or return to its pre–World War II owners.

Under these conditions, two areas of Sofia have changed most visibly. The first includes downtown and a few upscale neighborhoods near it (for example, Lozenetz and Iztok), which have experienced substantial infill in the form of upper- and middle-class housing. The second are the peripheral areas, particularly the foothills of the mountain of Vitosha,[77] where the dominant unit is the upscale single-family house with a yard. Since the late 1990s, the outskirts have also attracted a substantial number of large commercial uses, including hypermarkets, warehouses, and office parks.[78] For the first time in Sofia's history, then, one may truly speak of substantial upscale residential suburbanization and commercial decentralization. The first attempts to provide a new plan for Sofia began immediately after the end of communism. In 1990, the municipality organized a national planning competition in which twenty-six teams took part. Of those, fourteen teams sought urban dispersal—eight by building autonomous satellite towns separated by greenbelts, and the rest by expanding Sofia's borders and directing new low-density residential growth toward the green areas in the hilly outskirts. Despite the fact that no population growth was projected, some entries went as far as to advocate expanding the urbanized areas by 40 percent to allow for low-density living "amid nature," or even to erect a second large new center to counterbalance the existing downtown. Almost unanimously the proposals sought to decentralize downtown functions to peripheral districts or autonomous satellite towns, and thus create a polycentric metropolis.[79] Because of the unstable economic and political conditions in the early 1990s, however, the master-planning process was terminated. It was reinitiated in 1998.

The new master plan, *Sofia 2020*, was prepared from 1998 to 2003. In 2003, a coalition of citizen groups argued that implementing it would cause harm to the mountainous region surrounding Sofia and mounted a legal challenge to the plan's environmental impact assessment. The courts ruled against the coalition, and the city council adopted the plan, which was eventually approved by the National Parliament.

The process went through several stages.[80] Once the basic data were compiled, a national competition was held as in 1990. This time, thirty-four teams took part. Once again, around half of the teams proposed developing new green territories in Sofia.[81] A jury bestowed awards on several entries. Then an expert team synthesized the ideas from the winning entries, and split into two groups that would produce two competing scenarios: A and B.[82] Scenario A promoted urban infill, while scenario B favored spatial expansion.[83] The process thus recalled 1961, when the plan was the outcome of a competition between Neikov's compact and Siromahov's dispersed city.

The two alternatives shared the goal of transferring functions from the center to the periphery (that is, by relocating certain major civic buildings) and thus creating a polycentric metropolis. They disagreed, however, on the extent to which this should occur. The authors of scenario A argued that while both the center and periphery might benefit from some functional reorganization, no further residential decentralization was necessary. The existing urban areas, in their view, included vacant territory sufficient to allow the building of 260,000 new dwelling units—far more than necessary in conditions of limited population growth. Thus, they promoted policies to encourage urban infill. In contrast, using language strangely reminiscent of Frank Lloyd Wright, who sixty years earlier had linked dispersal to a new technological era (in his case, the "Machine Age"), the authors of scenario B argued for "dispersed living amid the natural environment, since it is an expression of new forms of spatial organization which correspond to information society." Such single-family living, the authors of scenario B further claimed, was appropriate for the growing upper classes and would enable Sofia to catch up with spatial trends in Western cities.[84] These excerpts from interviews with the team leaders illustrate the sharp contrast in their visions:

Team leader, scenario A: The premise that our group advocated was that Sofia needs to stop expanding. It has grown enough and from now on it must just become better organized. Under socialism, the city already incorporated too many vast new territories, which currently it can barely manage. . . . From now on, the focus must be on improving the assets we already have. This is the right, the sustainable thing to do—both economically and environmentally. And it is, I believe, the philosophy of Western cities at the moment.

Team leader, scenario B: Our alternative is the dispersed city. We want the region around Sofia to be inseparable from it and to adopt functions that would relieve the pressures now piling upon the compact city. There will be secondary centers of activity in what is now the periphery. Then the region around the city will be equal to the city itself. Dispersed urbanization is thus the regional and more equitable approach. And this type of new regional thinking is well known in the West. [Also] we want to encourage new types of dwellings, in a new type of environment of a totally different character, and encourage a lifestyle that is closer to nature, amid nature. People are totally fed up with this highly urbanized environment that is now offered in the compact city—an environment that contradicts the basic principles of sustainable development. . . . Our people long to live amid nature. In socialist times, the government had an interest in cramping people into high-density housing projects because this would save money. But in a market economy, in an information-type society, in a democracy, the compact city is no longer the right choice.

The debate between proponents of the two scenarios was resolved in 2002, when the urban-dispersal model was adopted as the basis of the plan's final draft.[85] Following the ideas of scenario B, this draft recommended: "Dispersed living amid nature, an expression of new forms of spatial organization inherent to the information society and enabled by advanced communication technology, should be encouraged. It is not necessary to utilize the whole potential of the existing territory. The growth of residential areas should be related to the growth in the standard of living rather than to population growth. The existing overpopulated urban areas should just be renovated, keeping in mind that the correlation between high density and poverty is so obvious that it needs no further proof."

Behind the difference in visions—one for a compact city, which was dismissed, and one for a dispersed city, which was endorsed—lurks a theme that permeates Sofia's planning history. Both visions aimed to position themselves within the framework of popular current Western ideological constructs. These ideologies were, however, endowed with contested meanings. The authors of scenario A linked them to compact form, while the authors of scenario B linked them to dispersal. But how can such interpretations coexist? How can the authors of scenario B claim that sustainability means dispersal amid nature, in conflict with the common interpretation? The first logical explanation—that they are unaware of international ideas—can be easily refuted. Based on the interviews, it is clear that they are highly educated individuals with a firm grasp of international planning theory. A more plausible explanation was given by one of the advocates of urban dispersal: "Obviously, we are familiar with this new trend in the West—to try to limit growth of the urban areas and encourage people to come back to the compact city. But we are simply not there! . . . We are all for sustainable development and regionalism. But what those things mean there, they may not mean here." Tapping into popular rhetoric for sustainability and regionalism, the authors of the dispersed-city model thus endowed the concepts with a meaning different from the one common in the Western planning literature: equitable regionalism for them meant transferring people and functions from the center to the periphery; sustainability meant dispersal "amid nature." This, however, is exactly the interpretation of regionalism and sustainability that prevailed in Western planning thought earlier in the twentieth century. That this interpretation should find strong support in Sofia is not surprising, if we take into account that the urban context of today's Sofia is reminiscent of that of Western cities in the earlier part of the twentieth century. Despite the incipient residential and commercial decentralization, Sofia is substantially more compact than cities farther west.[86] The downtown is densely populated[87] and is a thriving business node.[88] Housing demand in the center is strong, as evidenced by the fact that housing prices there exceed those even in the most affluent new suburbs.[89] Thus, Sofia today is far from having a weak center and a sprawling rich periphery—the context within which Western notions about the benefits of compact forms developed.

Sofia's current planning debates thus offer us a rare glimpse into a condensed history of Western planning thought. We observe the simultaneous juxtaposition of contested interpretations of fundamental planning concepts for the correct relationship between city and nature, and city and region. In Western planning thought, there has been a clear ideological evolution as one notion has gradually taken precedence over the other. In the early twentieth century, the prevalent idea was that the urban forms should disperse amid nature and the central city should distribute resources to other settlements in a polycentric region. In the early twenty-first century, the dominant idea seems to be the opposite—that human settlements should be compact and the nature around them left untouched. In a city like Sofia, however, which is heavily influenced by current Western ideas in all aspects of life but has local conditions closer to those of Western cities in the past, the two polar visions exist contemporaneously, side by side. Both visions seek legitimacy using Western rhetoric. But while one builds on current Western ideas that favor compact form, the other carries on historic Western notions of the benefits of dispersal. These conflicting notions arise from foreign traditions of the past and local conditions of the present. The fact that ultimately the vision of dispersal was endorsed in Sofia shows that foreign ideas, no matter how well known or progressive, cannot be easily forced upon the local context in a country that has developed differently from many Western nations.

Conclusion

This essay has reviewed the evolution of planning ideas on Sofia's form, the influence of foreign theories, and their interplay with local conditions. The evidence suggests that Sofia's planners broadly followed the main international paradigms and, much like their colleagues abroad, struggled to define the proper union between city and nature, and city and region. These two principal notions—of city and nature, and city and region—in fact provided the framework within which debates over Sofia's form evolved. There was a remarkable consistency in planning attempts to promote a polycentric metropolis, as well as to integrate city and nature, although the strategies of how to achieve this differed widely—by promoting single-family living; by providing public green space between "towers in the park"; or by creating garden cities, satellite towns, or upscale suburbs.

Current debates over Sofia's form provide evidence for the persistence of the dilemmas of how to relate city to nature, and city to region. They also manifest the multiplicity of meanings with which fundamental notions such as environmentalism or regionalism can be endowed. Because of the conflict between local aspirations to adopt Western ideological prescriptions and local conditions that do not exhibit the same set of problems that the Western ideologies attempt to solve, Sofia's latest plan exhibits a rhetoric following current Western ideologies while endowing them with alternative meanings. This amalgam holds little promise for the betterment of Sofia's form.

As Nedovic-Budic argues,[90] eastern European cities in the 1990s were "at a stage that Western European and U.S. cities have long passed, but which the West would like to re-achieve in the future." They are still relatively high-density and compact, have vibrant downtowns, and are characterized by a distinct urban contour. Clearly, under these conditions, Western ideas about strengthening the city center and limiting urban sprawl have a limited appeal. However, as residential and commercial decentralization are on the rise throughout the cities of eastern Europe, it is important to realize that compactness, a clear urban edge, and unspoiled nature around it are advantages that can be lost. Post-communist planners have a unique opportunity to observe the consequences of planning policies that encourage urban decentralization—consequences that are quite visible in many sprawling Western metropolises, most notably in the United States. While there may be some benefits to a policy that encourages the transfer of selected functions from the center to the periphery, post-communist planning should not replicate Western mistakes of the recent past.

Notes

I would like to thank the International Research and Exchanges Board, the American Council of Learned Societies, and the American Councils for International Education for supporting the research on planning and suburbanization in post-communist contexts through the Title VIII Program of the U.S. State Department. None of these organizations is responsible for the views expressed in this essay. A version of this article was published previously by Sage Publications as "The Compact vs. the Dispersed City: History of Planning Debates on Sofia's Urban Form" in the *Journal of Planning History* 6 (2007): 138–65.

1. P. Hall, *Cities of Tomorrow: An Intellectual History of Planning and Design in the Twentieth Century* (New York, 1988).
2. M. C. Boyer, *Dreaming the Rational City: The Myth of American City Planning* (Cambridge, 1983).
3. J. Nasr and M. Volait, "Introduction: Transporting Planning," in *Urbanism Imported or Exported: Native Aspirations and Foreign Plans,* ed. Nasr and Volait (Chichester, 2003), xi–xxxviii. See also S. Ward, *Planning the Twentieth-Century City: The Advanced Capitalist World* (Chichester, 2002); and S. Ward, "Reexamining the International Diffusion in Planning," in *Urban Planning in a Changing World: Twentieth-Century Experience,* ed. R. Freestone (London, 2000), 40–55.
4. See A. Yerolympos, "Urbanism as Social Engineering in the Balkans: Reform Prospects and Implementation Problems in Thessaloniki," in *Urbanism Imported or Exported,* ed. Nasr and Volait, 109–28.
5. R. Daskalov, *Mezhdu Iztoka i Zapada: Dilemi na Bulgarskata kulturna identichnost* (Sofia, 1998; in Bulgarian).
6. D. Jeleva-Martins, "Bulgarskoto gradoustrojstwo kato krustoput na Iztochnia i Zapadnia Avangard," *Arhitektura* (2000, in Bulgarian): 21–24.
7. M. Kaika, *City of Flows: Modernity, Nature and the City* (New York, 2005).
8. For example, see G. Marsh, "The Study of Nature," in *American Environmentalism: The Formative Period, 1860–1915,* ed. D. Hall and D. Howe (New York, 1973).
9. Boyer, *Dreaming the Rational City.*
10. For example, see C. Eliot, "The Reformation of the City Dweller and His Habitat," in *American Environmentalism,* ed. Hall and Owe, 179.
11. R. Herrick, *The Gospel of Freedom* (New York, 1898), cited by W. Cronon, *Nature's Metropolis: Chicago and the Great West* (New York, 1991), 18.
12. Eliot, "The Reformation of the City Dweller"; and F. L. Olmsted, "The Urban Planners as a Civilizing Force," both in *American Environmentalism,* ed. Hall and Owe.
13. Kaika, *City of Flows.*
14. E. Howard, *Garden Cities of Tomorrow: A Peaceful Path to Reform* (London, 1898).
15. See P. Hall, *Cities of Tomorrow;* J. Barnett, *The Elusive City: Five Centuries of Design, Ambition and Miscalculation* (New York, 1986); and Boyer, *Dreaming the Rational City.*
16. Barnett, *The Elusive City.*
17. Le Corbusier, *The City of To-morrow and Its Planning* (New York, 1987), 24.
18. Barnett, *The Elusive City.*

19. Le Corbusier, *The City of To-morrow*, 177.

20. R. Fishman, *Bourgeois Utopias: The Rise and Fall of Suburbia* (New York, 1987).

21. L. Mumford, *The Culture of Cities* (New York, 1938).

22. P. Geddes, *Cities in Evolution* (London, 1949). See also S. Wheeler, "The New Regionalism: Key Characteristics of an Emerging Movement," *Journal of the American Planning Association* 68 (2002): 267–78; and R. Fishman, "The Death and Life of American Regional Planning," in *Reflections on Regionalism*, ed. B. Katz (Washington, 2002).

23. For example, R. Pope, 1909, cited by M. Sies and C. Silver, "Conclusion: Planning History and the New American Metropolis," in *Planning the Twentieth-Century American City*, ed. Sies and Silver (Baltimore, 1966), 462.

24. R. Stites, *Revolutionary Dreams: Utopian Vision and Experimental Life in the Russian Revolution* (Oxford, 1989).

25. F. L. Wright, *The Disappearing City* (New York, 1932).

26. See P. Self, "The Evolution of the Greater London Plan, 1944–1970," *Progress in Planning* 57 (2002): 145–75; and S. Wheeler, "Planning for Metropolitan Sustainability," *Journal of Planning Education and Research* 20 (2000): 133–45.

27. See Fishman, *Bourgeois Utopias*.

28. Jane Jacobs, *The Death and Life of Great American Cities* (New York, 1961), 19–20.

29. See Wheeler, "The New Regionalism"; Fishman, "The Death and Life of American Regional Planning"; and Sies and Silver, "Conclusion."

30. See S. Hirt, "Toward Post-modern Urbanism: Evolution of Planning in Cleveland, Ohio," *Journal of Planning Education and Research* 25 (2005): 27–42.

31. See H. Rolston, *Environmental Ethics: Duties to and Values in the Natural World* (Philadelphia, 1988); and T. Regan, "The Nature and Possibility of an Environmental Ethic," *Environmental Ethics* 3 (1982): 19–34.

32. I. McHarg, *Design with Nature* (New York, 1971).

33. Wheeler, "The New Regionalism." See also P. Healey and R. Williams, "European Urban Planning Systems: Diversity and Convergence," *Urban Studies* 30 (1993): 701–20.

34. See Wheeler, "The New Regionalism"; E. Talen and G. Knaap, "Legalizing Smart Growth: An Empirical Study of Land Use Regulation in Illinois," *Journal of Planning Education and Research* 22 (2003): 345–59; and Congress for New Urbanism, *New Urbanism: Comprehensive Report & Best Practices Guide* (Ithaca, 2001).

35. S. Campbell, "Green Cities, Growing Cities, Just Cities? Urban Planning and the Contradictions of Sustainable Development," *Journal of the American Planning Association* 62 (1996): 296–312.

36. Wheeler, "Planning for Metropolitan Sustainability."

37. European Environment Agency, *Environment in the European Union at the Turn of the Century* (Brussels, 1998); American Planning Association, *PAS Report 479: Principles of Smart Development* (Chicago, 1998); President's Council on Sustainable Development, *Sustainable America: A New Consensus for Prosperity, Opportunity, and a Healthy Environment for the Future* (Washington, 1996); United Nations, *Agenda 21* (New York, 1992).

38. D. Jeleva-Martins, "Bulgarskoto gradoustrojstvo po putya na modernizma," *Arhitektura* 2 (1994, in Bulgarian): 36–39.

39. C. Staddon and B. Mollov, "City Profile: Sofia, Bulgaria," *Cities* 17 (2000): 379–87.

40. D. Jeleva-Martins, "Horizontalna organizacia na grada: Sinhronen analiz," *Arhitektura* 3–4 (1991, in Bulgarian): 25–28.

41. A. Ishirkov, "Naselenieto na Sofia," *Jubilejna kniga na grad Sofia* (Sofia, 1928; in Bulgarian).

42. G. Labov, *Arhitekturata na Sofia* (Sofia, 1979; in Bulgarian).

43. J. Lampe, "Interwar Sofia versus the Nazi-Style Garden City: The Struggle over the Muesmann Plan," *Journal of Urban History* 11 (1984): 39–62.

44. D. Yurdanov, "Sofia kato industrialen center," in *Jubilejna kniga na grad Sofia.*

45. According to Lampe, "Interwar Sofia," war refugees made up 11 percent of the city population in 1934, excluding their children born in Sofia.

46. Stolichna Goliama Obshtina, *Izgrajdaneto na Golyama Sofia: Kakvo predvijda Musmanovia
plan* (Sofia, 1938; in Bulgarian), 6.

47. Lampe, "Interwar Sofia."

48. The so-called "regulation" plans, or plans of the street network of various parts of the city,
were prepared in 1892, 1897, 1903, 1907, 1910, 1914, and 1928 (see A. Kovachev, *Zelenata
sistema na Sofia: Urbanistichni aspekti* [Sofia, 2005; in Bulgarian]; and S. Hirt, "Planning the
Post-Communist City: Experiences from Sofia," *International Planning Studies* 10 [2005]:
219–39).

49. Jeleva-Martins, "Bulgarskoto gradoustrojstvo."

50. T. Goranov, "Pulni avtentichni obyasnenya po Musmanovia Plan," *Zora*, May 15, 1938.

51. Lampe, "Interwar Sofia."

52. D. Jeleva-Martins, "Doktrinata na modernizma: Interpretacia na Musmanovija plan na
Sofia," *Arhitektura* 5 (1998; in Bulgarian): 36–39.

53. See I. Ivanov, "Rech na stolichnia kmet Ingener Ivan Ivanov po gradoustrojstvenia plan na
Sofia, izraboten ot Professor Musman, proiznesena pred Stolichniya Obshtinski Suvet na
18 maj 1938 g.," in Stolichna Golyama Obshtina, *Izgrajdaneto na budeshta Golyama Sofia.*
See also Stolichna Golyama Obshtina, *Izgrajdaneto na budeshta Golyama Sofia*, 41; and
A. Muesmann, "Gradoustrojstevenite problemi na Sofia," *Spisanie na Bulgarskoto Injenerno-
Arhitekturno Drujestvo* 17/18 (1936; in Bulgarian): 169–72.

54. Goranov, "Pulni avtentichni obyasneniya," 30.

55. Stolichna, *Izgrajdaneto na Golyama Sofia*, 29.

56. Lampe, "Interwar Sofia."

57. Ibid.

58. Stolichna Obshtina, *Izgrajdaneto na Golyama Sofia*, 43.

59. Protokoli ot Sreshtite na Ingener Ivanov s Grajdanska Delegacia Dokladvashta Opozicia
kum Musmanovia Plan (Protocols from the Meetings of Engineer Ivanov with the Citizen
Delegation Reporting Opposition to Muesmann's Plan), Sofia Archives, Source 1K, Part 3,
Archival Unit 482, July 27, 1938 (in Bulgarian), 3.

60. Hirt, "Planning the Post-Communist City"; Lampe, "Interwar Sofia."

61. Kovachev, *Zelenata sistema na Sofia.*

62. "Naredba-zakon za izmenenie na Obshtija Gradoustrojstven plan na Sofia i Stolichnata Goliama Obshtina," *Durjaven Vestnik* (state newspaper), issue 291, 1945 (in Bulgarian).

63. P. Tashev, *Sofia: Arhitekturno i gradoustrojstveno razvitie, etapi, postijenija i problemi* (Sofia,
1972; in Bulgarian), 30.

64. L. Tonev, "Golemite greshki na plana Musman," *Po putya na bulgarskoto gradoustrojstvo: Iz-
brani nauchni trudove* (Sofia, 1987; in Bulgarian).

65. Jeleva-Martins, "Doktrinata na modernizma," 36–39.

66. L. Tonev, "Za Generalnia Plan na Sofia ot 1945 godina," *Arhitektura* 7–8 (1992; in Bulgarian): 17–20.

67. J. Tangurov, "Modernata arhitektura, 1944–1990," *Arhitektura* 2 (2000; in Bulgarian):
46–48.

68. Kovachev, "*Zelenata sistema na Sofia*"; D. Mushev, "Za stolicata i nejnite proektanti," *Arhitektura* 7–8 (1992; in Bulgarian): 21–23; Labov, *Arhitekturata na Sofia.*

69. *Durjaven Vestnik* 89, "Zakon za priemane i prilagane na Obshtija Gradoustrojstven Plan na Sofia" (1961, in Bulgarian).

70. D. Smith, "The Socialist City," in *Cities after Socialism: Urban and Regional Change and Conflict in Post-Socialist Societies*, ed. G. Andrusz et al. (Oxford, 1996).

71. Kovachev, *Zelenata sistema na Sofia*.

72. G. Andrusz, "Structural Change and Boundary Instability," in *Cities after Socialism*, ed. Andrusz et al.

73. R. Buckley and S. Tsenkova, *Strategia za razvitie na grad Sofia: Predvaritelna ocenka* (Sofia, 2001; in Bulgarian).

74. Since then, Bulgarian GDP growth rates have been consistently around 5 percent.

75. By 2000, the private-sector share of the GDP reached 70 percent starting from 9 percent in 1990 (see A. Yoveva, D. Dimitrov, and R. Dimitrova, "Housing Policy: The Stepchild of the Transition," in *Housing Policy: An Era or a New Beginning*, ed. M. Lux [Budapest, 2003]).

76. A. Elbers and S. Tsenkova, "Housing a Nation of Home Owners—Reforms in Bulgaria," in *Housing Change in East Central Europe*, ed. S. Lowe and S. Tsenkova (Aldershot, 2003).

77. The Vitosha District in fact experienced a 50 percent increase in the number of dwelling units in less than a decade (see Nacionalen Statisticheski Institut, *Sofia v cifri* [Sofia, 2001; in Bulgarian]; and Nacionalen Statisticheski Institut, *Statisticheski sbornik—Sofia* [Sofia, 1993; in Bulgarian]).

78. S. Hirt and A. Kovachev, "The Changing Spatial Structure of Post-Socialist Sofia," in *The Urban Mosaic of Post-socialist Europe: Space, Institutions and Policy*, ed. S. Tsenkova and Z. Nedovic-Budic (Heidelberg, 2006); Staddon and Mollov, "City Profile: Sofia, Bulgaria"; G. Genov, P. Slavejkov, and H. Ganev, "Urbanizirani teritorii," in *Sofia: 120 Godini Stolica* (Sofia, 2000; in Bulgarian).

79. Jeleva-Martins, "Doktrinata na modernizma"; A. Alexandrov, "Noviyat Generalen Plan na Sofia mejdu vchera i dnes," *Arhitektura* 7–8 (1992, in Bulgarian): 30–48.

80. Hirt, "Planning the Post-Communist City."

81. N. Karaddimov, "Konkurs za budeshteto na grada: Dumata na jurito, " *Grad v polite na Vitosha* 2 (2001, in Bulgarian): 2–6.

82. P. Dikov, "Scenarii za socialno-ikonomichesko i prostranstveno razvitie na Sofia i Stolichnata Obshtina v perioda do 2020 g," *Arhitektura* 4 (2001, in Bulgarian): 29–31; V. Troeva, "Vajen etap ot podgotovkata na Obshtija Ustrojstven Plan na Sofia," *Arhitektura* 4 (2001, in Bulgarian): 32–33.

83. Stolichna Obstina (Sofia Municipality), *Obsht Ustrojstven Plan na grad Sofia i Stolichnata Obshtina: Faza predvaritelen proekt, etap 2, Scenarii za socialno-ikonomichesko i teritorialno razvitie na grad Sofia v perioda do 2020 g* (Sofia, 2001; in Bulgarian).

84. Ibid.

85. Stolichna Obshtina (Sofia Municipality), *Obsht Ustrojstven Plan na grad Sofia i Stolichnata Obshtina: faza predvaritelen proekt, etap 3, idejni proekti za teritorialno razvitie na grad Sofia i Stolichna Obshtina—bazov variant* (Sofia, 2002; in Bulgarian).

86. According to Stolichna Obshtina (Sofia Municipality), *Obsht Ustrojstven Plan na grad Sofia i Stolichna Obshtina: sintez i sukraten doklad* (Sofia, 2003; in Bulgarian), Sofia has an average density of 23 persons per acre (57.5 persons per hectare). This compares to 17 persons per acre in London, 18.8 in Paris, 19.7 in Amsterdam, and 21.5 in Stockholm. It makes Sofia's built-up areas more than ten times as dense as those of U.S. cities like Houston or Atlanta (see J. Kenworthy and F. Laube, *An International Sourcebook of Automobile Dependence in Cities, 1960–1990* [Boulder, 1999]).

87. As of 2000, the highest residential density in Sofia, 73 people per acre, is within a radius of

0.6 square miles (1 kilometer) of the heart of downtown. Densities tend to decrease toward the periphery with the partial exception of the socialist housing estates (see Buckley and Tsenkova, *Strategia za razvitie na grad Sofia*).

88. According to data made available to the author by *Colliers International*, as of 2003, Sofia's center holds around half of the total office space in the metropolis.

89. According to real-estate outlets (*Nedvijimi imoti*), in July 2005, housing prices in Vitosha averaged 61 euros per square foot, while in the center (e.g., Oborishte District) they were 71 euros per square foot (www.imot.bg).

90. Z. Nedovic-Budic, "Adjustment of Planning Practice to the New Eastern and Central European context," *Journal of the American Planning Association* 67 (2001): 38–52.

Green and Modern

Planning Mexico City, 1900–1940

Alfonso Valenzuela Aguilera

During the early decades of the twentieth century, a group of visionary planners undertook the physical transformation of Mexico City. They reinterpreted the concepts of nature presented in Ebenezer Howard's garden cities, Jean Claude Forestier's *systèmes de parcs,* and Patrick Geddes's regional planning ideas in order to provide green public spaces and comprehensively enhance the quality of life in the city. In Mexico City in the twentieth century, the concept of nature continued to evolve, with the Científicos—a circle of scientifically oriented politicians and intellectuals during the Porfirio Díaz regime—linking the "greening" of the city with their aspirations to modernize infrastructures in response to health concerns. Miguel Angel de Quevedo, Carlos Contreras, and José Luis Cuevas Pietrasanta established urban planning frameworks, addressing social, functional, and environmental issues. Thereafter, policies promoting industrialization radically transformed urban planning into an instrument for achieving economic development rather than for promoting the public welfare. In the early twentieth century, Mexico City embraced modernity, although views of social order, material and cultural progress, and the role of the nation-building project changed substantially over time. During this period, key planners shaped the capital according to planning practices originating in Europe and the United States which were later transfigured to foster a new national identity.

Haussmann, Howard, and Forestier: Their Influence on City Planning in Mexico City

There is little doubt that Haussmann's interventions as prefect de la Seine in Paris garnered him widespread influence on planners in Latin America.

The baron's spectacular transformation of Paris was quickly embraced as unquestioned urban savoir faire, which strengthened the French predominance not only in Latin American social and political thought but also in the fine arts and urban design. Mexican elites worshipped Haussmann's Paris as the ultimate model to follow in their effort to modernize the urban infrastructure and join the circle of world-class capital cities.[1]

Urban planning in Mexico City has been used to manipulate and legitimize political power structures over time. Planning first became part of the political agenda under the rule of Porfirio Díaz (1876–1910) at the end of the nineteenth century. Díaz was surrounded by his group of Científicos and eminent specialists in planning, such as Miguel Angel de Quevedo and Jesus Galindo y Villa, who were concerned about the quality of life in the city and the provision of public open spaces.[2] Even more decisive for the undertaking of such *grands travaux* was the intervention of José Yves Limantour, state secretary of finance, who described in his memoirs how he worked toward the realization of his development projects: "In politics, when you want to achieve an objective, it is always necessary to move ahead in zigzag or in curves. . . . It is not the case as in management where the only way to achieve good results is the straight line."[3]

In 1901, Miguel Angel de Quevedo attended the National Congress on Climate and Meteorology where he presented his work on the environmental risks of desertification. As a result of his participation, he was later appointed by President Díaz to head the Junta Central de Bosques (Central Forest Authority). From this platform, Quevedo advocated for the creation of urban parks that followed international standards.[4] To promote his idea, he identified key government officials willing to support his environmental agenda.

Quevedo was appointed as head of Mexico City's Department of Parks and Gardens in 1903. He created more than forty parks, which increased the amount of public space to up to 15 percent of the city's total area and provided open spaces within a 1,640-foot (500-meter) range from any given point in the city. Trained as a civil engineer specializing in hydraulics at the École Polytechnique in Paris, Quevedo became aware of a range of techniques for preventing the effects of desertification in the woodlands as well as on the seacoast. Later concerned with the deforestation of Mexico City's remaining forestlands and the associated environmental risks, he argued along with Humboldt that "deforestation in the Valley of Mexico was responsible for the increasing levels of documented floods."[5]

Quevedo was heavily influenced by the ideas of Jean Claude Nicholas

Forestier's *systèmes de parcs* and Ebenezer Howard's garden cities.[6] Howard was a distinguished member of the National Association of Planners of the Mexican Republic, and Forestier was Quevedo's mentor and intellectual advisor in his environmental enterprises. Moreover, Quevedo, whose extensive reforestation campaigns earned him the moniker the "tree apostle," was convinced that cities needed healthier environments that served their citizens' basic needs. He stressed the importance of comprehensive planning that addressed social welfare and public health issues and that acknowledged the cultural significance of new green open spaces.[7] Modeled on similar organizations around the world, he founded the Liga de la Defensa Urbana (Urban Defense League), which aimed to protect and preserve parks and gardens within the city. The group's initial efforts were directed toward renovating public landmarks such as Alameda Park as well as the Santo Domingo, El Carmen, and the Vizcaínas plazas. "Our Alameda is a place which provides great benefits to a large number of citizens who feel overwhelmed by urban stress, every time more intense, sickening and annoying. This park may help citizens to restore a healthier physical and mental equilibrium."[8] Quevedo would later, at the outbreak of the agrarian revolution (1911), present an influential paper entitled "Issues in Urbanism and its Relation to Open Spaces, Woodlands and Forest Reserves"[9] in which he voiced concerns about the dangers of urban "agglomerations" for human health and well-being.[10] Praising country life and the continuous circulation of air, Quevedo aimed to introduce open space and building standards concerning the city as a whole (building height and road width ratio) and individual dwellings (room size and natural ventilation).[11] Besides using Haussmann's Paris as the main reference, Mexicans also praised Berlin's Unter den Linden and Vienna's Ringstrasse as smart urban interventions that elevated living standards and the environmental quality in cities. In his public address, Quevedo also referred to data regarding the number of inhabitants per hectare of open space in cities such as Washington, San Francisco, Vienna, and Paris to demonstrate Mexico City's shortcomings and the need to duplicate (at least) the existing green open areas. Moreover, and probably thinking of Idelfons Cerda's works in Barcelona, he proposed the *Ensanche* of the city (urban growth through in-fill strategies), while at the same time also including open spaces, parks, and boulevards along with housing. As part of the same study, Quevedo proposed the creation of a series of playgrounds and "pocket parks" inspired by British squares that would serve not only the central core but the suburbs as well.[12] To that end, he also anticipated the creation of land reserves, partly by converting former military camps. At the *Centenario* celebrations,[13] the 238-acre (96-hectare) Balbuena Park was inaugurated as a living testimony that "not only health concerns were being addressed but also issues in the moral and social domains."[14]

Quevedo looked to Frederick Law Olmsted's interventions in Boston (Emerald Necklace), New York (Riverside Drive and Ocean Parkway), and Chicago (South Park System) for inspiration when designing metropolitan parks. He praised the American model of park systems and joined Forestier in exalting its hygienic virtues. Through his colleague José Luis Cuevas Pietrasanta, Quevedo was also influenced by Ebenezer Howard's garden city and its provision of working-class housing. Even though many of Olmsted's designs had been realized by the turn of the century and although Howard's famous treatise on garden cities was first published as "To-morrow: A Peaceful Path to Real Reform" in 1898, these works provided inspiration for planners worldwide for many years to come. Howard's garden city inspired the suburban working-class neighborhoods envisioned for the El Buen Tono project in Mexico City and the Colonia Ferrocarrilera in Orizaba. Following the latest theories in England and the United States, suburban neighborhoods were intended to form integrated self-sufficient enclaves with workplaces as well as community and recreational facilities. Therefore the seminal idea of an industrial and commercial center connected to the residential periphery was present in the minds of planners and public officials all over Mexico.

Although Ebenezer Howard's ideas had a significant impact on planning at the time, it was Jean Claude Forestier who influenced Miguel Angel de Quevedo earlier and to a greater extent. As a keynote speaker at the hygiene exposition of 1911, Quevedo acknowledged his debt to Forestier, drawing his attention to the case studies he presented in his address. Quevedo argued for green open spaces in Mexico City using the same rationale offered in Forestier's book *Grandes villes et systèmes de parcs*. He strongly advocated creating proper hygienic and sanitary conditions in the city, but he did not go as far as Forestier, who had promoted the use of open spaces to lessen the risks of vice, crime, and physical and mental illness. Forestier himself was influenced by the garden city movement and also advocated the return to the countryside, praising the creation of parks, gardens, and playgrounds not only because of their benign and healthy features but also because of their potential to raise the land's value.[15] However, planning influences went further back to Haussmann's Paris at the beginning of the twentieth century, when residential "colonias" including public open space and modern infrastructure and services were built. The Roma, Juárez, Hipodromo Condesa, and Santa Maria la Rivera districts were developed by private international investors who profited from the government's provision of licenses and tax breaks aimed to foster real-estate development.

It was José Luis Cuevas Pietrasanta who was directly influenced by Ebenezer Howard. Cuevas was familiar with Howard's early writings on greenbelts encompassing small farms and agricultural industries. A planner in Mexico City, Cuevas also was very active in the academia, teaching city planning and civic design at the National School of Fine Arts, and later introducing urbanism as a required course in the architecture program at the National University of Mexico. Later in 1938, he joined Enrique Yañez and the former Bauhaus director Hannes Meyer in creating a socially oriented graduate program in planning and urbanism at the new Instituto Politécnico Nacional.

Cuevas was a knowledgeable and well-traveled man. He traveled to England in 1920 to study Unwin's garden cities and to attend a special exhibition organized by the city of Bruges on the reconstruction efforts after World War I. He also was impressed by leading European planners such as Patrick Abercrombie, whom he met at a conference at the University College London, where Abercrombie was teaching at the time. In a speech addressed to young Mexican architects, Cuevas presented them with an up-to-date international bibliography. It included the major texts by the prominent professionals Patrick Geddes, Camilo Sitte, John Nolen, and Raymond Unwin, as well as the titles of a few English, American, and French planning journals.[16]

Drawing on Howard, Cuevas wrote about the importance of characterizing the garden city not as residential but instead as predominantly industrial and commercial. Moreover, he stressed the benefits of capturing the surplus exceeding 5 percent of the capital interest of investment for improving the community. In this spirit, Cuevas designed the Colonia Ferrocarrilera in Orizaba for railroad workers (which apparently never materialized) and later undertook the construction of the first two garden cities in Mexico: Chapultepec Heights (1922) and the Hipodromo Condesa (1929). However, these developments were not intended to house industrial workers or provide an alternative to the city, but rather to showcase upper-middle-class development projects featuring wide open green spaces. The Hipodromo Condesa was built in an art deco architectural style on the former grounds of a hippodrome; it featured a magnificent park in the center ringed by single-family houses. This development benefited from the extension of Insurgentes Avenue, a major boulevard that traversed the city along a north-south axis and provided access to public and private transportation. In the case of Chapultepec Heights, British, American, and Mexican investors created a corporation to realize the project, which was portrayed as an idyllic environment for the modern man:

> The modern city suburb is not country in the old sense: it is a transformation of a city into a country or the fusion of the two. It is a city built over roomier space, patterned with gardens and flower-bedded boulevards, combining all modern comforts of city life and excluding all of its undesirable features. It offers the ideal, most sensible, most healthful as well as economical manner of living. The proof of this is the fact that every large American city today is surrounded with lovely, garden-like suburbs inhabited by a healthy, happy, hard-working population, and there is an eloquent proof that such a population might also live in Mexico City. This proof is the remarkable success of Chapultepec Heights, the first Garden City of Mexico.[17]

Environmental Advocacy: The Miguel Angel de Quevedo Vision

As a result of the stable economy the nation experienced during the dictatorship of Porfirio Díaz, Mexico City was prepared to participate in the global economy, even though income disparities and social inequalities were developing and strengthening a *dual* socioeconomic system. Before the revolution began in 1910, planning was characterized by hierarchical decision making, the legitimization of plans by a group of technical "experts," and international businessmen taking a leading role. While industries were established in the northern part of the city, zoning led to the spatial segregation of the population: lower-income citizens lived in the north and east, middle-income in the center, and higher-income citizens found homes in the west. As the nation's economic engine, Mexico City attracted many people from other parts of the country. They mainly settled in rental housing known as *vecindades* in the worst areas of the inner city, or as tenants in the adjoining suburbs.

Influenced by the work of Frederick Law Olmsted, planners such as Nicolas Mariscal, Jesus Galindo y Villa, and Miguel Angel de Quevedo are credited with introducing nature into the urban planning practice in Mexico.[18] They adopted a comprehensive approach that integrated concepts of public hygiene, economy, ecology, and leisure. Mariscal championed landscape architecture as the only way to integrate issues of hygiene, sanitation, and beauty, asserting that only "an architect educated in *relational* architecture [would be able to develop] an architecture which harmonically blended agronomy, hydraulics and horticultural issues."[19] Moreover, he endorsed the preservation of large tracts of land for plazas and green open space. This way the "soft" lines of nature would interrupt the "hard" geometry of the urban fabric.

Miguel Angel de Quevedo accomplished his goal of winning public interest for public open space. As a result of his initiative, open areas increased from representing 2 percent of the territory at the time of the proposal to 16 percent by the end of the decade. However, the implementation of his ideas required the intense lobbying of politicians such as Finance Secretary José Yves Limantour. He was responsible for backing Quevedo's proposal to enlarge the Viveros de Coyoacan, where an annual quarter-million trees were produced to reforest urban areas. Quevedo was also acquainted with the political uses to which parks and gardens could be put. He claimed that the construction of parks, boulevards, and tree nurseries was material evidence of Mexico being a civilized country. Quevedo was determined to institutionalize environmental protection. To support this venture, he founded the first National School of Forestry in 1908, completed the first Forest Inventory (with preliminary data and statistics from Mexico City's considerable forestlands), and continued his efforts to preserve the southern water basins of the city.

A city planning concept that would be a recurrent theme throughout the century was the use of "greenbelts"—protected conservation districts around the cities—as green barriers to prevent further urban growth. Apparently Quevedo came in contact with this idea at the Second International Conference on Public Hygiene and Urban Issues held in Berlin in 1907, where he was invited to see recent interventions around the city where wetlands had been drained and replaced by forestlands.

Quevedo's international experiences did not stop there. He also traveled to Algeria to learn about the French projects to stabilize seafront dunes with pines and acacias, a technique he subsequently employed in Veracruz, in a project commissioned by Díaz in 1908 and completed in 1914. He also attended meetings such as the International Conference for the Conservation of Natural Resources in the United States in 1909, for which he received a personal invitation from President Theodore Roosevelt. At this meeting, he got acquainted with Gifford Pinchot, the first appointed chief of the United States Department of Agriculture (USDA) Forest Service, with whom he shared an interest in conservation, although the men differed in their motivations. Pinchot was mainly interested in avoiding lumber shortages, while Quevedo was concerned with the environmental effects of deforestation on agricultural productivity and hydrological cycles.[20]

Soon after the conference, President Díaz authorized the use of eminent domain to preserve forestlands and natural springs as a matter of
public interest. Díaz also supported Quevedo's initiative to create a greenbelt around the city in order to prevent floods and to guarantee the city's
supply of freshwater. It is worth noting that even though the climate change
caused by deforestation had not yet been sufficiently researched, Quevedo
used scientific methods to demonstrate that reforestation efforts carried out
under his supervision had a positive impact on preserving water reserves
and preventing flooding.

The Mexican Revolution was declared on November 20, 1910, and Porfirio Díaz was removed from power in 1911. After this, Francisco I. Madero,
a Berkeley graduate in agronomy, took office and expressed his intention to
support environmental conservation initiatives such as the drying of wetlands and their replacement with forestlands. As a result of the miasma
theory at the time, wetlands in coastal areas such as Veracruz were believed
to be a major threat to people's health in nearby urban areas; for instance,
the first forestland reserve was created on the former wetlands in the southern territories of Quintana Roo. However, before more work could be undertaken, political events forced Quevedo to go into exile. Conservationists like
him had come to be seen as a potential subversive threat after Victoriano
Huerta had murdered Madero and seized power in 1913.

In this menacing atmosphere, Quevedo headed back to Europe. During his compulsory *séjour,* Quevedo nevertheless learned a great deal from
the French Forestal Service operation, which received a fixed 10 percent of
the profits from wood-related products in order to restore and reforest the affected areas. When he returned to post-revolutionary Mexico in 1917, he saw
the profound environmental impact that the civil war had had on the national territory. Whole forestlands had been devastated in order to use the
wood as natural fuel. Nonetheless, he went back to work, becoming acquainted with the public works minister, Pastor Rouaix, and succeeding
in persuading the incoming president, Venustiano Carranza, to designate
the first national park at the Desierto de los Leones reserve. He also per-
suaded Carranza to include a conservationist clause in the crucial Article 27
of the new 1927 constitution, which read as follows: "The Nation shall always
maintain the right to impose on the private property the rules which ema-
nate from the public interest, as well as regulating the use of its natural resources, which are bound to be expropriated in order to distribute the public
wealth with equity and look after its conservation."[21]

During the 1930s, Quevedo headed the Mexican Committee for the Protection of Wild Birds and founded the Mexican Society of Forestry, which later published *Mexico Forestal,* a popular magazine featuring educational articles on climate change, water and soil protection, ecology, and public welfare. The publication influenced environmental awareness; as the first issue, dealing with the conservation of forestlands, stated: "[Woodlands] are not restricted to the narrow limitations of bordering frontiers since they are beneficial for humanity as a whole and represent key elements in sustaining a climatic equilibrium as well as the global wide-ranging flora and fauna."[22]

Miguel Angel de Quevedo's ideas proved to be visionary, although he also addressed the pragmatic side of their implementation: in order to institutionalize environmental practices, he advocated for legislation that would provide "official" support for them, such as the Law of Forestry (1923–26) with its operational regulations (1927).[23] Regarding the importance of the availability of land reserves, he pointed out: "It is the present generation's duty to secure adequate land reserves for the sake of the capital city. If our Nation is to achieve the amount of wealth and progress that we strive for, it is mandatory to endorse its growth not only in extension, but because of its environmental, health and comfort features, providing places for recreation and leisure which will attract both tourists and wealthy migrants worldwide."

Another remarkable point in Quevedo's vision was that he embraced the construction of parks in low-income areas at the periphery of the city, along with the traditional aristocratic parks in the center of the city: "The avenues along the greenbelt complement the road network that connects the center of the city with its periphery."[24]

When Plutarco Elias Calles took office in 1928, he endorsed Quevedo's environmental concerns, enacting the designation of areas with high biologic, scenic, and recreational value as Zonas Forestales Protegidas (Protected Forestland Areas). The Forestry Service was launched again, the School of Forestry was reopened after it had been closed in 1927 due to the lack of federal funding, and several tree nurseries were created. However, these good intentions didn't go far since crucial decrees to designate national parks were not enacted, projects were inadequately funded, and a legal framework to protect the environment was not developed. Quevedo realized then the limited value of legislation without enforcement and objectives without fixed deadlines or citizens' support.

It was not until the Lázaro Cardenas government (1934–40), during which Quevedo was appointed head of the Forestry, Fishing and Hunting Department, that he finally assumed charge of managing the natural resources of the country. Cardenas put the preservation of natural resources high on his administration's list of priorities, just as his peer Franklin Delano Roosevelt had. Interestingly, both administrations treated natural resources as a matter of public interest since they were facing serious environmental problems such as the deforestation and desertification of entire regions.[25]

At the time, Carlos Contreras was appointed to coordinate the Development Plan for Mexico City 1935–1985, which centered around six priorities: (1) to preserve the historic center; (2) to be transit- and transportation-oriented; (3) to be capable of controlling growth; (4) to protect ecological reserves; (5) to create industrial districts; and (6) to guarantee the city's food supply. It is worth noting that although the plan addressed the spatial arrangement of urban functions (physical planning), it overlooked the cultural and social components of urban life. Furthermore, transportation planning was limited to connecting functional hubs rather than developing a comprehensive transportation network for the city.[26]

As Lázaro Cardenas was engaged in providing social welfare, he envisioned and endorsed conservation practices as possible means to provide a regular income for the rural population.[27] Moreover, he stressed the important role of scientific research and education in achieving sustainable practices as well as in the rational and regulated administration of resources. To this end, Cardenas established the National System of Forestland Reserves, which was responsible for restoring and protecting nonurbanized land all over the nation. Furthermore, 6 million trees were planted during his administration (2 million in the Valley of Mexico and 4 million in the rest of the country).

Even though Cardenas has been criticized for granting lower-income groups the right to exploit part of the woodlands for self-subsistence, his conservation program was later revealed as a groundbreaking initiative since social and economic policies were oriented to address environmental equilibrium and were aimed at achieving "sustainable development," a concept that conservationists would reappraise in the 1970s. Moreover, Cardenas and Quevedo were responsible for the creation of 294 tree nurseries and forty national parks,[28] stressing the *therapeutic* value of such parks and regarding them as indicators of the level of civilization attained.[29]

Green and Modern: Carlos Contreras's Master Plan

If, at the turn of the twentieth century, Quevedo led the way in integrating nature and modern planning, Contreras grounded the planning practice within the city's legal and procedural frameworks. These two key planning figures worked as co-editors of the journal *Planificación* for several years as well as working for the transformation of Mexico City, with Quevedo greening the city as chief director of the national natural resources office, and Contreras as the preeminent figure in the urban planning scene.

Carlos Contreras is credited with having introduced modern planning in Mexico. Educated at the University of Columbia and a delegate at the various international housing and planning conferences, Contreras advocated for the need of urban legislation and construction codes. In a period in which the ideas of the Bauhaus and Le Corbusier were praised around the world, Contreras followed the idea of automobile-oriented cities connected through road networks and highway systems. While at Columbia University, Contreras prepared an ambitious plan to restructure the entire country, called "La Planificación de la República Mexicana" (1925). It was intended to draw attention to planning as a means to organize and manage growth in a broader sense.[30]

Contreras's national plan featured the institutionalization of planning practices, "national zoning" of specialized regions, a national system of roads, ports, seafronts, and national parks. Roads and highways were high on the agenda, as Contreras stated emphatically that "one of the urgent needs Mexico has at this time is building and developing its communications. . . . We need roads and we shall have them." The road system included the creation of internal highways linking the principal cities as well as "transversal" roads cutting across the country. Contreras supported his advocacy of road expansion with U.S. data on vehicle ownership: in fewer than twenty-five years, an initial stock of 28,000 vehicles in the United States had reached 15 million automobiles in 1924; therefore, if Mexico already had 14,000 vehicles, an exponential increase could be expected in the following two decades.

Another important feature of the initiative was the creation of national parks and reserves, in support of which Contreras stressed not only the parks' natural and scenic features, but also their economic benefits. Quoting from a report from the American Association for the Scenic and Historic Transformation of the United States (1924), in which the financial revenues from the national parks were highlighted, Contreras convincingly argued that national parks such as Yellowstone, Yosemite, Glacier, Crater Lake, Sequoia, General Grant (now Kings Canyon), Rocky Mountain, Mesa Verde, and the Grand Canyon reported a combined annual profit of $1 billion.

A final innovation of the plan was the proposed development of "model cities" featuring a distribution of residential and industrial areas reminiscent of the early experiments of the garden city movement. However, the creation of public gardens, nature reserves, parks, and playgrounds was motivated more by hygiene and health principles than by environmental awareness and the protection of natural resources. Zoning was highly praised by Contreras as a tool to "protect everybody's interests," to address the "sacred rights of the community," and to create the conditions that would foster the "citizens' trust in justice." This technocratic rationale dominated the planning discourse and hid the sociopolitical interests underlying the zoning.[31] That rationale, however, was very powerful when combined with the logic of capital; Contreras elaborated on the plan, defining it as a "intelligent investment scheme" to carry out public works and improvements, which, besides having a positive impact on the community, would improve public hygiene and help to raise the standard of living.

In 1927, Contreras founded *Planificación,* an influential planning journal featuring, in its fourteen issues, essays by Raymond Unwin, Thomas Adams, Ebenezer Howard, John Nolen, and Miguel Angel de Quevedo, among others. The journal also served as a platform for Contreras to advocate for establishing regulatory zoning, as well as for forming a committee in charge of designing a long-term Regional Plan for Mexico City and its Environs (1928). The committee was later appointed to undertake the *Plano Regulador del Valle de Mexico,*[32] the first planning device introducing scientific research based on geographical and topographical data, industrial and economic trends, as well as on social and qualitative assessments.[33]

At the time, planning was portrayed as a scientific discipline: "City planning is much more than the scattered ideas and opinions of residents put together. Planning is a science, or even better, an assemblage of sciences devoted to the city, understood as a physical organism as well as a moral entity."[34] Interestingly, the concept of "planning" was grounded in an *organicist* approach that related the city's functions, including human and spiritual dimensions, to human organs. Therefore, planning was presented as "the physiology of the city or the region, similar to an organism with particular functions in which planning scientifically guarantees its operation"; furthermore, planning would "solve social issues . . . raising the moral standards of its inhabitants through education and through the welfare it creates."[35]

Carlos Contreras was also the founder and chair of the National Planning Association of Mexico, which was intended to be instrumental in the institutionalization and implementation of planning practices. The association included as honorary members such luminaries as Ebenezer Howard, Raymond Unwin, John Nolen, Arturo Soria y Mata, and Thomas Adams.[36] Notwithstanding the members' notoriety, it is conspicuous that no local groups, community associations, or citizens were included in the picture.

Influenced by the *Regional Plan of New York and Its Environs* (RPNYE) of 1929,[37] Contreras's plan embraced suburban cities for both middle-class residential compounds and working-class units, with Colonia Balbuena appearing in 1933 as the first experiment in affordable garden suburbs.

The RPNYE emerged as a planned response to metropolitan problems in North America. It radically restructured "the city according to functional zoning and decentralization." Thomas Adams, as appointed director of the plan, stressed the role of New York City as the cultural and economic center of the region and proposed a "diffused re-centralization" aimed at managing sprawl while containing urban industries at the core of the region. Carlos Contreras was to adopt regional zoning as a "tool for increasing efficiency and integrating work and residence through the careful planning and creation of garden cities."[38] He criticized the disorganized growth of the city and suggested the creation of a more defined and rational organization of space, similar to the RPNYE. This plan was concerned with avoiding what Haig defined as "friction of space" (or spatial diseconomies), which was believed to prevent the correct functioning of cities.[39]

The RPNYE definition of the region and the role of regional planning synthesized Ebenezer Howard's vision along with the urban ecology approach of the Chicago school of sociology.[40] Park and Burgess's famous diagrams presented a spatial hierarchy as the result of the social configuration of the city.[41] However, Adams would turn the description of human ecology into a prescription in the RPNYE, proposing "a community where industrial, residential, and recreational areas are distributed in well-balanced proportions."[42] Furthermore, the RPNYE proposed the integration of satellite cities made up of neighborhood units, business, industries, and open spaces connected by overlapping systems of parkways, canals, and walkways.[43] The plan explained that "neighborhoods were based on the Radburn principle but were accessible to adjacent offices and factories by public transportation."[44] It also stated: "What is called a well-balanced community is one in which these functions [industry, business and residence] are so related as to produce the highest efficiency, the most wholesome living conditions, and the greatest economy in work and travel."[45]

In this period, zoning principles heralded by the International Congresses of Modern Architecture (CIAM) had already attracted attention in a number of countries. The official statement of its preparatory congress of

1928 read: "Urbanism is the organization of all forms of collective life within the city and the countryside. Urbanism cannot be determined by aesthetic considerations but rather exclusively by functional demands. It is the prime duty of urbanism to order functions: housing, working and leisure."[46] Likewise, Contreras referred to the urban plan as a document expressing the "functional life of the city" using biologistic analogies: "the flow through arteries" for roads, boulevards, and canals; the possibility of "breathing" through parks, gardens, forestlands, and reserves; and "digestion and disposal" for food and water supply as well as sanitation and sewage. However, Contreras adopted a rational, official explanation of development and planning, and contributed to equating the latter with the "growth and flourishing of cities within an equilibrated fashion dictated by the regulatory plan." On the other hand, Contreras's vision of participatory practices in planning relied heavily on the residents' "cooperation," possibly related to the nation-building spirit of postrevolutionary times. In his view, each major planning initiative built upon the concerns of small citizen groups engaged in the transformation of the city: "It is only through the organization of active citizens of goodwill, eager to serve their city and country, that we shall bring up private investments to the city."[47]

Contreras considered the issue of identity and modernity, criticizing the relocation of the working-class population into brand-new functionalist homes. He argued that before deciding what kind of housing models to use, it was particularly important to address the "idiosyncrasy of the people, the needs of the Nation [and even] of the Mexico City question."[48] Carlos Contreras advocated for the creation of public spaces and provided a set of creative solutions: from an agricultural park in Texcoco to the creation of extended parkways along the main avenues like Insurgentes and Tlalpan. He also proposed the expansion of major existing parks such as Chapultepec and the Alameda, the creation of new plazas and parks that—surprisingly for the time—involved public and private initiatives. A major concern for Contreras was the establishment of a major system of forest conservation districts within the city (including Coyoacan, Xochimilco, and Mixcoac) as well as a park system surrounding the metropolitan area (Desierto de los Leones–Los Remedios–Milpa Alta–Xochimilco–Texcoco). The rehabilitation of landscape features was another way to conserve them. Contreras therefore proposed to recover the city's canal network and fluvial transportation system (at the time a real option), to turn old railroads into linear parks, and to create promenades along existing creeks in Chapultepec Park.

In 1933, he authored a master plan for Mexico City that has been highly influential ever since. Although the plan was only partially implemented at

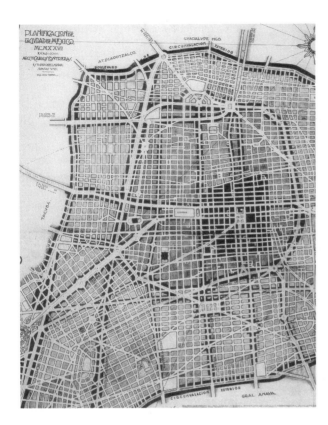

Carlos Contreras's master plan for Mexico City, 1933. ("Estudio preliminar para la planificación de la Ciudad de Mexico, 1927," in Carlos Contreras, *Plano regulador del distrito Federal* [Mexico City, 1933].)

the time, many of the proposals were built in later stages such as the Circuito Interior highway, the extension of Pino Suarez and 5 de Febrero avenues, as well as the construction of several parkways. Contreras proposed electrifying the train system to nearby Cuernavaca in order to foster suburban residential developments along the way, particularly in Lomas de Chapultepec, Mixcoac, San Angel, and Tizapan. He paid special attention to the provision of public spaces, plazas, parks, and forests. Private parks were incorporated into the public domain; new parks were created from scratch or resulted from land-use changes. This was the case with Noche Buena Park, which was created on the grounds of a former brick factory. Cemeteries were labeled "commemorative parks"; old parks such as Chapultepec and Balbuena were remodeled; reforestation programs in the outskirts of the city were implemented (Lomas de Tacubaya, Santa Fe, Ajusco, Lomas de Chapultepec); and sports clubs flourished. The role of the state in reinforcing the master plan was to improve the city's infrastructure as a basis for industrialization. It is widely acknowledged that the physical infrastructure played a crucial role in achieving the Mexican miracle of the *steady growth* period (1940s to 1970s).

"The embellishment of a major city, capital of a Nation, is not an issue of academic or abstract beauty, but suggests a cultural element with which to assert our national identity."[49] These opening remarks of Mayor Aaron Sáenz revealed the planning agenda immediately after the impasse of the agrarian revolution. They expressed an explicit commitment to aesthetics, culture, and identity and portrayed a heartfelt desire to define what it meant to be Mexican.

In this context of postrevolutionary Mexico, Carlos Contreras represented the international approach to planning that drew ideas from ongoing plans and programs around the world and promoted the establishment of urban legislation, construction codes, and regulations within the Mexican legal framework. He organized the Sixteenth International Congress on Planning and Housing in 1938 by direct appointment of the president Lázaro Cardenas, which served to elevate the status of planning to the highest levels of public policy in the country.

Conclusion

Green public spaces played a substantial role in the transformation of Mexico City in the early decades of the twentieth century. The planners who had a long-lasting impact on the configuration of Mexico City's urban fabric envisioned nature as an instrument with which to achieve modernity. Their aspiration to modernize the city was grounded mostly on practical concerns for public health and welfare and on ideological interests. Quevedo's vision of modernity, for example, was closely linked to the conservation of nature because it could provide the metropolis with representative grandeur and would preserve nature for future generations. He consistently advocated for environmental awareness and was Mexico's foremost environmentalist, even if this type of activism did not exist when he started his public service at the turn of the twentieth century.

Quevedo's, Contreras's, and Cuevas Pietrasanta's visions for the city pushed the limits of planning and urban politics in order to integrate nature in the form of parks and gardens into the urban fabric.

Notes

1. Arturo Almandoz, "The Emergence of Modern Town Planning in Latin America—After a Historiographic Review—," paper presented at the Finnish Research Seminar on Latin America, Helsinki, 2003.
2. Cuevas Pietrasanta was influenced by Ebenezer Howard and by Patrick Abercrombie, at-

tending several of Abercrombie's conferences in London and later incorporating these ideas into his own proposals.

3. José Ives Limantour, *Apuntes sobre mi vida pública 1892–1911* (Mexico City, 1965), 97.

4. The international standard for urban area devoted to open spaces was 15 percent.

5. Memoria sobre el Valle de México, su desagüe y saneamiento. Presented to the H. Junta Directiva del Desagüe and sent to the Secretaría de Fomento to be exhibited at the International Exposition of Paris (Mexico City, 1889).

6. Forestier also designed parks and open spaces in Buenos Aires and Havana in the mid-1920s, while Howard had influence only on various garden suburbs for middle and working classes in the 1930s.

7. In fact, his primary concern was health and infrastructures as Quevedo attended international conferences on hygiene in Paris (1900) and Berlin (1907), where he collected ideas on systems of parks and public spaces.

8. Miguel Angel de Quevedo, "Los espacios libres en las ciudades y su adaptación a parques, jardines y lugares de juego," *Revista Planificación* 2, no. 5 (1934).

9. M. A. de Quevedo, *Espacios libres y reservas forestales de las Ciudades: Su adaptación a jardines, parques y lugares de juego. Aplicación a la Ciudad de México* (Mexico City, 1911).

10. He even shared Jean-Jacques Rousseau's moral concerns about human congestion as a source of corruption.

11. The size of the room should be between 215–377 square feet (20–35 square meters), the maximum height for buildings was 66 feet (20 meters), while the corresponding road width had to be at least 72 feet (22 meters).

12. An ideal scheme of having a park not farther away than 1,640 feet (500 meters) from any given point in the city was sought.

13. For a detailed account of the celebrations, see M. Tenorio Trillo, "1910 Mexico City: Space and Nation in the City of the Centenario," *Journal of Latin American Studies* 28, no. 1 (1996): 75–104.

14. Quevedo, *Espacios libres*.

15. J. C. N. Forestier, *Grand villes et systèmes de parcs, France, Maroc, Argentine* (1908; Paris, 1997).

16. "Las primeras hiladas para nuestro arte cívico," in *Anuario de la Sociedad de Arquitectos de Mexico, 1922–23* (1923).

17. *Mexico City Monthly Review*, supplement, *El Pulso de Mexico*, La Tolteca, Compañía de Cemento Portland, 1925, 20–21.

18. In 1902, Quevedo, Mariscal, and Galindo worked together on the "Embellishment Commission," and in 1903, Galindo was appointed as chief director of the Public Works Division.

19. N. Mariscal, "Arquitectura del paisaje," *Arte y Ciencia* 11 (1905): 154–57.

20. Quevedo stressed the scenic and recreational value of landscape and forestlands, while also considering these ecosystems to be biologically indispensable.

21. *Constitución Política de los Estados Unidos Mexicanos* (Mexico City, 1917).

22. *Mexico Forestal* 1 (1923): 1.

23. In Mexican legislation, a preliminary law embodies the broad guidelines while the Reglamento (code of norms) addresses the specific operation of such a law.

24. Quevedo, *Espacios libres*, 395–96.

25. Such as the "dust bowl" phenomenon, which became a major concern for subsequent administrations in the United States.

26. As Manuel Perló notes, during the Cardenas administration it is estimated that more than

100,000 people lived in illegal settlements and were not considered or mentioned in the planning realm.

27. For example, through the endorsement of indigenous forestry cooperatives.

28. Representing 75 percent of the actual national parks system and selected for its scenic beauty, recreational potential, and environmental value.

29. In a letter to Cardenas, Quevedo expressed his satisfaction at "having positioned the country among the most civilized."

30. Translated as "Planning the Republic of Mexico."

31. Even Adams and Mumford mentioned at the time that zoning was to be considered as a "preliminary step in planning."

32. Translated as "Regulatory Plan of the Valley of Mexico."

33. It is worth noting that the chief planning consultants for this plan were Edward H. Bennett (assistant to Daniel Burnham in the plan for Chicago), and Jacques H. Lambert (consultant for the New York, Chicago, and Washington plans).

34. Carlos Contreras, *Revista Planificación*, no. 3 (November 1927).

35. Ibid.

36. An important event was the International Planning Conference held in New York in 1925, which was attended by a high-profile delegation from Mexico, including Federico Mariscal, Vicente Lombardo Toledano, José Luis Cuevas Pietrasanta, Carlos Obregón Santacilia, and Carlos Contreras.

37. Contreras acknowledged that "from April 1919 to April 1925, I've been studying and documenting planning issues related to the *Regional Plan of New York and Its Environs.*"

38. T. Adams, ed., *The Regional Plan of New York and Its Environs*, vols. 1–7 (New York, 1929).

39. Robert M. Haig, "Major Economic Factors in Metropolitan Growth and Management," in *The Regional Survey of New York*, vol. 1 (New York, 1927).

40. Andrew A. Meyers, "Invisible Cities: Lewis Mumford, Thomas Adams and the Invention of the Regional City, 1923–1929," *Business and Economic History* 27, no. 2 (Winter 1998): 294.

41. Ernest Burgess, "The Growth of the City", in *The City*, ed. R. Park, Burgess, and R. Mckenzie (Chicago, 1925).

42. Ibid, 546–47.

43. Ibid, 327.

44. Ibid, 569.

45. Ibid, 340–41.

46. Eric Mumford. *The CIAM Discourse on Urbanism, 1928–1960* (Cambridge, Mass., 2000).

47. Carlos Contreras. *Plano regulador del distrito Federal* (Mexico City, 1933).

48. Carlos Contreras, "El problema de la habitación rural, urbana y semiurbana," *Revista Mexicana de Ingeniería y Arquitectura* 17, no. 5 (1939).

49. Saenz Aarón, *Gobernar a la ciudad es servirla*, Informe del C. Jefe de Gobierno del Distrito Federal a la (Mexico City, 1934).

Part II

Nature and Urban Identity

Mediterranean Reflections

Reconstructing Nature in Modern Barcelona

Gary McDonogh

The sea has been for Catalonia the principal artery of its very blood. Thus, Catalonia appears powerful in times when it enjoys preponderance over the sea, and decadent when the Mediterranean ceases to be the central sea of the known world.
—Joaquim Pla Cargol, *La terra Catalana*

Among the most striking transformations of contemporary Barcelona, in both urban culture and urban nature, is the city's "return" to the Mediterranean. Barcelona long has been a port city whose commerce, politics, and culture have depended on the Mediterranean. Its early links to Carthage and Rome were followed by its medieval and early-modern status as the capital of a maritime empire, and its nineteenth-century renaissance as a commercial-industrial metropolis tied to Havana, Manila, and New York. Over the centuries, artists, journalists, scientists, planners, and politicians have invoked the sea and its littoral ecosystem in both pragmatic activities and abstract visions. Nevertheless, in the last four decades, Barcelona's leaders and citizens have transformed the former working port into a focal point, "a new '*plaça mayor*' for leisure activities in the city."[1]

Renovated and expanded parks, and miles of beaches reclaimed from industrial pollution have redefined the spaces of city and nature. They have been amplified by a vivid pedagogy of "nature" in the city's museums—including a 2009 museum focused on sustainability—in multiple publications, and through an active Web site (www.bcn.es).[2] Barcelona's leaders evoked the Mediterranean visually and metaphorically in the opening ceremonies of the 1992 Summer Olympiad; a decade later, the 2004 Universal Forum of Cultures showcased redeveloped coastal spaces as ecological exhibits and prime real estate, presenting the Mediterranean as a global foundation from which to envision the twenty-first-century city.[3]

Barcelona Harbor 2009. (Photo by the author)

Yet, this "cara al mar," as many Barcelonans have pointed out, also my-thologizes the Mediterranean, distancing the imagined city from its ecologi-cal history. It conceals, for example, the transformation of the industrial city that had used the sea as its highway and sewer into a tertiary metropolis dominated by consumption, leisure, international exchanges, and migrant labor. For centuries, Barcelona's walled seafront revealed citizens' long-standing ambivalence toward the Mediterranean as a source of traders *and* pirates, food *and* armadas. Even the port now seen as a ludic space was de-scribed more darkly a century ago: "The Port of Barcelona is worthy of the second capital of Spain. Its most sumptuous feature is the water of the sea. Its principal adornment, the filth floating on its surface."[4]

Modern imagery, pedagogy, and planning entail specific albeit diverse constructions of what nature is in and for the city. These discourses often value selected elements of "nature"—especially climate, water, mountains, and cultivated vegetation—while overlooking fundamental transformations in fauna, fire, soil, and geological formations created by millennia of human interactions.[5] Interpretations of nature also reinterpret processes that have united "city" and "nature" for centuries. The very port that embraces the Mediterranean has entailed centuries of construction, surrounding and tam-ing the sea. Other urban terrains have shifted from agricultural lands to fac-tories to real estate. Over time, nonetheless, the lives of the city and its citi-zens have been intertwined with the sea and the Mediterranean littoral, its geography, climate, social organization, and cultural meanings. The region's ecology, filtered through social and cultural transformations, has shaped the form, lives, and policies of the city. Barcelona's claims as the capital of a maritime geographical region are different, yet enmeshed with nationalist claims for rights and sovereignty in this political territory.

This essay explores Barcelona's changing relationships with the Mediterranean as physical space, social place, and cultural imaginary since the Industrial Revolution. It first contrasts evocations of the Mediterranean as form and cultural statement in the work of two architects of the nineteenth and twentieth centuries. Antoni Gaudí (1852–1928) explored the Mediterranean in *modernista* monuments for patrons of a renascent economic and cultural elite who participated in the rebirth of Catalan nationalist politics. Nicolau Maria Rubió Tudurí (1891–1981), better known as a landscape architect, exemplifies a subsequent movement, *noucentisme,* which both embellished the modern city and reenvisioned its global presence. In both cases, erudite discourses arose in counterpoint to claims of other classes including anarchists who used the sea and land in their everyday life and considered the garden city as a space of social transformation. Finally, I compare these forms and discourses with twenty-first-century representations of the Mediterranean that incorporate scientific and architectural discussions of ecology and lifestyle, exemplified in the 2004 Universal Forum of Cultures. A Mediterranean identity has become integral to the international marketing of global Barcelona. Yet, this discourse of nature intersects inevitably with the Mediterranean as a social space and with ambiguous meanings of class, nation, and power in Barcelona, the Spanish state, and the European Union. Here, contemporary issues of humans in nature resonate with earlier working-class claims to nature and justice.

These analyses derive from my anthropological fieldwork in Barcelona since 1975 and readings in history, philosophy, architecture, geography, sciences, literature, art, and journalism of that city as well as broader discussions of the city and nature worldwide.[6] Within this discussion, Barcelona, as a city rich in localized literate cultural debates in Catalan (and Castilian) and in concrete expressions of art, politics, and identity, proves particularly instructive. The city offers a relatively circumscribed world of discourses in which scientific, aesthetic, political, and social discussions of nature have been created and used by diverse agents, and toward divergent ends.[7]

Debating the Mediterranean as a Space of Historical Identity

While Barcelona had achieved an important position as a Mediterranean capital in the Middle Ages and Renaissance, its fortunes declined over the centuries of its unification into a Spanish state increasingly dominated by

Castile.[8] As Catalonia reemerged in the nineteenth century as a European industrial power in a backward Spanish state, renewed nationalist identities coalesced around history, language, culture, and place. A sense of place, in the most literal sense of the natural environment, pervaded the urbane recovery of mountain and maritime traditions, Pyrenean Romanesque architecture, rural law, and folklore studies as well as elite landscapes, arts, literature, and politics. Relations of nature and place shaped everyday life whether in the scientific analysis of weather through voluntary collection of data mapping Catalan territories or in the bilocalism of bourgeois families who traded residences in the hot city for summer mountain retreats.

These relations of nature and the city underscored fundamental conditions of power as well. Scientific knowledge differed from proverbs based in centuries of practice and religious calendars. While elites escaped for months with baggage and servants, workers and shopkeepers reached only the nearby slopes of Montjüic.[9] Finally, claims about ownership and experience in Catalonia differed from nationalist claims to speak for and rule Catalans who lived there.

Industrializing Barcelona, in fact, occupied an uneasy position within Catalonia, which stretched from the Pyrenees to southerly coastal points. In nineteenth-century revivals, the "truly natural" Catalonia resided in the saw-edged rocks sheltering the patronal Abbey of Montserrat or the familiar household customs and cuisine of rural Pyrenean *masies* (homesteads) enshrined in Catalan folklore, not in the city.[10] Barcelona sullied its oceanfront, paved its streambeds, carved up its mountains, and swallowed farms and other green spaces with reckless abandon. By the mid-nineteenth century, Barcelona, strangled by its early-modern walls, became known for urban congestion and its attendant diseases. Hence, Pere Felip Monlau (1808–1873), a Barcelona physician, in his influential pamphlet *Abajo las murallas!!!* (Down with the Walls!!!) characterized cities as "monsters of nature" (mónstrous de la naturaleza) where "the air is noxious, the water corrupt, the land weakened and exhausted for large distances. Life in them is necessarily shorter, the sweetness of abundance little known and the horrors of necessity and misery extreme."[11] Later, the planner-reformer Ildefons Cerdà began his geometric revisions of the urban fabric with a survey of the mortality decimating working-class neighborhoods, proposing a new, expansive city of green spaces, air, health, justice, and modernity.[12]

Meanwhile, nineteenth-century elites translated their economic success into political demands for local control and respect within the Spanish state. They also sought to make Barcelona—the *cap i casal* (head and hearth) of a

Mediterranean nation dominated by the Spanish state—into a more fitting European capital. One strategy of embellishing the city entailed the creation of boulevards, gardens, and parks, reading "formal nature" into the city. Another cosmopolitan model entailed the planning and expansion of the city, evident in the Eixample (expansion), where regular green spaces and healthy, aesthetically appealing blocks were designed to catch salubrious sea breezes (and Cerdà's egalitarian plans fell victim to real-estate markets).[13] A third strategy, intimately linked to these, was to reenvision the Mediterranean as a mythic landscape for a renewed Barcelona and Catalonia, to claim nature for the nation.

The architect Antoni Gaudí (1852–1926) synthesized concrete and ideological interpretations of the revitalized Mediterranean city within the movement labeled *modernisme*.[14] His patrons comprised the new social elite of the era: families whose wealth had developed through consolidation of industrial and financial entrepreneurship in the mid-1800s. These families negotiated the rights and meanings of Catalonia vis-à-vis the state while defending their own position against a growing working class. Thus, Gaudí built palaces and apartments but also created a chapel for the mill town known as Colonia Güell, sanctifying a domain of familial capitalism. At the same time, his Temple Expiatori de la Sagrada Família (Expiatory Temple of the Holy Family) purported to atone for working-class sins and to reconsecrate Catalonia under the model of the Holy Family (and bourgeois patriarchy).[15]

Throughout his career, Gaudí combined studied craftsmanship and his search for rational structures with his Catalanism, his Catholicism, and his exaltation of Mediterranean nature as a source of structural and decorative inspiration. Gaudí himself wrote of the Mediterranean: "On its shores with their average light—that of 45 percent inclination—which best defines bodies and reveals their form—is the place where the great artistic cultures have flourished because of this equilibrium of light: not too much and not too little because the extremes are blinding and blind men do not see."[16] His Casa Batlló (1905–7) reminds us of the sea in its serpentine curves and dappled azure tiles. In the Sagrada Família, the Mediterranean landscape is sere and chthonic, soaring from an otherwise ordinary block of Barcelona's Eixample toward heaven, exalting real and mythical Mediterranean mountains, humans, flora, and fauna. The viewer's imagination travels easily from this church's towers to the rocks cradling the Abbey of Montserrat, while the garden and pool reflecting the temple (designed later by Rubió Tudurí) evoke the rocky coast and vegetation of Mediterranean shorelines.

Gaudí worked with the elite Güells and their family network on many

Reconstructed nature: the Park
Güell 2009. (Photo by the author)

projects around Barcelona and Spain.[17] Perhaps the best known is the garden
city project known as Park Güell (1900–1906). This 37-acre (15-hectare) hill-
side domain, roughly 5 miles (8 kilometers) from the port, opens to the city
with fairy-tale gatehouses and a ceremonial staircase leading to a market
space and an undulating polychrome plaza above. Beyond this central complex, winding avenues cross the park, sustained by multilevel arches and columns that recall the rocky peaks of the Pyrenees. Petrified paths and Mediterranean palms overlook the striking contrast of the ordered development
that the Cerdà plan had imposed on the plain below, guiding the observer
toward the sea. Imitating Mediterranean nature, Gaudí re-created it as an
aesthetic space as well as a social and political one. The emphasis on air
and movement in the garden city, for example, allowed elite escape from the
pathogenic city.[18] Still, this park failed as a development project, whether
because of difficulties of access or due to its motifs of nationalist identity
that were too strong for the Catalan bourgeoisie.[19] After short-term use as a
suburban residence, the Güells donated it in 1922 to the expanding city. Yet,
questions about the garden city as natural and political space endured.

Mediterranean nature took on different urban dimensions for Nicolau Maria Rubió Tudurí, another architect and political collaborator of Catalan elites. Like Gaudí, Rubió looked to the Mediterranean for inspiration, which he translated into private gardens and public parks. He was involved early on with the ideological currents of *noucentisme,* literally "1900-ism," a term coined by the philosopher and author Eugeni D'Ors around 1906 to characterize a new spirit and political will in Catalonia that followed its early industrialization, labor unrest, and artistic *modernisme.* While generally seen as an artistic and literary movement, *noucentisme* was intimately linked to twentieth-century Catalan bourgeois politics. As such, it fell into disfavor with the dictatorship of Miguel Primo de Rivera (1923–30) and with subsequent right-wing regimes, forcing Rubió into many years of exile.

As an artistic movement, *noucentisme* emphasized order, serenity, clarity, and reason. It took its mythical charter not from the bursting Mediterranean energy of Gaudí but from the ordered Mediterranean of classical Rome, epitomized in an appeal to *Llatinitat*—latinness. (For Catalans, this could also be seen in a fundamental human contrast between *seny* [common sense] and Gaudí's *rauxa,* or demonic spirit.) As Rubió Tudurí designed elegant gardens, created public spaces to frame Sagrada Família, and reformed Barcelona's park system, "Mediterraneanness/ Llatinitat" infused the city with local flora that were hardy, aggressive, and straining to survive, poised against the fundamental elements of water and an ordered geometry of paths and walls. The Mediterranean garden celebrates an extreme ecosystem. It is dry, with plants that withstand the scorching summers and low rainfall of the Mediterranean: succulents, bushes like rosemary, hardy pines, and cypresses (an Islamic touch). Water is necessary to survive, whether bubbling in fountains like at the Alhambra or reposing in still pools (the Catalan *safreig*), but water does not yield lushness. The Mediterranean garden turns silver, green, and brown against a blue sky, and it is rich in odors and sounds. Other colors might be introduced in tiles or furniture, especially if these recalled earlier Arab elements in Spain. Plantings convey a sense of wildness constrained, as in the Garden of Eden, by walls and walkways.[20]

Rubió's garden at Santa Clotilde, for example, was carefully traced "through the chromatic effect of green masses of the trees and minor plants, almost always perennials, acquiring a tone of rigorous homogeneity only broken by the marble whiteness of the statues and busts that fix for us different visual focal points."[21] Unlike the winding exuberance of Gaudí's dry landscape in Park Güell, in Santa Clotilde, simplicity, order, reason, and clarity converge in nature under a Mediterranean sun, while "the apparent naturalness of its landscape plays a part in referring to its place, the Mediterranean."[22]

Rubió Tudurí also brought *noucentista* ideals into the wider spaces of Barcelona in his work on public gardens like Montjüic. As director of parks and gardens for Barcelona from 1917 to 1937 and founder of the city's Escola de Jardineria (1933), he also transformed the park system that shapes the city today. "Any maritime city," he wrote, "can be considered a half city, from the point of view of open spaces, the shore forming the divider of another half city—all of it open space, all open air, field of aquatic games, space of diffusion and healthy exercise. The vital center of the maritime city is next to this middle line, next to the port, not in the geometric center of urbanized space."[23] Rubió's vision placed the Mediterranean at the physical and cultural heart of Barcelona.

Noucentisme as a political movement also extended the Mediterranean beyond Catalan shores. Just as *modernisme* coincided with the Catalan revival within the Spanish state, Oscar Costa Ruibal has shown that *noucentistes* also saw the Mediterranean as a zone of commercial and colonial expansion that recalled Catalunya's medieval glories.[24] Rubió Tudurí brought landscape and pan-Mediterranean culture together in his book *Del paraíso al jardín latino* (1981), which traces the history and meaning of what constituted the Latin garden from Eden through Middle Eastern derivatives and Rome. In it, he claimed that "the genius, the capacity and the force of Latinidad are not simple records and phantasms of the past. They are realities that belong as well to the future and that thus form integral parts of our hopes."[25]

In another work, *La patria llatina: De la Mediterrània a Amèrica,* which Rubió published while in exile in France, he posited Latin identity as a beacon for a new spirit of confederation in Europe, replacing parties and states. Here, as in Gaudí, the Mediterranean became the wellspring of a universal vision, embracing nature and politics and turning them into a new spirit.[26]

While elites debated and re-created abstract Mediterraneans, the sea and land provided livelihoods for fishermen (already moving to smaller ports away from urban contamination), workers around the port, and farmers and vineyard workers outside the city. While it is hard to balance fragmented documentation of their perceptions of the Mediterranean against elite texts, anarchist claims to nature and social justice in this period remind us of alternative visions that existed within a complex city. In his 1992 work on urban planning among Catalan anarchist thinkers between the consolidation of metropolitan Barcelona and the end of the nineteenth century and the Spanish Civil War (1936–39),[27] Eduard Masjuan Bracon argues that activists such as the lawyer Cebrià de Montoliu and the engineer Alberto Martínez Rico sought to use their political beliefs and support among politicized workers to remodel the relations of citizens and nature. Their discourse on nature and health was global, drawing on the ideas of Patrick Geddes, Peter Kropotkin, Elisée Reclus, and Ebenezer Howard. Yet, it also engaged with local problems and nationalist politics in proposing the elimination of central governments, communal ownership of land, and equal rights, offering a new vision of the Mediterranean garden city: as the site of social transformation.

For anarchist Cebrià de Montoliu (1873–1923), for example, the garden city was not a site for bourgeois repose but rather for reformulating human relations. Garden cities, with their small scale and connection to local nature, challenged the dense, highly governed city. The healthy reformation of country life would be further supported by communal ownership, whose stewardship would safeguard community and land. From 1901 onward, Montoliu propagated these ideas in his writings and educational efforts. He also sought, unsuccessfully, to bring them into practice in Catalonia, collaborating with elites like the Güells and the architect-politicians Josep Puig i Cadafalch, Rubió Tudurí, and Lluís Domènech i Muntaner in the Garden City Civic Construction Society (1918–1920). Within two years (during a period of intense class conflict), however, he angrily abandoned his associates and left for the United States. Like Park Güell, this reformist project collapsed shortly before the Primo de Rivera dictatorship (1923–31).

During and after the repression of this dictatorship, nonetheless, alternative ecocommunal ideas continued to influence scientists like the geologist and hydrologist Albert Carsi (1876–1960) and the astronomer Joan Comas (1868–1937). Carsi argued for sustainable development with regard to water as early as 1910. He carried this fight into his role in the Catalan republican government and exile. Masjuan thus suggests rereading science not only as a technical field but also as politicized discourse (which perhaps foreshadows the technocratic ecologism of socialist Barcelona in the 1990s).[28] The garden city model, meanwhile, was distorted to open land to the south into bourgeois developments, where any gardens were strictly private.

Throughout the industrial period, Barcelona's citizens re-created their city as an economic power and political actor, while debating, sometimes violently, their own political divisions. For many, the Mediterranean figured as nature *in and for* the city in multiple ways. For Gaudí, it was place, inspiration, and foundation, intrinsic to his Catalan and Catholic identity and embodied in buildings like Sagrada Família. For his patrons and other adherents of conservative Barcelona nationalism, the Mediterranean shaped the private space of the garden, the civic space of a glorified city, and the ideal albeit political space of a revitalized Catalonia in Spain and the world. An architect and thinker like Nicolau Maria Rubió Tudurí balanced capitalist and political interests with a wider vision. Yet, plans to let these values of the Mediterranean filter down to a wider working-class population and unite them with bourgeois experiences failed, from Cerdà's reforms to Montoliu's plans to claim the garden city for a wider and liberated public. Still, these contests illuminate the multiple origins of public and private constructions of nature in Barcelona today.

The Mediterranean and Barcelona Today: Ecology and Society

After the intense struggles and rapid transformations of the Second Spanish Republic (1931–39) and the Spanish Civil War (1936–39), Francisco Franco's victory imposed a conservative Catholic and "Castilian" regime on Barcelona, Catalonia, and the rest of Spain from 1939 until 1975. This regime changed the conditions of local nature as well as the fora, discourses, and rights through which urban nature might be discussed. While scientists continued to work on climate, architects constructed local housing and buildings, and poets praised the sea and mountains from which many Catalans derived sustenance as well as satisfaction (albeit sometimes doing so in Castilian), any discussions that posited Catalan ownership, distinctiveness, or national rights to nature were severely constrained. At the same time, industrialization, migration, tourism, and unregulated development damaged the water, fouled the air, and scarred the landscape of the city and surrounding areas.[29]

Even under Franco, the new global vision of "nature" offered possibilities for change. While Catalan elites had explored quaint fishing villages and rocky coasts for years, these spaces changed after the 1950s and 1960s as tourists from northern Europe began to frequent Spanish beaches in large numbers. The attire and behavior of these visitors initially scandalized some local residents, but over generations, coastal towns such as Sitges, Lloret del Mar, and Roses boomed while tourists sometimes bypassed Barcelona. Over time, local citizens have accommodated this influx with massive construction, time-share housing, cheap imported souvenirs, and their own claims to a Mediterranean of sea and sun.

Development, however, forced a reconsideration of environmental stewardship, a stance that gained voice and power with a reconstitution of local authority after the death of Franco. In 1976, the early days of Spain's transition to more democratic institutions, Ramon Folch Guillén edited an

800-page tome on the management of nature in Catalonia—*Natura¿ Us o abús?*—that raised questions about the Mediterranean as a zone of conflictive uses. Folch and his colleagues demanded increasing local action to control growth, to manage sewage and infrastructure, and to preserve an environmental heritage for the future.[30]

Concerns about overdevelopment surfaced in local and provincial debates, increasing awareness of the Mediterranean as an ecology threatened by global (and Spanish) development. After the Franco era, the elected socialist mayors Narcís Serra and Pascual Maragall and the autonomous government of the Generalitat developed strong environmental agendas that infused renewed political, scientific, journalistic, and pedagogical discussions.[31] Working with planners, architects, geographers, environmentalists, and citizens' groups, Barcelona administrators have sought to transform "nature's footprint" in the city. Barcelona opened its waterfront and beaches, cleaned the air, and also re-created and expanded the city's park system, opening the "lungs" of the "civic body."[32] Throughout these efforts, the influence of Rubió Tudurí's Mediterranean has once again become clear, especially in the reorientation of the city to the seafront as *plaça mayor*.

Barcelona leaders displayed a transformed industrial port and a new maritime port linking the Olympic Village to the Mediterranean as the city claimed global attention with the 1992 Olympiad. Spatial shifts have been accompanied by newly global environmental discussions as well. In 1997, for example, Barcelona's Centre de Cultura Contemporània sponsored a major exhibit entitled The Sustainable City. Displays juxtaposed high-tech representations of consumerism, massive stacks of postindustrial detritus, and computer imagery that excoriated sprawl and pollution. At the end of its didactic presentations, the exhibit turned to environmental action and policy: a computer lab showcased Barcelona projects and offered Web interaction with other European cities. Thus, the ideological message about threats to and the value of nature became a statement of Barcelona's postmodernity, Europeanness, and civic technology.[33]

Europeanness framed local discourses after the Aalborg Declaration (1994), the charter produced by a pathbreaking meeting in which representatives of European towns and cities assembled to rethink environmental policy and dedicate themselves to sustainable planning.[34] In Barcelona, this agreement resonated with socialist campaigns to modernize and sell the city. The Sustainable City exhibit also contrasted problems from outside with the values of the Mediterranean city, including compactness, decentralization, and climate. Indeed, "Mediterraneanness" itself set Barcelona apart from northern European models: "The Mediterranean city is the perfect terrain for rethinking urban ecosystems in terms of sustainability."[35]

In the late 1990s, as Barcelona leaders began promoting the 2004 Universal Forum of Cultures, sustainability took on even wider meanings through its linkages with social diversity and dialogues about global peace in a renovated industrial site along the Mediterranean.[36] For those who attended the Sustainable City exhibit or the 2004 Universal Forum of Cultures, however, admonitions about recycling, sustainability, and harmony inevitably competed with other visions of nature as an object of consumption in real estate and travel magazines and in materials touting Catalan golf courses or beaches for European visitors. In fact, the designer/consumer ethos that has reshaped Barcelona since the Olympics represents a sustainability paradox: a world's fair selling sustainability to tens of thousands of visitors while using it as a launching pad for further urban expansion.[37]

New valuations of Barcelona as a Mediterranean eco-city thus have regenerated contradictory discourses about the uses, balance, and meanings of nature. The apparently paradoxical positions of autonomous socialists championing tourism and consumption in the name of nature for concerned citizens who drive cars on crowded highways to sprawling seaside developments remind us that the elements and themes from past events, policies, and writings distilled more complex everyday contradictions. In grappling with human nature as another facet of the Mediterranean, Barcelona has also produced incomplete and conflictive readings.

Noucentistes saw the Mediterranean Sea as a field of expansion for Barcelona, physically and economically. The Olympic opening ceremonies brought thousands of Barcelonans dressed in Gaudí-esque wavy blue collars onto the field of the Olympic Stadium to represent the sea through which Hercules marched to a new land. Later in this highly abstract, orchestrated piece, a ship crossed the sea, battling oceanic demons of plague, war, and famine before finding safe harbor. Here, the Mediterranean as a place of danger converged with the Mediterranean as a channel of communication and culture, linking older civilizations to newer ones, claiming that heritage and pedigree for the host city. These images were broadcast to audiences around the world.

After millennia of war, pirates, trade, and human movements, Catalonia has sought to reclaim primacy in the human Mediterranean. Modern Catalan politicians have looked to the Mediterranean as a southern space that balances both the politics of the European Union—dominated by countries to the north—and the formerly centralized Castilian governance of the

Spanish state. Conferences like the Generalitat de Catalunya's 1989 International Symposium on Human Movements in the Western Mediterranean, sponsored by the Institut Català d'Estudis Mediterranis, highlighted these themes in academic and political terms. There, Jordi Pujol, then president of the Generalitat (from the conservative Convergencia i Unió Party), welcomed visitors by noting that "the privileged geographic situation of Catalonia permits it to aspire to being a bridge between Spain and Europe, between the Mediterranean and the center of Europe."[38] As the site of yet another conference, Barcelona lent its name to the Barcelona Process and Barcelona Declaration of 1995 that established circum-Mediterranean governmental commitments to peace and stability, an emergent free-trade area, and sociocultural exchange. The Universal Forum of Cultures in 2004 vaguely drew on Arab architectural influence to create a social space, the *haima*, that showcased exhibits on war, water, biodiversity, and fair trade, as well as a food court. It also sponsored entertainers, visitors, and dialogues on immigration and other cultural issues. As in the ideology of the sustainable Mediterranean city, cultural and design links to the south provide a counterweight to the power of the north.

While contemporary conferences, declarations, and public events have evoked the Mediterranean as shared social and cultural space, trajectories in the Mediterranean passage remain profoundly unbalanced. Barcelona tourist agencies tout travel to North Africa, and the Catalan fishing industry has made good use of fishing grounds off Tunisia to supplement the dwindling bounty of its own littoral. But migration in the opposite direction has evoked concern and restriction. In fact, Maghrebi migrants became a social and political issue in Barcelona at the same time that urban leaders were reinventing the city as a cosmopolitan center. Since the 1970s, appeals to universality and diversity have contradicted complaints about Arabs (*"moros"*) crowding poorer areas of the city, taking on menial jobs and introducing crime and drugs as well as differences of religion, culture, and society, a debate playing out across Spain and Europe. Ironically, many of these new immigrants settled in portside zones like the Raval or the Ribera.

Over subsequent decades, trans-Mediterranean migration and tens of thousands of North Africans in and around Barcelona (whose province is home to 20 percent of all Moroccans in Spain) have met varied responses. Schools and government agencies have promoted efforts to integrate new migrants, especially children and women, including their incorporation into Catalan nature through sports and excursions into the countryside. Some have expressed concern about the possible threat to Catalan cultural values in such a global city. Meanwhile, gentrification has tended to eliminate areas of concentrated settlement like the Raval, sometimes replacing tenements with more "open" spaces where "nature" acts as a buffer. As Barcelona public agencies celebrate diversity in ritualizations of ethnicity, immigrants themselves continue to raise questions about their employment, medical care, and civil rights. In this sense, the human Mediterranean continues to create many local issues in Barcelona.[39]

Responding to these long-term issues, another group, the Fòrum Social del Mediterrani, an offshoot of Porto Alegre's World Social Forum, posited an image of the human Mediterranean that recasts the image of the garden to overcome social contradictions: "How can we make the Mediterranean into a new Andalusian garden for the twenty-first century? A garden where flowers from here and there mix, where odors mingle to exhale a strong, exquisite aroma. A garden where the joy of living, of equality, of conviviality, of fraternity, of liberty and democracy open perfectly?"[40] Here, the malleability of discourses of nature and the city appears once again as leaders grapple with the city's position in the human and physical Mediterranean of the future, and as Barcelonans debate what natures and cities they may own, must protect, or might share.

Conclusion

Interpretations of nature and the city in Barcelona, whether through *modernista, noucentista,* or anarchist prisms of the early twentieth-century or contemporary debates and manipulations of ecosystems and human flows, prove complex and contradictory. These cultural constructions are embedded not only in the sea, climate, rocks, and flora of Barcelona and its environs, but also in its human formations—class, race, culture, gender, architecture, and politics of the nation, state, and world—that shape the valuation of the natural world as a whole or in different, abstract parts. Permeating these discussions, nonetheless, are three primary themes: the tension between nature as a source of danger and one of wealth, the constructions of divisions between the natural and human world, and the changing location of the Mediterranean in a global context.

Within the first theme, Barcelona's history as a Mediterranean city has included many dangers—pirates, invading navies, storms, drought, fire, and diseases. Yet, Mediterranean ecosystems also provide the basis for healthy livelihoods and the creation of wealth through fishing, agriculture, trade, and, more recently, tourism (whether or not this is sustainable). These polarities are meshed through the human ability to "control" nature, whether by harvest, defense or the technological and visionary re-creation of the city. Even so, "nature" often appears to defy these controls, whether in historic plagues, recent droughts, or the fires that sweep Catalonia each summer.

In many texts and buildings, nonetheless, the separation of nature from humans contraverts the rich symbiosis described by scholars of the Mediterranean and the admonitions of urbanists and ecologists who have eschewed such artificial boundaries. The land, sea, and air around Barcelona have been re-created through centuries of human care and exploitation. These features have become conceptually separated in perceptions and policies of the Mediterranean and in their implications for culture, planning, and human rights. Furthermore, the Mediterranean region does not correspond to political and social boundaries that determine its governance and the re-creation of its cities and ecologies. This has led to the problems that current administrations and pedagogies now face.

Finally, the Mediterranean, over centuries, has weathered its own changing positions in global cultural geography. Beyond its values as highway, plain, and boundary, this *mare nostrum* occupied the center of a "world" for millennia, but has become peripheral in political and economic terms in recent centuries. As Joaquim Pla explained decades ago in the textbook for Catalan schoolchildren from which this essay's epigraph is taken: "The sea has been for Catalonia the principal artery of its very blood."[41] This onetime image for schoolchildren resonates with today's Catalan strategies in European politics and with Catalan attempts to embrace the Mediterranean in cultural pursuits.

Images and meanings of the Mediterranean in Barcelona thus recall historical discourses, reshaping and transcending them. Although Barcelonans' readings of the city and nature embody divergent local and global positions and strategies, the continuity of "nature" in these readings underscores continuities in Barcelona society, culture, and politics. Through this analysis, the discourses of nature and the interventions to shape nature in the city appear as convergent ways of seeing and acting on city and nature. The analysis reveals multiple Mediterraneans evolving with complex Barcelonas and their worlds.

Notes

Epigraph in the original Catalan: *El mar ha estat per a Catalunya com l'artèria principal de la seva sang. Per això Catalunya apareix potent en els temps en què arribà a gaudir de pre-*

ponderànci en el mar, i apareix decaiguda quan el Mediterrani deixà d'ésser el mar central del món conegut.

1. Pascual Maragall, *Refent Barcelona* (Barcelona, 1986), 14.
2. See Ajuntament de Barcelona, *Urbanisme a Barcelona: Plans Cap al '92* (Barcelona, 1986); Ajuntament de Barcelona, *Barcelona: La Segona Renovació* (Barcelona 1996); and Joan Busquets, *Barcelona: The Urban Evolution of a Compact City* (Cambridge and Rovereto, Italy, 2005).
3. Richard J. Williams, *The Anxious City* (London, 2004), 88–106.
4. Manuel Angelón, *Guia satírica de Barcelona* (1854; Barcelona, 1946), 61. (Original quotation: *El Puerto de Barcelona es digna de la segunda capital de España. Lo más suntouso que en él se observa es el agua del mar. Su principal adorno, la inmundicia que vaga por su superficie.*)
5. This reading draws on a framework from Fernand Braudel, *The Mediterranean and the Mediterranean World in the Age of Philip II* (New York, 1973); Anne W. Spirn, *The Granite Garden* (Philadelphia 1984); Michael Hough, *Cities and Natural Process* (London, 1996); Stephen Pyne, *Vestal Fire* (Seattle, 1997); Peregrine Holden and Nicholas Powell, *The Corrupting Sea* (London, 2000); and L. Leontidou, "Postmodernism and the City: Mediterranean Visions," *Urban Studies* 30, no. 6 (1993): 949–65.
6. In addition to the sources cited above, general Catalan writings on nature that I have found important include Francesc Carreras Candi, *Geografia general de Catalunya* (Barcelona, 1913–18); Carles Carreras Verdaguer, ed., *Geografia general dels Països Catalans* (Barcelona, 1992); C. Carreras Verdaguer, *Barcelona: Temps mediterrani, espai europeu* (Barcelona, 1993); Ramón de Folch Guillén, *Natura ¿Us o abús?: Llibre blanch de la gestió de la natura als Països Catalans* (1976; Barcelona 1988); Margarida Parés, Gisela Puo, and Jaume Terrada, *Descobrir el medi urbà: 2 Ecologia d'una ciutat* (Barcelona, 1985); Salvador Rueda Valenzuela, *Ecologia urbana: Barcelona i la seva regió metropolitana com a referents* (Barcelona, 1995); and Ignasi Aldomà, *La lluita per l'aigua a Catalunya* (Lleida, 2007). I have also learned from the reflections of Richard Forman on Barcelona in *Urban Regions: Ecology and Planning beyond the City* (Cambridge, 2008).
7. Despite these wide-ranging examples, this brief exploration still must omit much of the history, arts, cuisine, science, and political economics of Barcelona. A fuller reading of Mediterranean nature and the Mediterranean city should also incorporate the poetry of Salvador Espriu, the paintings of Picasso and Miró, the nostalgic *habaneres* of coastal towns, and the enraptured performances of Balearic folksinger Maria del Mar Bonet. Food is also a compelling arena of Catalan identity and everyday life, in which ecology and human invention have played out in ingredients, recombinations, and banquets.
8. See J. H. Elliott, *The Revolt of the Catalans* (Cambridge, 1963); James Amelang, *Honored Citizens of Barcelona* (Princeton, 1986); Gary McDonogh, *Good Families of Barcelona: A Social History of Power in the Industrial Era* (Princeton, 1986); as well as Busquets, *Barcelona*, for general background, among many other Catalan, Castilian, and English-language sources.
9. Santiago Russinyol depicts such an expedition from his own ironic upper-class vantage in the classic *Auca del Senyor Esteve* (Barcelona, 1902). This remains an important area for future investigation.
10. See McDonogh, *Good Families.*
11. Pere Felip Monlau, *Abajo la murallas!!!* (Barcelona, 1841), 12. (Original quotation: *[E]l aire es infecto, las aguas corrumpidas, el terreno desustanciado y exhausto hasta largas distancias; la vida es en ellas necesariamente mas corta, las dulzuras de la abundancia son poco conocidas y los horrores de la necesidad y la miseria extremos.*)

12. Ildefons Cerdà, *Teoria general de la urbanización y aplicación de sus principios y doctrinas a la reforma de Barcelona* (1867; Barcelona, 1968–71). See also Ramon Grau, coord., *Cerdà i els altres: La modernitat a Barcelona, 1854–1874* (Barcelona 2008).

13. Ana Cabré and Francisco M. Muñoz, "Ildefons Cerdà and the Unbearable Density of Cities," in *Cerdà: Urbs i territori* (Barcelona, 1996), 37–46; Gary McDonogh, "Discourses of the City: Policy and Response in Post-Transitional Barcelona," in *Theorizing the City*, ed. Setha Low (New Brunswick, N.J., 1999), 328–76; Stéphane Michonneau, *Barcelona: Memòria i identitat: Monuments, commemoracions I mites* (Vic, 2001-).

14. Literally "modernism," but akin to art nouveau throughout Europe and not the twentieth-century International Style (see Fundación Caja de Pensiones, *Antonio Gaudí* [Barcelona, 1993]; J. J. Lahuerta, *Antonio Gaudí* [Barcelona, 1993]; and Gijs Van Hensbergen, *Gaudí: A Biography* [New York, 2001]).

15. McDonogh, *Good Families*, 38–58.

16. From George Collins, *The Drawings of Antonio Gaudí* (New York, 1977): 42, cited in Van Hensbergen, *Gaudí*, 143.

17. McDonogh, *Good Families*. The Güells, however, were not involved in Sagrada Família.

18. McDonogh, "Discourses of the City."

19. Eduardo Rojo Albarrán, *Antoni Gaudí, aquest desconegut: El Park Güell* (Barcelona, 1986).

20. Francisco di Castri and Harold Mooney, *Mediterranean Type Ecosystems* (New York, 1973); Nicolau M. Rubió Tudurí, "De como vaig renovar un jardí, envellint-lo," *Claror* (June 1936); Nicolau M. Rubió Tudurí, *El jardí obra d'art* (Barcelona, n.d.).

21. Josep Bosch Espelta, M. Rubió Boada, C. Dominguez, and Ignasi de Solà-Morales, *Nicolau M. Rubió i Tudurí (1891–1981)* (Barcelona, 1989), 115. See Josep Bosch Espelta, "Rubió versus el paisatgisme llatí," *Quaderns* 151 (1982): 85–90.

22. Ibid., 115–16.

23. Nicolau M. Rubió Tudurí, *El problema de los espacios libres* (Barcelona, 1929), 82.

24. Oscar Costa Ruibal, *L'imaginari imperial: El noucentisme català i la política internacional* (Barcelona, 2002).

25. Nicolau M. Rubió Tudurí, *Del paraíso al jardín latino* (Barcelona, 1981), 11. Earlier, Rubió also had published a work that linked this heritage with Barcelona's future and imperial *noucentisme: Barcelona capital Latina: Historia de una nueva latinidad*, in which he envisioned a confederation of Latin states whose logical capital would be Barcelona (see Bosch Espelta et al., *Nicolau M. Rubió Tudurí*, 110).

26. Nicolau Maria Rubió Tudurí, *La patria llatina: De la Mediterrània a Amèrica* (1945; Montserrat, 2006).

27. Eduard Masjuan Bracons, *Urbanismo y ecologia en Cataluña* (Móstoles, 1992).

28. Ibid.

29. Eduardo Moreno and Manuel Vázquez Montalbán, *Barcelona ¿cap a on vas?* (Barcelona, 1990); Oriol Bohigas, *Barcelona entre el plan Cerdà y el barraquismo* (Barcelona, 1993); Gary McDonogh, "Discourses of the City."

30. Folch Guillén, *Natura*.

31. For example, Rueda, *Ecologia urbana;* and Maria Boada and Luisa Capdevila, *Barcelona: Biodiversitat urbana* (Barcelona, 2000). Decades of pedagogical materials have brought this knowledge into the classroom and to civic action (Parés et al., *Descubrir el medi urbà;* Joan Vilà-Valenti, coor., *Recerques i reflexions sobre el medi ambient a Catalunya* [Barcelona, 1997]; Ajuntament de Barcelona). The city's frequently updated Web site also promotes ecological issues, among many other presentations of the Barcelona model (www.bcn.es). Yet, complaints continue, for example, Ramón Suñé, "Bahía 'cochinos,'" *La Vanguardia Digi-*

tal, March 30, 2006, www.lavanguardia.es/web/20060530/51262594090.html. For discussions of the city's transformation, see McDonogh, "Discourses of the City"; Tim Marshall, ed., *Transforming Barcelona* (London, 2004); Busquets, *Barcelona*; and continuing publications of the Ajuntament (city hall). The Mediterranean perspectives of Francesc Monclús's "Barcelona Planning Strategies: From 'Paris of the South' to the 'Capital of the Western Mediterranean,'" *Geojournal* 51 (May 2000): 57–63, are also of interest.

32. The relationship of city, body, and disease invokes other parameters of city and nature I have explored in Gary McDonogh, "Constructing the Civic Body in Barcelona: Planning, Metaphors and Digressions," *Eleventh Conference of the International Planning History Society Conference Book* (Barcelona, 2004).

33. La Ciutat Sostenible (The Sustainable City), conference, Barcelona, 1998.

34. The Aalborg Declaration, or Charter, became a call throughout Europe for strategic action to promote sustainable growth in cities and towns, to which many Catalan municipalities have agreed (see www.gencat/mediamb/engl/sosten/aalborg.htm for explanations, chronology, and impact in Catalonia).

35. Ibid., 116.

36. www.barcelona2004.org (accessed November 2004; no longer present as a Web site in 2010).

37. See Gary McDonogh, "Learning in Barcelona: Sustainability as Myth and Practice," paper presented at the American Anthropological Association Meeting, Philadelphia, 2009. Here, I have been influenced by work such as Erik Swyngedouw's "Impossible Sustainability and the Postpolitical Condition" (13–40) and other works in *The Sustainable Development Paradox,* ed. Rob Krueger and David Gibbs (New York, 2007).

38. Jordi Pujol Soley, "Discurs d'obertura: Catalunya i la Mediterrània," in *Els moviments mumans en el Mediterrani Occidental,* ed. M. A. Roque (Barcelona, 1989), 33.

39. Walter Actis, Carlos Pereda, and Miguel A. de Prada, *Marroquins a Catalunya* (Barcelona, 1994); Alex Seglers, *Musulmans a Catalunya* (Barcelona, 2004); Gaspar Maza, Gary McDonogh, and Joan J. Pujadas, "Barcelona, ciutat oberta: Transformacions urbanes, participació urbana i cultures de control al barri del Raval," *Revista d'etnologia de Catalunya* 21 (November 2002): 11–131; Gary McDonogh, *Iberian Worlds* (New York, 2008).

40. Fòrum Social del Mediterrani, www.fsmed.info/ct/FSMED-comcult-ct.rtf.

41. Joaquim Pla Cargol, *La Terra Catalana* (Girona, 1936), 38.

German Ideologies of City and Nature

The Creation and Reception of Schiller Park in Berlin

Stefanie Hennecke

Today public parks are an essential part of every big city, and it is hard to imagine city life without them. Often they are described as a retreat from the urban jungles of today's postindustrial cities. Many of these public parks were established in the nineteenth and early twentieth centuries. A park provides evidence of the social conditions and cultural values of its time, and its layout even today can reveal how the relations between city and nature were envisioned by contemporaries. This essay reconsiders the creation and reception of Schiller Park, planned in 1907 in the north of Berlin as an example of linking city and nature under uniquely German conditions. In early-twentieth-century Germany, the ideal of a new union between nature and city or culture was usually connected with a conservative point of view. This ideal was based on a critical attitude toward the contemporary social conditions in industrialized cities like Berlin. The idea of reconciling city and nature thus was still based on the old conviction that modern cities were not reconcilable with nature. If a house or a park was planned and designed in the context of the all-embracing life reform movement (*Lebensreformbewegung*), it was often done not only to bring about social progress and to make life more comfortable but to fundamentally reconfigure society. Today we can appreciate these projects (for example, parks and housing developments) as a benefit to city life. But the conservative character of the vision of a new "natural" society that the authors of these works often advocated is inconsistent with our contemporary ideas of democracy. The horrific consequences—or inherent dangers—of such reform ideas became manifest in National Socialism. In light of this, it is important to analyze the ideological basis of the German reform movement, especially since this ideology, which remained powerful in city planning and open space development throughout the twentieth century, continues to exercise influence to this day.

Schiller Park is still considered the first "people's park" in Berlin and is generally seen as a turning point in the shift toward the modern and functional design of public parks. The process of creating the park, from the first public discussions in 1898 until its completion in 1913, was accompanied by intense debates about the reform of garden design and the inherent social benefits of public open space. The innovations of Schiller Park can be discovered not only in the design itself but also in the process of planning the park and realizing its design. The details of the planning process reveal how a holistic ideal found its way into politics and administration.

Thus far, studies of Schiller Park have concentrated on the external conditions of its genesis, for instance on economic conditions, social and political affairs, and on formal questions of design. For example, since the 1970s, the aspects of the park reflecting social reform have been stressed, while its design and reception history have been neglected. But how did contemporaries envision the place of nature in the city? To answer this question, I analyze and interpret original sources from the professional journals of that time. I examine the discursive structure of the professional debates to elucidate the conception of nature held by the park's planners. What emerges is a striking contrast between the retrospective analyses, which stress the social, political, and aesthetic meanings of Schiller Park, and the contemporary point of view held by its designer and supporters, who anticipated that Schiller Park would contribute to the establishment of a new social order. I describe the status of "nature" within the discourse of city planners, garden designers, and local politicians at the time Schiller Park was planned. In so doing, I hope to add an important dimension to the understanding of how Schiller Park was received by contemporaries and to take a critical look at the possible connections between city and nature from a sociopolitical perspective.

The Retrospective Point of View

Across Europe, industrialization brought about enormous social upheavals, a dramatic increase in urban populations, and the expansion of city limits. Recent scholarly literature describes social conditions in Berlin at the turn of the twentieth century and assumes that the development of public green space was brought about by the poor living conditions of the working class, and by the lack of opportunities in the city for walking, playing, and exercising, for breathing fresh air, and for enjoying the rejuvenating effects provided by natural surroundings.[1] Politicians and landowners, however, are portrayed as being motivated by a desire to increase land values and to ensure social stability.

In 1898, members of the Berlin City Council (Stadtverodnetenversammlung) proposed the creation of a new park in the north of the expanding city.[2] Economic and social motives were also a factor in the planning of the so-called "Park of the North" since industrial problems were especially prevalent in the north of the city. As space was limited, industries had to move farther out of the city, finally settling in what were then still independent communities neighboring Berlin. To compensate for the declining tax yield, the city government had begun to develop the area northwest of the city center to build living quarters for the industrial workforce.[3] A rendering plant and a malodorous garbage dump, as well as bare sand dunes causing windborne sand that was harmful to men and machines, were located on the proposed site for the new park.[4] These factors hindered development of the site. In the context of the planned city expansion, the plan for the "Park of the North" has been interpreted as a way of raising the prices of building sites. The building of parks had already been a useful instrument of speculation to increase the value of the surrounding lots during the period of industrial expansion in Germany and in cities of Europe and North America as well.[5]

Aside from these economic considerations, social, hygienic, and political motives played an important role in the planning of the new park. A 1979 study of the value of preserving Schiller Park offers the following description: "In the beginning of the century social concerns emerged suddenly and strongly. It was recognized that living in densely populated areas was unhealthy and had to be balanced by green open spaces. For the first time meadows had been created for various uses by the people, including the petite bourgeoisie; however in return the state demanded loyalty, something badly needed by the declining upper class of the German Empire of Wilhelm II."[6] Also, several authors argue that the fact that the construction of Schiller Park occurred within the scope of a job-creation program suggests that the park project may have been seen as a way to fight unemployment and thereby promote social stability.[7]

The socially critical attitude toward the planning of the park can be gleaned from these retrospective assessments. The park itself and its assumed social benefits, however, have been viewed almost exclusively in a positive light. Karl Thomanek, for example, writes: "With the creation of Schiller Park an era of public green space began. It was motivated by social concerns and characterized by simple, functional principles of design, which

The "meadow of the schoolchildren" around 1913, shortly after the completion of the park. The stone terrace is in the background. (Bezirksamt Wedding von Berlin, Abteilung Bau- und Wohnungswesen—Gartenbauamt, ed., ". . . wo eine freye und gesunde Luft athmet . . .": Zur Enstehung und Bedeutung der Volksparke im Wedding [Berlin, 1988], 45)

reached its high point in the big People's Parks [Volkspark] of the Weimar Republic in Berlin."[8] The two big meadows, which could be used without restriction, are always described as an innovative or even "revolutionary" novelty of this park.[9] Until then, walking in park meadows was either completely forbidden or strictly regulated. The photos shown in the secondary literature underline this social benefit of the park. Playing children are seen in the "splashing meadow,"[10] in the sandbox, and on the big meadow.[11]

The interpretations of the creation of Schiller Park offered by authors from the 1970s until today represent an external point of view. Their interpretations of nature in cities reflect their own worldview more than that of the planners of Schiller Park. The emphasis on the social benefits of the park can be understood today as being typical of the German literature on city planning of the 1970s and 1980s. The authors use discussions of Schiller Park and its historical context to voice their own interest in the emancipatory aspects of open space development.

The Contemporary Point of View

I would like to interrogate this positive view of Schiller Park as an example of reform-oriented garden design. I do not wish to deny its qualities of use

The "splashing meadow" in Schiller Park around 1920. (Landesarchiv Berlin. F Rep.290–279018)

and design or the social benefit it provided and continues to provide. None-theless, I hope to show that Schiller Park did not represent a progressive view of society. This becomes apparent when we attempt to reconstruct the worldview of Friedrich Bauer,[12] the man who designed Schiller Park. Bauer's views of society were simultaneously informed by progressive and conserva-tive, even antimodern, impulses: his statements concerning garden design were progressive/modern; those concerning society were conservative/anti-modern. Bauer's antimodern-modern worldview is characteristic of parts of the city planning movement in general.

Young garden designers of the period, like Bauer, distanced themselves from the picturesque style of the nineteenth-century landscape garden. In investigating Bauer's statements regarding his own attitudes about plan-ning, I delineate the truly new and modern in so-called reformed garden de-sign and show that Bauer's view of society follows a conservative interpreta-tion of how people should live together. The structure of Bauer's worldview was inconsistent with social emancipation.

Friedrich Bauer used the annotations of his design proposal for the Schil-ler Park competition and several other articles in professional journals to set out some basic statements on garden design. Bauer's approach can be described as holistic. His ideas range from technical details to general state-ments about the state of society, and they are governed by a belief in the harmonic unity of nature and human culture. Bauer draws explicitly on the aims of the Heimatschutz movement (homeland protection movement), especially as articulated by the architect Paul Schultze-Naumburg, a leading figure in the movement. Schultze-Naumburg became famous for his book series *Kulturwerke* (Cultural Works), which appeared during the first decade of the twentieth century.[13] In nine volumes, Schultze-Naumburg confronted examples of good and bad architecture, landscape architecture, and garden design. His efforts were primarily directed at denouncing contemporary design as "empty," "artificial," or "against nature" and then setting examples of contemporary design in opposition to works from the past, which he called "alive," "real," or constructed "according to nature." Bauer fashions his critique of the contemporary state of society and its implications for garden design by referring to Schultze-Naumburg:

> No doubt, the question of gardening is closely connected with all problems of culture confronting our times, problems that demand the examination of conscientious, thorough men. Fortunately right now the understanding of the importance of historical cultural works is increasing, as has been proved by the formation of the Dürerbund and the Union for Heimatschutz. This is accompanied by recognition of the fundamental mistakes and faults of which our superficial time, in spite of its pride in its cultural works, is guilty. It is due to the great and inestimable merit of Schultze-Naumburg and like-minded people that the attention of all sensitive people has been drawn to the stark and glaring contradictions of character and expression between our forefathers' works and our own works. At sites of old and solid culture one can easily answer the question, an important one for us: "How [do] human works fit in nature in harmony, how do they agree?"[14]

Bauer then criticizes the focus of contemporary professional debate on the question of whether gardens should be designed "naturally" or "formally." This debate took place between the old-school garden designers and reform-minded "garden artists," whose views were supported by statements of architects, artists, and art historians.[15] In Bauer's opinion, such distinctions missed the point; he claimed, rather, that "the garden we need must be formal *and* natural, natural though in a different sense than it is understood today within the profession."[16] Bauer was strongly opposed to the picturesque-natural style of garden design. In addition to the usual reproaches that this style was nothing more than a cliché and could not meet the demands of a modern park, Bauer claimed: "I condemn [the natural style] not only as a friend of gardens and art, but also out of sincere love and sympathy for our native culture, with its genuine landscape [*Heimat-landschaft*], to which the natural style stands in crass opposition. Indeed, under the guise of land beautification and cultivation its products destroy much that is *natural* and therefore full of life and let 'landscape-gardens' take its place."[17] This quotation makes Bauer's desire for a unity of nature and human culture very clear.

Bauer's view accords with those expressed by advocates of the reform movement, which sought to connect cultural works with "higher" natural values. With this aim, the reform movement departed from the long-held position that human progress constituted the emancipation of man from his natural surroundings, offering instead the notion that the human capacity for progress was a "natural" ability. Nature had come to represent a lost unity. Furthermore, the unity of nature and man was closely connected to the idea of national uniqueness. Nature became synonymous with home (*Heimat*). Bauer assumed nature to be an "organic" or "harmonious" interplay of the specific locality and its "naturally" occurring living beings. In his writing, nature is the individual expression of single, "naturally" developed geographic localities, their soil, plants, and animals. The unity of nature and human culture depends on "understanding nature": if humans would adapt their cultural work to the individual natural circumstances, culture would grow out of the "nature" of the locality. In this vein, Bauer praises both Schultze-Naumburg and the "works of our forefathers" and their "solid culture." From this notion of cultural and natural peculiarity emerges Bauer's notion of "home-landscape" (*Heimatlandschaft*). A natural home (*Heimat*) develops only if humans yield to the natural geographic peculiarities of the local environment and cultivate cultural progress only as an expression of that "nature." In this way, nature and culture can create local organic entities. In keeping with this view, Bauer considers the nineteenth-century picturesque garden "false" since it was a universal style that had been realized everywhere in the same way without appreciation of the individual peculiarities of its respective location: "Above all," Bauer complains, "it is the garden-landscape's total appearance that shows little regard for the surrounding native landscape, that seldom fits into it without being forced, and that therefore almost always sticks out, lifeless and foreign, just like the vacuous, ostentatious buildings pervasive today. The template for winding paths continues to be forced into the sites of important and unimportant parks alike, and the terrain is embellished according to these curves."[18] "Gardeners don't work the soil according to the very old but forever valid principles," Bauer argues, but, "on the contrary, they deprive the ground of its local peculiarity, of its life because they think it is imperfect, uninteresting, and in need of improvement."[19] Whereas Bauer believes the style of the picturesque garden is "lifeless," "alien," "hollow," or "superficial," he himself aims at a garden design that fits into the nature of home (*Heimat*) "without being forced." He uses the words "simple," "unpretentious," and "functional" to characterize an appropriate garden design. With these words, he relates to the understanding of "functionalist" garden design that preoccupied many architects, artists, and designers at the time: "It is honestly not the point whether one should design straight or winding paths, whether preference should be given to an 'architectural' or a 'natural' ground plan. Rather it should be designed with proper care to be functional and appropriate to human buildings, without striving for effect, and without a glorification of woods; a garden should be designed simply as a *garden*, nothing else."[20]

It is significant that Bauer's argumentation emphasizes the "feeling," "real sense," and "intuitive understanding" of design. He is not talking about an intellectual discourse or about scientific knowledge; rather, he is discussing a sentimental, intuitive harmony of men and nature, a harmony only the sensitive man of culture is able to achieve if he is receptive to the local nature and culture. According to Bauer, cultural achievement is "born," by itself; it "grows" and looks as if it were "natural." Bauer praises medieval buildings in similar terms: "It happens that these old buildings weave tenderly together with the surrounding plants, have grown together in the nourishing maternal soil, their roots strong like those of trees, and for this reason they seem indigenous, so genuinely native and so natural in the true sense. The landscape gardener should look in this direction, and feel, realize, and learn!"[21] Thus Bauer looks not for professional expertise but for the right attitude toward nature. He does not oppose the fact that architects, artists, and other men of culture critiqued garden design because he didn't consider them "unqualified dilettantes," but rather like-minded people engaging in a stimulating dialogue in their search for the new unity of nature and culture: "It should be made clear without prejudice, that architects and painters are not using their professional skills to show off their ability or to extend their sphere of activity into other disciplines, but that as artistically and naturally inclined people, they protest energetically against those so-called gardens that are antithetical to art and nature and act against this intolerable abuse."[22]

This holistic attitude toward a renewal of culture and society can also be seen in Bauer's detailed descriptions of practical garden design: woods should be produced from "few forms of trees and shrubs, expressive of native character. . . . The cultivated trees should be as strong and natural as possible. . . . The flowers . . . must be arranged so as to fit into and submit organ-ically and harmonically to the most significant aspects of form."[23] Bauer's view on people's use of open space fits "organically" into his worldview, even if this is not immediately apparent. In the design for Schiller Park, Bauer calls for a range of possible uses: "This Schiller Park should be dedicated to the necessary recreation of body and soul of the city dweller; it should pro-vide opportunities for walks through fresh greenery, for play, for sporting ac-tivities, for an enjoyment of nature often missed. But it should also offer the chance for serious contemplation and quiet solemnity, and, last but not least, full delight in the exquisite splendor and beauty of the plants."[24]

With this statement, Bauer makes clear that his design concentrates on people and their need for nature, for activity and recreation within nature. This seems to go along with the interpretation of Schiller Park as a project of social reform by scholars writing in the 1970s and later. But there is an obvious difference between Bauer's view of society and the one expressed by later interpreters of his work: As shown, Bauer believes in an organic interplay between nature and culture. "Organic" in his sense means to be expressive of a holistic but hierarchical order, which attains perfection only through the peculiarities of its subordinate individual parts. For this rea-son, in Bauer's view, human cultural activity must comply with the higher measure of nature.[25] This belief results not from rational understanding but from intuition and "true" sensitivity. Indeed, nature in this sense is not a model that can be discussed in a rational way, but rather something that has a metaphysical presence. Nature is seen as a given and not to be questioned. This "organic" worldview has politically conservative foundations and op-poses the democratic ideal of social emancipation.[26] Bauer is not interested in a rational discourse about political equality, freedom, and emancipation. Instead, he wants to recall the "old" knowledge of the forefather's natural way of life. But this act of remembrance should, in his view, not be accom-panied by the restoration of premodern life and societal order. Instead, he argues for what he sees as a "modern" fundamental reform of life and social upheaval. But this modernization has to be done "right," and "right" in Bauer's sense means "natural." In fact, with his design for Schiller Park, Bauer aims for much more than merely social advancement for the working class. He strives for the realization of indigenous culture as a vital contribu-tion to a new, intrinsically German community. For Bauer, man is only a part of a higher entity symbolized by German nature.

The interpretations of Schiller Park written in the 1970s and 1980s were motivated by a desire for improved urban living conditions. They were based upon democratic ideas of freedom and equality, including unimpeded access to and use of public space for everybody. I would argue, however, that this latter concern for social emancipation in the 1970s and 1980s was fundamentally opposed to Bauer's conservative understanding of society, while at the same time it was consistent with his imagined use of open space. The conservative and the progressive ideas of social reform thus overlap in their demand for the free, unregulated use of green space. But the motivations underlying these ideas were very different: conservatives (like Bauer) promoted the integration of man with nature. They believed that nature could heal body and soul. "Correct" and "natural" attitudes and behavior, for example, sports and movement in the fresh air, comfortable clothes,[27] and a healthy diet could enhance nature's benign effects.[28] While the progressives supported many of the same things, they also argued against the discrimination and restriction imposed by a hierarchical society and lobbied instead for equality in everyday life as embodied in the free access to and use of open space.

The Schiller Park Competition of 1907

The public design competition for Schiller Park represented the first such event in the history of Berlin's green-space development.[29] Members of the Berlin City Council most likely used this procedure in order to neutralize the influence of Hermann Mächtig,[30] then the garden director of Berlin. Mächtig was an old-school garden designer and an adherent of the picturesque style considered by then as antiquated and conservative. This so-called "Lenné-Meyer school," or "mixed style," is based largely on naturalistic design that integrates geometric forms.[31] In 1899, Mächtig had already presented a design for the new "Park of the North" that reflected the conventional nineteenth-century approaches. At the turn of the twentieth century, it was common practice for employees of the public park administration to design and supervise the construction of city parks. The change in planning procedure to an independent design competition suggests an open critique of the park administration and the type of garden design it supported. Moreover, the members of city parliament pushed for the "consultation of experts in artistic urban development—even from outside of Berlin—in the jury, in order to thwart the influence of the park administration."[32] Of the fifteen jury members, only four were professional garden designers, a fact that was criticized in the trade press.[33] Apart from Berlin's garden director, Hermann Mächtig, two reform-oriented garden directors, Freiherr von Engelhardt from Düsseldorf and Fritz Encke from Cologne, were invited as well as a number of representatives of other branches of the reform movement: Paul

Schultze-Naumburg; Alfred Lichtwark, art historian, director of a Hamburg art gallery, and a supporter of garden design reform;[34] Max Liebermann, artist and the chairman of the Berlin Secession; Theodor Goecke, editor of the journal *Der Städtebau*; and Ludwig Hoffmann, Berlin's municipal building surveyor and a reform-oriented architect of numerous public buildings in Berlin.[35]

The competition brief did not favor a particular style: "Regarding the design of the park (natural, architectonic etc.) the competitors are completely free." However some innovations in the uses specified for the park were stipulated: "If possible in the south part one should set aside a 3½-hectare (8½-acre) meadow for playing fields for schoolchildren. . . . In the appropriate location a larger meadow (about 3 to 6 hectares) (7½–15 acres) should be set aside for the citizens' general use. The provision of an ice-skating rink should also be made possible."[36]

Out of 105 design entries, the jury awarded the first prize to Bauer for his proposal entitled *Freude schöner Götterfunken* (Joy, Fair Spark of the Gods), a quotation from Schiller's "Ode to Joy." Two submissions with a similar stylistic orientation shared second prize. The jury's deliberations turned into a fundamental referendum on modern garden design. Hermann Mächtig was the most vociferous in defending his point of view, here reported by Alfred Lichtwark: "The old Mächtig, garden director of Berlin, tried everything to derail the decision of the jury. He is a dyed-in-the-wool fanatic, but at the same time a modest man who sees himself as a disciple and, so to speak, defender of his famous predecessor, Garden Director Meyer. [Mächtig's] attitude toward this technically gifted and important designer has hardened into dogma. Within the park commission of Berlin he has an adversary in Liebermann, who has already swept the lukewarm [jury members] toward the new ideas."[37] Lichtwark saw the award to Bauer's work as a compromise between the two tendencies represented by the jury:

> The naturalists like [Bauer], because he relies on meadow and forest edge, and they turn a blind eye if the terrace seems perhaps too severe to them. The stylists are happy that even in the natural part there is a sense of space and because the terrace is a great success. . . . The plan is as simple as Good Morning. No messing around with rocks and ponds and islands, no arrangements that are expensive to maintain except for the flower garden; the whole park open to the public . . . only a great sense of space.[38]

Hermann Mächtig did not submit silently to the jury's decision; only a day later, he submitted his own layout for Schiller Park, a proposal that differed only marginally from his first design of 1899. His proposal still bore the hallmarks of the nineteenth-century style, with its winding paths, groups of trees clustered at the intersections of paths, and numerous little ponds. While naturalistic design characterized the main parts, geometric design forms created the representative surroundings for monuments or ornamental buildings, like a little temple. The meadow playground required in the competition brief here is as small as possible, and is described as meeting the conditions "demanded by the commission for physical education"; in this way, Mächtig justified its presence although it contradicted his aesthetic ideals. Mächtig saw the main purpose of the park he designed as affording a strolling—and therefore genteel—clientele with a spiritually edifying experience: "The park will also serve the higher purpose of cultivating a better understanding of life as opposed to the ever-increasing crass materialism."[39] But Mächtig's efforts to promote his design were not successful.

In January 1909, Mayor Reicke, who had also been part of the jury, supported Bauer's plan and simultaneously rejected Mächtig's proposal by declaring in the Berlin City Council: "Without a doubt, Berlin has the right to be proud of the parks it has created until now. . . . But surely, in matters of art, stagnation runs the risk of regression, and we have said to ourselves: there is no real reason that we should repeat once again what we have already done well in our other parks in Berlin."[40]

With the backing of the municipal politicians, Bauer's plan had the chance to be realized. What was the plan in detail? Compared to Mächtig's competing plan, Bauer's design looks very modern. It follows the instructions of the competition: he planned two large meadows, one for schoolchildren (Schülerwiese) in the east, and one for citizens in the west (Bürgerwiese). The paths and sidewalks encircling the central meadows connect to the surrounding streets. The tree-lined avenues and the monumental terraced garden built on a large sand dune appear as the geometrical elements in the plan. In his commentary, Bauer emphasized how his plan differed from traditional garden design by referring to his choice of plants and to the arrangement of the paths and meadows. The edges of the paths no longer needed to be parallel, and grass did not have to be cut at the edges of the walkways: "The often superfluous and false scrupulousness and excessive maintenance should be limited, and the flawlessness of the path edges and their exact linearity shouldn't be looked after too rigidly. One should carry out the plan without constraint and naively without any exaggeration. Only misuse should be prohibited, but never naturally legitimate and reasonable use."[41] Here we see Bauer's understanding of the "naive" and therefore intuitive

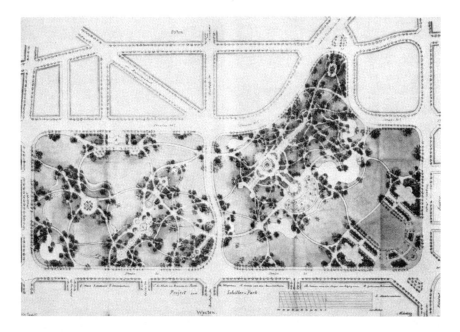

Schiller Park design by Hermann Mächtig, 1899 or 1907–8. (Norbert Schindler, "Gartenwesen und Grünordnung in Berlin," in *Berlin und seine Bauten* [Berlin, 1972], 73)

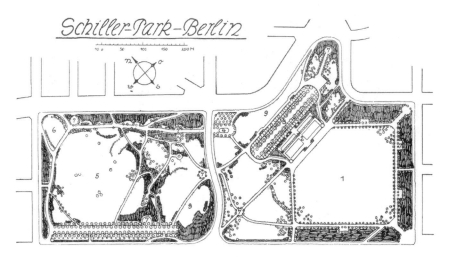

Schiller Park design by Friedrich Bauer, 1908 (Bezirksamt Wedding von Berlin, Abteilung Bau- und Wohnungswesen—Gartenbauamt, ed., *". . . wo eine freye und gesunde Luft athmet . . .": Zur Enstehung und Bedeutung der Volksparke im Wedding* [Berlin, 1988], 38)

Perspectives of Schiller Park design by Friedrich Bauer (1908). *From left to right and from top to bottom:* West of the terrace, clock-tower at the terrace, the edge of the terrace, the rose garden, playground, playing field. (Bezirksamt Wedding von Berlin, Abteilung Bau- und Wohnungs-wesen—Gartenbauamt, ed., *". . . wo eine freye und gesunde Luft athmet . . .": Zur Enstehung und Bedeutung der Volksparke im Wedding* [Berlin, 1988], 39)

inclination of man to associate himself with nature. For Bauer, the human need of nature is an unconscious "healthy" desire: "And what harm is there, finally, if the park in areas of intensive use does not look very 'manicured,' if it only meets the noble purpose of benefitting the healthy and vital instincts of the city's citizens, old and young, and if it gives pleasure to its 'owners.'"[42]

The choice of plants draws heavily on "German species, with only the

The "meadow of the schoolchildren" today with the stone terrace in the background. (Photo by the author)

most sparing and careful use of foreign or exotic trees."[43] Bauer's call for the use of native species was a new issue in professional debates and should be seen as part of the general reformist agenda. Criticism of cluttered decorations and the overuse of exotic plants brought with it increasing calls for the use of native plants. Along the same lines, reformers opposed overbred and highly cultivated flowers and plants and called for a return of the simple and natural forms of herbs and plants. The garden architect Reinhold Hoemann wrote in the journal *Gartenkunst:* "Take the beautiful columbine (aquilegia) with its numerous varieties. Isn't the double breed actually a caricature compared to the noble wonderful form of the simple species?"[44] In the same article, however, Hoemann reveals the ideological superstructure of his views on the choice of plants, which corresponds with Bauer's own ideas on the use of native plants and herbs:

> The new man looks again for an inner correspondence between himself, work and leisure, serious purpose and happy enjoyment of life. All should be united again in one totality; it should be harmonious, in short: life should be lived and experienced truly and honestly. And a life lived in this new way seems to me to become larger and more noble and intrinsic and independent and vital and therefore more worthwhile, even while becoming outwardly *simpler.* . . . Fundamentally it becomes natural like this, because simplicity, plain noble simplicity, seems to me part of the *German character.*[45]

Without suggesting that Bauer offensively supported racist ideas, there is no denying that the superstructure of his theory is consistent with the widespread conservative and nationalistic movement of social renewal that was a precursor of racist National Socialist theories of blood and soil.[46] That Bauer's ideas and designs were received positively by National Socialist ideologists can be seen in his obituary in 1937:

> Bauer helped to consolidate and spread the belief in a German garden, which is the garden created from the experience of the always victorious plant. . . . With his Schiller Park in the north of Berlin he gave to the working comrade for the first time a real "German" park, in which he designed only with the wealth of German flora and in which he created, by sculpting the ground and arranging the plants, a masterpiece that captured, like a folksong, the spirit of German landscape down to the smallest detail.[47]

How exemplary Bauer's thought was for his time can be seen in the similar ideas to be found in the second-prize designs for Schiller Park. Both second-prize entries seek to distance themselves from the much-criticized "picturesque-natural" style by referring to simplicity, functionalism, and an appreciation of the existing terrain. In the proposal entitled *Los vom alten Schema* (Away from the Old Scheme), by Paul Tilsner and Fr. Holoubeck from Düsseldorf, the "usual schematic system of curved paths" should be replaced by pathways along the "existing directions of public traffic through the place" without heavily affecting the "existing unevenness of the terrain." In addition, the edges of the paths did not have to be cut off sharply, the meadows should be enriched by "known native herbs," and the woods should contain mainly native species with "matching undergrowth."[48] The other second-prize plan, titled *Feierabend 2* (After Work 2), by Wille Petznick und Johann Schneider from Essen, refers to the "character of our true home-landscape," which should lead to "pure natural beauty."[49] Thus the jury clearly expressed itself in favor of the "modern"—what I would call antimodern/modern design.

Conclusion

Today Schiller Park is an often-frequented, well-functioning park in a densely populated quarter of Berlin. The park is largely preserved in its original condition of 1913.[50] Giving the impression of a spacious landscape with the massive terrace in its center, the park is easily recognized as a work of the early twentieth century. The "meadow of the schoolchildren" is always full of people playing soccer; the "meadow of the citizens" is used for picnicking and sunbathing. The social problems of the surrounding area can certainly be seen in the graffiti on the walls and the vandalized benches. But, in total, the park seems functional enough to offer space for current recreational needs and robust enough to bear abuse. The existence of a well-functioning Schiller Park one hundred years after its creation might lead one to the conclusion that the problematic ideology of its designer and promoters is interesting today only as a historic peculiarity. After all, the park itself and the types of activities it supports are the decisive criteria for its assessment. Nevertheless, I believe that it is important for us as urban planners, sociologists, and citizens to confront the ideological underpinnings of the garden reform movement played out in Schiller Park.

Let me point to one final example: the competition for the design of another "Park of the North" in Berlin, the so-called Mauerpark, eighty-five years after the Schiller Park competition. Free access to and use of parks and open space has become a given for the people of the twenty-first century. It also has become quite usual to view the role of a city park as more than offering recreational space. Increasingly, city parks are also seen as ecosystems that provide a space for nature, a habitat for flora and fauna. In the 1992 announcement of the Mauerpark competition, the desired ecological effects of the park were enumerated before the recreational needs: "This park will decisively improve the ecological situation and range of recreation areas in this highly dense urban area."[51] The rules of the competition made clear that plants should be "native" and "genuine": "Vegetation of the proper kind for the location, preferably native vegetation, is to be used."[52] Although similar expressions of preference for native plants can be found in nearly all German landscape-architecture competitions, the word "native" no longer carries its former ideological freight. Rather, the emphasis on native plants relates to the plants' ecological viability.[53]

Notes

I would like to thank David Yearsley for his helpful comments and editorial remarks on the English version of this essay.

1. See, for example, the description of Dietmar Land and Jürgen Wenzel in the first part of their monograph about the garden designer Erwin Barth, *Heimat, Natur und Weltstadt: Leben und Werk des Gartenarchitekten Erwin Barth* (Leipzig, 2005); Walter Kieß, *Urbanismus im Industriezeitalter—Von der klassizistischen Stadt zur Garden City* (Berlin, 1991); Bezirksamt Wedding von Berlin, Abteilung Bau- und Wohnungswesen—Gartenbauamt,

ed., ". . . *wo eine freye und gesunde Luft athmet* . . .": *Zur Enstehung und Bedeutung der Volks-parke im Wedding* (Berlin, 1988); and Norbert Schindler, "Gartenwesen und Grünordnung in Berlin," in *Berlin und seine Bauten*, vol. 11, *Gartenwesen*, ed. Architekten- und Ingenieur-Verein zu Berlin (Berlin, 1972).

2. For a reprint of the inquiry, see Grit Hottenträger, "Kommunales Grün—Schillerpark: Nach 1900," in *Zur Enstehung und Bedeutung der Volksparke im Wedding*, ed. Bezirksamt Wedding von Berlin, 34. Among the members of city parliament who conducted the in-quiry was Dr. Rudolf Virchow, professor of medicine at Humboldt University. Virchow was an influential public figure in questions of hygiene and spoke in favor of the building of hospitals and the canalization in the city.

3. Karl Thomanek, "Der Schillerpark," in *Stadt Grün: Berliner Topographien*, ed. Vroni Hampf-Heinrich and Goerd Peschken, vol. 3 (Berlin, 1985), 67–69.

4. Ibid., 67. See also Hottenträger, "Kommunales Grün," 34.

5. Goerd Peschken, "Schmuckanlagen des 19. Jahrhunderts," in *Stadt Grün*, ed. Hampf-Heinrich and Peschken, 50–55.

6. Wolfgang Liedtke, *Untersuchung des Denkmalwertes von Grünflächen in Berlin (West): Schil-lerpark (Berlin-Wedding)*, on behalf of Senator für Bau- und Wohnungswesen of Berlin (Berlin, 1979), 3.1. (This and all subsequent translations are my own.)

7. Thomanek, "Der Schillerpark," 69. Thomanek also mentions the bad working conditions at the construction site and the low wages for the workers.

8. Ibid., 67. Similar quotes can be found in Rainer Stürmer, *Freiflächenpolitik in Berlin in der Weimarer Republik: Ein Beitrag zur Sozial- und Umweltschutzpolitik einer modernen Industri-estadt* (Berlin, 1991); and in a recent work on the value of preserving Schiller Park: Bettina Bergande, *Der Schillerpark in Berlin—Mitte (Ortsteil Wedding): Gartendenkmalpflegerische Analyse und Konzeption*, on behalf of Landesdenkmalamt Berlin, Referat Gartendenkmalp-flege (Berlin, 2003) (e.g., "Schiller Park . . . represents the change from representative and decorative green to social green in the beginning of twentieth century" [9]).

9. Bergande, *Der Schillerpark in Berlin*, 8.

10. Even if the "splashing meadow" had been part of the original Schiller Park design, it was not realized until the idea of establishing public bathing was promoted by the big city planning exhibition in Berlin in 1910. Examples of people's parks in Chicago with "splash-ing meadows" especially impressed the visitors. The Schiller Park design also was shown in this exhibition as an example of a modern city park (Anonymus, "Allgemeine Städtebau-ausstellung Berlin 1910," *Die Gartenkunst* 12, no. 9 [1910]: 155–59; Bergande, *Der Schillerpark in Berlin*, 16).

11. For example, Hottenträger, "Kommunales Grün," 44–45; Thomanek, "Der Schillerpark," 64–65; Marie-Louise Plessen, ed., on behalf of Senator für Stadtentwicklung und Um-weltschutz, *Berlin durch die Blume oder Kraut und Rüben: Gartenkunst in Berlin-Brandenburg* (Berlin, 1985), 165.

12. Friedrich Bauer, garden architect (1872–1937), was very successful in various competi-tions before 1913, winning first and second prizes, for example, for the cemetery in Berlin-Lichterfelde, the cemetery in Mannheim, and the prototype of a private garden, but only his Schiller Park design has been realized. A contemporary describes Bauer as the "inspiration of the garden designers between 1905–1913" (Carl Heicke, "Zum Scheiden Friedrich Bau-ers," *Die Gartenkunst* 50, no. 9, supplement [1937]: 5).

13. Paul Schultze-Naumburg radicalized his critique of culture during the 1920s and 1930s, finally arriving at a racist theory of "German design" elaborated in *Die Kunst der Deutschen*,

ihr Wesen und ihre Werke (The Art of the Germans, Their Character and Their Works) in 1934; and in *Rassengebundene Kunst* (Race-Based Art) in 1937. With these publications, he became a successful ideologist of National Socialist blood-and-soil propaganda. For a list of his publications, see Gert Gröning and Joachim Wolschke-Bulmahn, *Grüne Biographien: Biographisches Handbuch zur Landschaftsarchitektur des 20. Jahrhunderts in Deutschland* (Berlin and Hannover, 1997), 354.

14. Friedrich Bauer, "Gartenbau und Landschaft," *Die Gartenkunst* 8, no. 6 (1906): 110.

15. The "natural" style represented by the old-school garden designers also could be characterized as "picturesque." For a description of the garden style of the nineteenth century in Germany, see the next section of this essay.

16. Bauer, "Gartenbau und Landschaft," 110 (emphasis in original).

17. Ibid., 110 (emphasis in original).

18. Ibid., 111.

19. Ibid.

20. Ibid., 110–11 (emphasis in original).

21. Ibid., 112.

22. Ibid., 111.

23. Friedrich Bauer, "Haus- und Villengärten," *Die Gartenkunst* 7, no. 4 (1905): 53–54.

24. Friedrich Bauer, "Explanation of his Schiller Park design *Freude schöner Götterfunken*," *Die Gartenwelt* 12, no. 39 (1908): 464.

25. For a detailed description of the "organic" view of the world, see the anthology edited by Annette Geiger, Stefanie Hennecke, and Christin Kempf, *Spielarten des Organischen in Architektur, Design und Kunst* (Berlin, 2004), especially the essays by Stefanie Hennecke, "Berlin soll 'wachsen'—Kritik an einem organischen Stadtmodell," 149–64; and Annette Voigt, "Die Natur des Organischen—'Leben' als kulturelle Idee der Moderne," 37–50.

26. For the political implications of the "organic" view, see Martin Greiffenhagen, *Das Dilemma des Konservatismus in Deutschland* (Frankfurt am Main, 1986).

27. For example, Schultze-Naumburg wrote a book about women's clothing: *Die Kultur des weiblichen Körpers als Grundlage der Frauenkleidung* (The Culture of the Female Body as Basis of Women's Clothing) (Jena, 1902).

28. This attitude is encapsulated in a quote from the contemporary youth movement (*Jugendbewegung*), which was not interested in questions of design but in a new orientation of young people's way of life. A statement from a famous meeting, the festival at the mountain Hoher Meißner in 1913, read: "We oppose naturalness, genuineness and straightforwardness to all artificial and unnatural attitudes; we oppose the serious, free feeling of responsibility to all small-mindedness! Instead of petty ambition, upright conviction! Instead of smugness, the joy of youth and receptivity; education of body and strict self-discipline instead of squandering the power of youth!" (quoted in Werner Kindt, ed., *Grundschriften der deutschen Jugendbewegung* [Berlin, 1963], 93).

29. Liedtke, *Untersuchung des Denkmalwertes*, 1.2.

30. Hermann Mächtig succeeded Gustav Meyer as the garden director of Berlin and, by the end of the nineteenth century, had designed numerous ornamented squares and Viktoriapark (Berlin-Kreuzberg).

31. Peter-Joseph Lenné and Gustav Meyer, royal and municipal garden directors, were the designers of Berlin's most important nineteenth-century parks (see, for example, Dieter Hennebo, "Der deutsche Stadtpark im 19. Jahrhundert," *Das Gartenamt* 71, no. 8 [1967]: 382–91).

32. Hottenträger, "Kommunales Grün," 36.
33. See, for example, the critique of Felix von Hartrath, municipal garden director of Mönchen-Gladbach: "I consider the composition of the competition jury consisting largely of non-experts is not unobjectionable" (*Die Gartenwelt* 12, no. 49 [1908]: 584).
34. For Lichtwark's influence on modern garden design, see Helmut Klausch, "Beiträge Alfred Lichtwarks zu einer neuen Gartenkunst in seiner Zeit" (Ph.D. diss., Technical University Hannover, 1971).
35. The members of the jury are listed in *Die Gartenkunst* 10, no. 6 [1908]: 108.
36. Quotes from the advertisement of the municipal park deputation for the Schiller Park competition of September 23, 1907, reprinted in Hottenträger, "Kommunales Grün," 36.
37. Quotes from a letter from Lichtwark to a commission of the Hamburg art gallery (Kunsthalle Hamburg) from Klausch, *Beiträge Alfred Lichtwarks*, 102–3.
38. Lichtwark quoted in Klausch, *Beiträge Alfred Lichtwarks*, 103.
39. Quoted from the design-explanation of Hermann Mächtig, reprinted in Hottenträger, "Kommunales Grün," 41.
40. Quoted in Rainer Stürmer, "Vom Friedrichshain zum Volkspark Rehberge—Kommunales Grün in Berlin," in *Berlin durch die Blume oder Kraut und Rüben: Gartenkunst in Berlin-Brandenburg*, ed. Marie-Louise Plessen, on behalf of Senator für Stadtentwicklung und Umweltschutz (Berlin, 1985), 165.
41. Bauer, "Explanation of His Schiller Park Design," 464.
42. Ibid., 465.
43. Ibid., 464.
44. Reinhold Hoemann, "Die Einfachheit in der Gartenkunst," *Die Gartenkunst* 10, no. 9 (1908): 152.
45. Ibid., 147 (emphasis in original).
46. I refer to the critical analysis of the German discussion of native plants by Gert Gröning and Joachim Wolschke-Buhlman (for example, Gröning and Wolschke-Bulmahn, "The Native Plant Enthusiasm: Ecological Panacea or Xenophobia?" *Arnoldia, The Magazine of the Arnold Arboretum* 62, no 4 [2004]: 20–28).
47. Werner Jänicke, "Friedrich Bauer ist tot!" *Die Gartenkunst* 50, no. 9, supplement (1937): 5.
48. See the commentary by the authors in response to the proposal *Los vom alten Schema* in *Die Gartenwelt* 12, no. 39 (1908): 465–66.
49. See the commentary by the authors to the proposal *Feierabend 2* in *Die Gartenwelt* 12, no. 39 (1908): 466–67.
50. For a stocktaking of the present condition of Schiller Park and changes in it since 1913, see Bergande, *Der Schillerpark in Berlin*.
51. Senatsverwaltung für Bau- und Wohnungswesen Berlin, ed., *Realisierungswettbewerb Sporthalle im Friedrich-Ludwig-Jahn-Sportpark für Olympia 2000: "Mauerpark," Auslobung, Brief* (Berlin, 1992), 8–9.
52. Ibid., 79.
53. For an analysis of the ideological basis of ecology, especially regarding native plants, see Stefan Körner, *Das Heimische und das Fremde: Die Werte Vielfalt, Eigenart und Schönheit in der konservativen und in der liberal-progressiven Naturschutzauffassung* (Münster, 2000).

Race, Recreation, and the Conflict between Public and Private Nature in Twentieth-Century Los Angeles

Lawrence Culver

The growth of modern Los Angeles was inextricably connected to its promotion as a place of outdoor recreation. During the late nineteenth century, L.A. and Southern California utilized tourism as a strategy to foment regional development. Tourist leisure served an important economic function, but as tourists became resident recreationalists, leisure took on profound social and cultural meaning. In Southern California's regional resorts, such as Palm Springs, Santa Catalina Island, and Santa Barbara, leisure was usually contained within a private realm. In Los Angeles, leisure often occupied public space. In a city notorious for privileging private over public, recreation was one of the few things Angelenos did publicly and collectively. Leisure created a public space, sometimes shared, and sometimes contested. Here issues of race, class, and gender sometimes provoked social conflict. The history of recreation in twentieth-century Los Angeles is a history of conflicting conceptualizations of nature and recreation. One was shared and public, such as recreation at a public beach or park, while the other was fundamentally private, whether occurring at a private beach club or in the family backyard swimming pool.

This tension between public and private natures proved a hallmark of urban and recreational planning in Los Angeles. This city, unlike some others examined in this volume, never enacted large-scale plans for parks or public spaces to bring nature into the city. It might seem likely that a city promoted as a playground and as a pastoral retreat from eastern urbanism and industry would preserve open space and create urban parks. Instead, L.A. set aside less parkland than any other major U.S. city. Yet it created one of the nation's first municipal playground departments, made outdoor recreation and nature appreciation part of the city's school curriculum, and purchased beaches and mountain camps to ensure public access. In contrast to its reputation as a morass of unplanned sprawl, Los Angeles actually inaugurated one of the very first citywide zoning systems in the United States.[1]

Civic access to nature in Los Angeles was conceptualized as something domestic and democratic—access to outdoor recreation in the backyard of a bungalow home, or via a family automobile trip to the beach, or the mountain and desert areas of Southern California. This domestic, private form of nature in the city offered outdoor leisure to the middle class, promising a new and, in many ways, better kind of life than could be lived in a crowded tenement apartment neighborhood or on an isolated farm homestead. This mixing of urbanism and nature—which seemed new and unique in the late nineteenth century—became the basis for American suburbia in the twentieth century. Contained within this cheery and optimistic vision of democratic access to nature, however, were grimmer realities. Racism and poverty limited access to housing, private automobiles, and recreational space. This affected African American Angelenos most directly, but had consequences for others as well. Mexican Americans, who composed the largest minority population in the city, and who were expected to provide low-wage labor to support Anglo-American leisure in this metropolis in the U.S.-Mexico borderlands, also faced restrictions on housing and access to nature. Thus, while Los Angeles from the late nineteenth century to the mid-twentieth century encapsulated an idealized vision of suburban life, it also portended the future of a nation that would be increasingly suburban, and, long after racially restrictive housing laws were overturned, increasingly segregated.

Parks, Urban Planning, and Planning Play in Los Angeles

In the nineteenth century, recreational policy in American cities was primarily an issue of the acquisition and development of parkland. Green spaces offered urban residents a chance to enjoy the aesthetic contemplation of bucolic scenery without leaving the city. In the United States, this conceptualization of parks—as places of repose—motivated the development of parks as part of the City Beautiful movement in the late nineteenth century. This era witnessed the creation of parks, parkways, and green spaces in a variety of cities, such as Boston and Chicago. Many of these borrowed from the design of the nation's premier urban oasis, the naturalistic Central Park in Manhattan.[2]

The early growth of modern Los Angeles was not accompanied by similar purchases of open land, or of planning for an elaborate city park system.

This city, founded in 1781, remained a small community during the Spanish and Mexican era. Unlike San Francisco, which boomed immediately after U.S. annexation in 1848 due to the gold rush, Los Angeles remained a small regional center for Southern California, dominated not by mining but by agriculture. Beginning in 1885, however, when the Santa Fe Railroad arrived and ended the monopoly of the Southern Pacific Railroad, Los Angeles grew at a phenomenal rate. In the half century between 1880 and 1930, Los Angeles grew from a town of 11,000 to a city of 1.2 million, the fifth-largest city in the United States, with another 1 million residents living in other communities in Los Angeles County.[3]

This rapid growth, facilitated by cheap land, a balmy climate, and a massive regional publicity campaign, was certainly one reason why the city did not plan more extensively for parkland. Yet rapid growth was not the only reason Los Angeles lagged in park development. Local promoters and outside observers alike asserted that Los Angeles was a new sort of city, unlike those of the East or even other western cities. Some of them believed that this new city would not need an extensive park system for it had transcended the traditional urban ills that made parks necessary. Beyond climate, Los Angeles and Southern California sold a lifestyle—one that proved irresistible in a nation of growing affluence and longevity. This was to be a place where retirees—an entirely new demographic class—could enjoy an old age of leisure, rather than spending their dotage on a remote farm. Middle-class families, rather than living in rural isolation or in cramped city quarters, could instead have a bungalow, complete with a garden and citrus and palm trees. More affluent farmers could relocate to a Southern California citrus plantation, where they could enjoy all of life's luxuries—including inexpensive labor provided by Mexican Americans, Native Americans, and various Asian immigrant groups. Dispersed communities were connected by Henry Huntington's Pacific Electric interurban train system, which allowed the development of a sprawling, suburbanized landscape, neither city nor country, which seemed to combine the best qualities of both. Trains also provided access to beaches, resorts, and other attractions in the growing communities within Los Angeles County.[4]

Los Angeles did not adopt a City Beautiful plan, nor did it buy undeveloped landscapes for recreational purposes. A local political culture that unfailingly catered to the wishes of developers, allowing profits to take precedence over the public good, contributed to this outcome. Yet beyond material concerns was the matter of ideology. Surrounded by recreational amenities, it seemed that Los Angeles would not need to plan for parks or public space.

It was instead the southwestern pastoral that would serve as the antidote to industrialization, "un-American" immigration, and all the other urban woes of the East.[5]

The advent of the automobile only accelerated residential access to recreation and suburban growth. Residents of Los Angeles founded the Automobile Club of Southern California in 1900, and by 1910 the city had the highest per-capita rate of car ownership in the world. Automobiles allowed development to sprawl ever-farther outward, beyond the reach of Huntington's trains. It also allowed residents to escape the city, venturing up into the mountains or out into the desert for recreation. The car, like the bungalow, was an essential part of the projected Los Angeles lifestyle.[6] Many Angelenos, of course, did not have picturesque homes or automobiles. Many more would be discouraged or actively banned from recreational areas due to their race or ethnicity. What mattered, however, was the image. The proto-suburban, semi-fictionalized lifestyle Los Angeles marketed to the nation proved irresistible.

Accordingly, Los Angeles only haltingly accumulated a system of urban parks, most coming in the form of donations or created from preexisting city properties. The first public space in Los Angeles was the Plaza, created when the pueblo was founded in 1781. Subsequent to the annexation of California and the rest of northern Mexico into the new Southwest of the United States, the Plaza was officially designated a city park in 1856. Several other city parks, either in whole or in part, were also created from unsold communal pueblo lands. The new Charter of 1889, created to help the city cope with rapid growth, included provisions for a Park Commission. This commission, like those of eastern cities, conceptualized parks as places of genteel recreation for more affluent residents and tourists. As such, it largely concerned itself with picturesque plantings and pathways. In the early twentieth century, it also made arrangements for motion-picture companies to use city parks for filming, and operated a series of municipal auto camps for tourists.[7]

Aside from remaining pueblo lands, most early parks came through donation. These included Echo Park, donated in 1891, and Lafayette Park, given in 1899. By far the most significant donation came in 1896, when the local magnate Griffith J. Griffith gave the land for Griffith Park to the city in perpetuity. Griffith called the 3,500-acre park his "Christmas gift" to the City of the Angels. While the donation of the largest urban park in the United States might have seemed a boon, the response of local political leaders was underwhelming. The park languished for years, suffering the depredations of illegal squatters and timber harvesters. Film-production companies appropriated parkland for sets and film shoots.[8]

Local governments, institutions, and individuals did, however, produce reports, surveys, and studies that amply demonstrated the general paucity of parkland in the region, and the limited recreational opportunities for many of its residents. Perhaps the most comprehensive—and certainly the most elegant—of these was the 1930 Olmsted-Bartholomew study, *Parks, Playgrounds and Beaches for the Los Angeles Region*. Its authors called for the creation of vast urban parks, parkways, beach recreation areas, scenic drives, and a variety of other amenities that, if enacted, would have created a very different city and region from the one that actually came to be. Yet this plan did not propose the construction of some fanciful arcadia. It planned for a vast urban area, complete with a large network of traffic arteries that foreshadowed later freeways. The report gave primary consideration to lower-income residents, who, as the authors pointed out, made up a majority of the city's population, and had less leisure time and available recreational space than the more affluent. Yet the plan was never realized. Fears about taxes, expense, and the worsening Depression prevented the plan's adoption. The report was shelved without ever being released to the public.[9]

In contrast to their lax attitudes toward the development of parks, city leaders carefully planned the growth of their metropolis in many other respects. While critics of Los Angeles have condemned it as the epitome of unplanned sprawl, it was often intricately planned. The city was placed under a comprehensive zoning ordinance in 1908, one of the first such ordinances in the nation. New York City would not pass a similar one for another eight years. The 1908 ordinance, and others that followed, delineated the city into different areas. Industry was separated from recreation, and whites from nonwhites. The Westside was classified as "higher-class" residential only, with some allowances for commercial establishments. A linear swath of south Los Angeles, adjacent to the L.A. River, was classified as industrial. "Residential only," in reality, meant white—Anglo-Saxon and usually Protestant—only, and realtors and white homeowners' associations maintained this color line.[10]

In the same era that Los Angeles was subjected to a rigorous planning regimen, the city pursued a new avenue in recreational policy. In 1904, the city was one of the first in the nation to create a Department of Playgrounds and Recreation—a landmark in the national playgrounds movement. The playground movement asserted that parks could serve as places of physical recreation and interaction rather than just settings for aesthetic contemplation. This new movement, part of larger Progressive Era efforts to improve American life, did not completely abandon the elitist attitudes of earlier park proponents. The masses would now be encouraged to visit parks, but parks—and especially new playgrounds—were strictly controlled to ensure that everyone enjoyed recreation "properly." Far from just offering a place for play or relaxation, parks were charged with an essential mission. They were intended to keep the public physically and mentally active, ensuring their participation as productive members of society. Additional recreation programs, aimed not only at children but also adult workers, were designed to teach immigrants to socialize with the larger population. Thus recreation could "Americanize" immigrants by teaching them to play, dress, and live as middle-class white Protestants did.[11]

This agenda also influenced the public-school curriculum in Los Angeles. Students were taken on field trips to the La Brea Tar Pits, and on hikes to collect insects in the foothills and marine life in tidal pools. In the classroom, they were taught about conservation, and about hunting that was "proper" rather than wasteful. The goal of this instruction was to help each student "better know himself as part of nature." Exposure to the outdoors was also intended to promote health. To that end, the city's school system experimented with outdoor "teaching porches," akin to the "sleeping porches" attached to many houses of the era, and provided instruction in physical activity and hygiene.[12]

Like city planners who divided prosperous residential and recreational areas from lower-income or industrial ones, or codified racial restrictions in housing, the Department of Playground and Recreation took as its mission the separation of spaces for safe, productive play, removed from the dangers of urban life. For the employees of the new department, children's play was serious business. On a series of its annual reports, the playground department emblazoned the motto: "The test of whether a civilization will live or die is the way it spends its leisure."[13]

The important societal function that playgrounds could purportedly serve was depicted in a drawing printed in a 1930 Department of Playground and Recreation annual report entitled *The Playground—A Haven of Protection form Childhood's Dangers*. Within a square was a depiction of a safe playground. Outside the playground was a series of circles, each containing a scene of peril. These included lack of cooperation, lack of supervision, poor health, unhappiness, loneliness, delinquency, and "un-Americanism," which was depicted by an image of a crowd listening to a man talking on a soapbox in the street.[14]

The Segregation of Recreational Space in Los Angeles

California did not enshrine Jim Crow in its constitution, as happened in the American South. Nevertheless, racism could sometimes be as pervasive in Greater Los Angeles as in the cities of the South. A complex web of laws regulating housing, land ownership, labor, and marriage targeted people of color, and immigration laws added another layer of coercion to the lives of Mexican Americans and Asian Americans. Los Angeles, however, differed from southern cities, and indeed from almost all eastern cities, in its diversity. In the East, racial issues were almost always portrayed as a matter of black versus white, and systematized white racism in L.A., when manifested in recreational space, most consistently targeted African Americans. With the aid of national organizations such as the NAACP, African Americans combated the restriction of recreational space in a more systematic way than other nonwhites. Yet in Los Angeles, whites and blacks were only two groups within a racial and ethnic mix that included Mexican Americans, Japanese, Chinese, and Filipinos, as well as Native Americans. Boosters might try to sell Los Angeles and Southern California as a balmy version of the Midwest, but even they could not entirely ignore its remarkable diversity.[15]

The ordinances that governed Los Angeles city parks, playgrounds, and other recreational areas in the first decades of the twentieth century made no reference to race. Indeed, it appears that parks and pools were initially integrated, though that did not necessarily mean that they were always welcoming to people of all races and ethnic groups. The first publication of the Department of Playground and Recreation, an "annual report" from shortly after the founding of the department, depicts black and white children playing together. Later reports would occasionally show children who appear to be Mexican American, but black children would virtually disappear from the department's reports for decades. The reason for this remains unclear, but it seems likely that whites in Los Angeles were influenced by both national and local trends that were manifested in recreational policy.[16]

In the 1920s and 1930s, migration began to "southernize" parts of the American North and West. Large numbers of African Americans began the "Great Migration" out of the South in search of employment in the North and, to a lesser degree, the West. Though still small compared to the African American population of major eastern cities, Los Angeles's black community expanded. The African American population of the city grew from 15,579 in 1920 to 63,774 by 1940. Among these new residents was a significant number of incipient middle-class African Americans, who were drawn to the region for many of the same reasons as middle-class whites. Despite restrictions, they could buy homes and cars, vote, and live lives that seemed filled with opportunity, particularly compared to the prospects of blacks in the Jim Crow South. In fact, they were not subject to the harsh immigration laws that affected Mexican Americans and Asian Americans, or to restrictions on "alien" land ownership. These African American migrants, therefore, possessed the resources to enjoy life and leisure in Southern California, and the fact that they could stake a claim to the recreation and recreational space that stood at the core of the city's civic life and identity made them seem more of a threat to white dominance than the more impoverished migrants or immigrants.[17]

While "Okies" are associated with the Dust Bowl of the 1930s, significant numbers of poor whites from the South, Texas, and the Southwest began migrating to California and Los Angeles by the early 1920s, bringing their racial views with them. By 1924, the editors of the California Eagle, the first African American newspaper in the city, fretted that: "part of Texas seemed to have been transplanted in and near Los Angeles." The disappearance of blacks from printed representations of Los Angeles parks and playgrounds thus likely also represented a changing white population, and local white anxieties concerning the appearance of a growing African American presence by the 1920s.[18]

In Los Angeles, segregation and recreation collided over the issue of swimming at public pools and beaches. For segregationists, public bathing was a potentially explosive issue, mixing issues of race, gender, and the body in disturbing ways. For them, the prospect of males and females of different races swimming together in revealing swimming attire was unacceptable. Even among bathers of the same sex, sharing public changing rooms and showers forced a degree of physical intimacy that some whites found troubling. In 1920, the Playground Commission set aside Vignes Pool as the "Negro pool." By 1923, all city pools were segregated. In 1927, a group of African Americans asked that the Los Angeles City Council appoint an African American to the City Parks Commission, no doubt hoping to end racist policies. Their request was denied. When the National Association for the Advancement of Colored People became involved, Los Angeles built Central Pool exclusively for blacks, hoping to preclude court action.[19]

Swimming-pool segregation limited nonwhite access to one of the most popular forms of recreation in the city. One survey found swimming to be the single-most popular mode of recreation for men under the age of forty-five, and for women under the age of thirty-five. Neither backyard pools nor air-conditioning would be common among middle-class residents until the 1950s and 1960s. Pools, like an array of weekend, afternoon, and evening recreational programs offered by city and county parks, drew legions of residents in the decades before television began competing for Americans' free time. As a result, public pools were crowded oases during the heat of summer, and popular for much of the rest of the year.[20]

Yet pools were just one place where people of different races might swim together. A far larger subject of contention was the 75-mile coastline of Los Angeles County. This expanse of sand and surf was the premier recreational amenity for the entire region—an unofficial "park" that served as public recreational space. During the 1920s, the Department of Playground and Recreation estimated that on a summer weekend or holiday a half million people converged at local beaches—a number representing a quarter or more of the total population of Los Angeles County at the time. Beaches were also a primary tourist destination. Various cities in Los Angeles County had already taken steps to police beaches and maintain sanitation. By the 1920s, the City and County of Los Angeles began purchasing and managing beaches to ensure public access, and urging voters to support more beachfront purchases. Political leaders, however, also had another agenda. White politicians feared that private ownership could mean nonwhite ownership, and this was a possibility they could not countenance for the region's most important recreational and tourist asset.[21]

The money for such purchases, as well as the maintenance of public beaches, initially came from taxpayers in individual beach municipalities. Yet the realization that beaches were a regional resource led to new methods of assessment that more equitably spread the cost of the public beach system. Ultimately, all taxpayers in Los Angeles County paid for the beaches they enjoyed through either municipal or county taxes, and sometimes both. Yet at least one group of taxpayers was prohibited from the recreational resource for which they helped pay. African Americans were banned from almost all beaches in Los Angeles County. Worse yet, they were forced to pay taxes to buy up even more beach land that they would be expressly prohibited from using.[22]

This segregation appears to have happened at most beaches relatively early, whether through explicit ordinance or by "custom." Blacks who arrived at local beaches did not necessarily need to see signs or encounter police to know they had to leave. As was the case with white homeowners, white beachgoers did not hesitate to confront African Americans—and others—who dared to enter a "public" beach. At one time, the only beach in

Though the City and County of Los Angeles actively discouraged African Americans from bathing at local beaches, and segregation was widespread at beaches and public pools in the 1920s and 1930s, black Angelenos did in fact frequent the few beaches that welcomed them, as this group of young people enjoying a day at the beach illustrates. "Group of Young People at the Beach," ca. 1925. (Shades of L.A. Archives, Los Angeles Public Library)

Los Angeles County that African Americans could visit was Bruce's Beach. George Peck, the developer of Manhattan Beach, set aside two blocks along the waterfront for use by nonwhites when the city was incorporated in 1912. A black couple, Charles and Willa Bruce, bought the first two lots and began development of the resort known as Bruce's Beach. Peck assisted them in developing the beach area. Yet as the region's African American population grew, and the resort drew more and more black recreationalists, local whites became increasingly hostile. Members of the Ku Klux Klan tried to terrorize the Bruces by making threatening phone calls and attempting to set their house on fire. Blacks arriving for a day at the beach could face harassment, vandalism to their cars, and bogus signs proclaiming a ten-minute parking limit in the area. In spite of this, the resort endured.

In 1924, exasperated city officials who lacked Peck's enlightened views condemned the beach, claiming that it had been selected as the site of a park. The Bruces and others sued. While the court ruled that they were guaranteed the right to buy other land in Manhattan Beach with the compensation they received for eviction, they were not allowed to buy beachfront property. The Bruces took their financial settlement and left the city.[23]

Another African American beach, called the "Inkwell," was located in Santa Monica. It lay at the terminus of Pico Boulevard—the site of a sewer outlet—and ran only the width of the street. The beach became a black beach in 1924, likely in response to the impending closure of Bruce's Beach. Unlike Bruce's Beach, the Inkwell remained in operation for years; it was the only major beach area left open to African Americans. Even so, blacks who went to this beach could still face harassment from local whites and police, and the City of Santa Monica shut down clubs that catered to blacks within walking distance of the Inkwell.[24]

As they had with segregated swimming pools, African Americans fought back against their restriction from beaches. The NAACP even organized a "swim-in," akin to the sit-ins at segregated restaurants and other public facilities in the 1950s and 1960s. This resulted in the abandonment of an explicit policy of segregation at beaches and pools in the city of Los Angeles during the early 1930s. Yet the end of segregation at city beaches and pools by law did not mean the end of segregation of beaches in fact. For that matter, some other communities still maintained official segregation. In the 1940s, Mexican American high school students reported that some "public" beaches remained closed to them. Some such beaches were kept all white by aggressive local police or homeowners' associations. Others apparently tolerated Asian, Mexican, and African American visitors—but only as long as their attire and haircuts were "clean-cut" and their numbers remained small. This de facto segregation suggests the type of discrimination that was likely most common at city and county pools, parks, and playgrounds. While county or city policies might not explicitly ban nonwhites, local police, homeowners' groups, and average citizens could take on the role of self-appointed enforcers of white sentiment. This continued well after the U.S. Supreme Court struck down racially restrictive housing covenants in cases decided in 1948 and 1953.

While African Americans and other people of color fought back against white attempts to control recreational space, they also created their own places of leisure. Despite pollution and the dangers of sudden floods, Mexican American children swam in the Los Angeles River and other watercourses. Another favorite swimming spot for young Mexican Americans was a water-filled quarry called Sleepy Lagoon. This swimming hole grew popular as a place where they could enjoy swimming and socializing without the hostility they might encounter at Anglo-dominated public swimming pools. It would become best remembered for its association with the Sleepy Lagoon trial of 1942, at which seventeen Mexican American youths were convicted of the murder of another youth at Sleepy Lagoon in 1942. The convictions were later overturned, but the trial remains a landmark in the history of Anglo-American fears about "Mexican" violent crime.

Despite its efforts to restrict and segregate recreational areas, city government facilitated some sports competitions that included, and sometimes mixed, various races and ethnicities. Individuals of all races participated in the team sports leagues organized by the Department of Playground and Recreation, from basketball to baseball and soccer. These teams were often organized by race and ethnicity. They therefore functioned as a form of socialization within individual racial and ethnic groups, but could also facilitate socialization between different groups when they met on the court or playing field.

The segregation of recreational areas, or the outright banning of some groups, was certainly the most obvious variety of racial bias in the development of the Los Angeles city and county park and recreation systems. Yet more subtle forms of discrimination were far more pervasive, and just as damaging. The funding—or, more accurately, the lack of funding—for recreational spaces and amenities in nonwhite areas of the city and county functioned as a pernicious form of fiscal discrimination. Since neighborhood parks and playgrounds in the city were normally funded by neighborhood assessment, affluent neighborhoods could more easily pay for parks. An additional concern, particularly after World War II, was crime—fears among some white residents that parks, rather than spaces for leisure, were instead havens for crime.

One early example of this was the privileging of Pershing Square over the Plaza, and then Pershing's subsequent decline. While the Plaza originally served as the city's focal park, by 1900, government attention—and money—had shifted westward to the square called "South Plaza," or "Central Park," which lay in the heart of the new downtown, surrounded by office buildings and hotels. This park was subsequently renamed Pershing Square. The Plaza was retained as a part of the historicist makeover of Olvera Street, as the city attempted to transform what had been a center of the city's Mexican American community into a shopping and tourist attraction. Pershing Square's fountain and lush landscaping made it a favorite lunchtime gathering place for white-collar workers. As downtown declined, however, Pershing Square also lost its luster. The park became a focus of LAPD surveillance due to its popularity as a place for drug dealing, for activists to make speeches and stage protests, and as a covert meeting place for gay men. The city passed ordinances banning alcohol and vagrants, and ultimately gouged out the park in the 1950s, leaving only a sparse garnish of greenery atop a subterranean parking structure. The parking was intended for white professionals, and the removal of trees and foliage made it easier to police the park. It also made Pershing Square a far less pleasant place to

Before its excavation for an underground parking structure, Pershing Square was a lush oasis at the heart of the city's financial district. "Aerial View of Pershing Square," 1951. (Herald Examiner Collection, Los Angeles Public Library)

Stripped of trees, fountains, and foliage, Pershing Square now offered convenient parking, but proved a much less pleasant place to linger. "Pershing Square Garage," 1954. (Herald Examiner Collection, Los Angeles Public Library)

linger. The Department of Recreation and Parks described the new park design as a "see-through, walk-through park."[25]

Los Angeles, Leisure, and the Shaping of Postwar America

World War II brought new challenges to Los Angeles. The city's industrial base expanded as wartime munitions and aircraft factories opened. The war witnessed a huge influx of industrial workers and military personnel. The city had to accommodate these new arrivals, as well as plan for the future. Yet World War II did not simply increase the population of the Los Angeles region. It also accelerated the area's growing diversity, and demographic changes in various neighborhoods. The number of black Angelenos, for example, jumped from 64,000 in 1940 to more than 171,000 in 1950. Anglo Angelenos were on the move as well. They moved to new suburban developments in the San Fernando Valley and Orange County, where affordable land and Federal Housing Administration (FHA) and Veterans Administration (VA) loans made suburban home ownership feasible. The same government assistance—as well as the new federal freeway system—made the mass suburbanization of the United States possible. This new national suburban landscape owed much to Los Angeles.

The ubiquitous "ranch" house, which in the postwar era spread nationwide from the San Fernando Valley to New York's Long Island, incorporated hallmarks of the more exclusive homes constructed in Palm Springs and other Southern California resorts. The movement of family social life and leisure time into the backyard, and the construction of patios, barbecues, and swimming pools allowed suburbanites to live a resort lifestyle year-round, at least as long as weather permitted. Pattern books for ranch-style houses, published by *Sunset* magazine and other periodicals, proved widely popular. The spread of ranch houses demonstrated how a popularized form of outdoor leisure, first manifested in regional resorts and affluent neighborhoods, could influence urban and suburban development.[26] Perhaps the most striking manifestation of this was the backyard swimming pool, which before World War II had been a luxury for the wealthy. In 1949, there were 10,000 private swimming pools in the United States. In 1959, there were more than 250,000—and 90,000 of these were located in the city of Los Angeles.[27]

Postwar prosperity, at least for Anglos, ensured that private leisure and private nature, rather than public, would dominate Los Angeles. Backyards and residential swimming pools became the preferred leisure areas for middle-class homeowners. Yet the very same federal programs that facilitated home ownership for millions also encouraged residential segregation across the United States. While FHA and VA loans were theoretically available to all, the loans were managed not by the federal government, but by local banks—banks that refused to offer loans to African Americans or other nonwhites. As a result, the most famous postwar suburb in the United States, Levittown, on New York's Long Island, was the whitest city in America; it did not have a single black resident.

For the rest of the twentieth century, Los Angeles would remain profoundly shaped by the visions of its nineteenth-century boosters, who promoted Southern California as a pastoral frontier of leisure for middle-class Anglo-Americans. They conceived of Los Angeles as a place designed for recreation in nature. A public conceptualization of nature and outdoor recreation did provide a crucial, if contested, public space for Angelenos. Parks, pools, and beaches, no matter how restricted by racism or neglected by developers' greed or politicians' indifference, were public spaces where residents of the city met, sometimes quarreled, and sometimes mingled. Yet a private conceptualization of nature, and of private recreation, emphasizing middle-class Anglo-American leisure, could not accommodate massive population growth, nor could it provide for all those it excluded.

It was this limited vision that would guide recreational policy and urban planning in much of the suburban Sunbelt, designed around the automobile and the family home. By the end of World War II, the dream Los Angeles propagated—of car and home ownership, of outdoor leisure and family vacations—had become the white middle-class American dream, made attainable by rising prosperity and government assistance. Los Angeles, originally an escape from urban America, had instead become an urban model that reshaped the twentieth-century American landscape. That model prioritized a private conceptualization of nature and recreation over a public one. As a result, in much of American suburbia, parks and recreational space would be scarce, and suburbanization meant that funding for inner-city parks and recreation would decline as well. If, as the writer and urban historian Lewis Mumford observed, suburbs represented a contradiction—the collective effort to live a private life—then those suburbs inherited the contradictions of Los Angeles. Los Angeles had indeed been designed as a city of leisure and access to nature—a place that merged city and nature. It had not, however, been designed as a city for all.[28]

Notes

1. For more on the history of recreation in Los Angeles, see Lawrence Culver, *The Frontier of Leisure: Southern California and the Shaping of Modern America* (New York, 2010); and Law-

rence Culver, "America's Playground: Recreation and Race," in *A Companion to Los Angeles*, ed. William Deverell and Greg Hise (Hoboken, N.J., 2010), 421–37.

2. Galen E. Cranz, *The Politics of Park Design: A History of Urban Parks in America* (Cambridge, 1982); William H. Wilson, *The City Beautiful Movement* (Baltimore, 1989); Roy Rosenzweig, *The Park and the People: A History of Central Park* (Ithaca, 1992).

3. All population figures are taken from Leonard Pitt and Dale Pitt, *Los Angeles A to Z: An Encyclopedia of the City and County* (Berkeley, 1997), 576, 578.

4. Robert Fogelson, *The Fragmented Metropolis: Los Angeles, 1850–1930* (Cambridge, 1967).

5. Some of the national trends that helped produce the pastoral vision of Los Angeles are discussed in Peter J. Schmitt, *Back to Nature: The Arcadian Myth in Urban America* (Baltimore, 1969).

6. Scott Bottles, *Los Angeles and the Automobile: The Making of the Modern City* (Berkeley, 1987).

7. Al Goldfarb, *An Overview: 100 Years of Recreation and Parks* (Los Angeles, 1988); Burton L. Hunter, *The Evolution of Municipal Organization and Administrative Practice in the City of Los Angeles* (Los Angeles, 1933); Fred G. Crawford, "Organizational and Administrative Development of the City of Los Angeles, during the Thirty-Year Period July 1, 1925–September 30, 1955," School of Public Administration, University of Southern California, 1955, Los Angeles City Archives.

8. Griffith published a work arguing for the value of urban parks and bemoaning the condition of his gift to the city (see Griffith J. Griffith, *Parks, Boulevards, and Playgrounds* [Los Angeles, 1910], Rare Book Collection, Huntington Library, San Marino, Calif.).

9. The plan is reprinted in its entirety in Greg Hise and William Deverell, *Eden by Design: The 1930 Olmstead-Bartholomew Plan for the Los Angeles Region* (Berkeley, 2000). See also Mike Davis, *Ecology of Fear: Los Angeles and the Imagination of Disaster* (New York, 1998), 61–67.

10. For the history of urban planning and zoning in Los Angeles, see Greg Hise, *Magnetic Los Angeles: Planning the Twentieth-Century Metropolis* (Baltimore, 1997); and Greg Hise, "'Nature's Workshop': Industry and Urban Expansion in Southern California, 1900–1950," *Journal of Historical Geography* 27 (Spring 2001): 74–92; Becky M. Nicolaides, *My Blue Heaven: Life and Politics in the Working-Class Suburbs of Los Angeles, 1920–1965* (Chicago, 2002), 50; and Pitt and Pitt, *Los Angeles A to Z*, 93.

11. Dominick Cavallo, *Muscles and Morals: Organized Playgrounds and Urban Reform, 1880–1920* (Philadelphia, 1981); Goldfarb, *An Overview;* Hunter, *The Evolution of Municipal Organization and Administrative Practice in the City of Los Angeles.*

12. Charles Lincoln Edwards, "An Outline of Nature Study, Showing the Plan and Practice in the Los Angeles Public Schools," reprinted in *Popular Science Monthly*, April 1914. Edwards was director of nature study in the Los Angeles city schools. See also *Health Supervision in Los Angeles City Schools*, pamphlet, no date, Ephemera Collection, Seaver Center for Western History Research, Natural History Museum of Los Angeles County, Los Angeles.

13. George Hjelte, *The Development of a City's Public Recreation Service, 1904–1962* (Los Angeles, 1978); *Report, 1930–32*, City of Los Angeles Department of Playground and Recreation, Special Collections, Young Research Library, University of California, Los Angeles.

14. *Annual Report of the Department of Playground and Recreation, City of Los Angeles, 1930*, 33, Special Collections, UCLA.

15. For an analysis of race in Los Angeles, particularly of the experience of African Americans, see Susan Anderson, "A City Called Heaven: Black Enchantment and Despair in Los Angeles," in *The City: Los Angeles and Urban Theory at the End of the Twentieth Century*, ed. Allen J. Scott and Edward W. Soja, 336–64 (Berkeley, 1996); Quintard Taylor, *In Search of*

the Racial Frontier: African Americans in the American West, 1528–1990 (New York, 1998); Lawrence B. de Graaf, Kevin Mulroy, and Quintard Taylor, eds., *Seeking El Dorado: African Americans in California* (Seattle: Autry Museum of Western Heritage and University of Washington Press); and Walter Nugent, *Into the West: The Story of Its People* (New York, 1999).

16. "Annual Reports" of the Department of Playground and Recreation and later the Los Angeles Department of Recreation and Parks, Special Collections, UCLA; and Archive, City of Los Angeles Department of Recreation and Parks.

17. Taylor, *In Search of the Racial Frontier,* 223.

18. A total of 84,230 residents of the "Western South" states of Arkansas, Missouri, Oklahoma, and Texas are estimated to have relocated to California in the 1920s (James N. Gregory, *American Exodus: The Dust Bowl Migration and Okie Culture in California* [New York, 1989], 6; Charlotta Bass, *Forty Years: Memoirs from the Pages of a Newspaper* [Los Angeles, 1960], 55).

19. Andre Keil, *Swimming at the Park Pool: A History of Aquatics in the City of Los Angeles* (Los Angeles: City of Los Angeles, Recreation and Parks, 1992), 9; *Annual Report of the Board of Park Commissioners,* City of Los Angeles, 1928, Special Collections, UCLA; Los Angeles City Council Minutes, July 7, 1927, also 1929, Los Angeles City Archives; Douglas Flamming, Atlanta, Ga., telephone interview by author, October 31, 2002. At the time of this interview, Dr. Flamming was writing *Bound for Freedom: Black Los Angeles in Jim Crow America* (Berkeley, 2006). He generously shared his research on the history of segregation and black recreation in the city and region.

20. Stella Elizabeth Hartman, "A Study of Leisure-Time Habits of Young Men and Young Women in Los Angeles," master's thesis, University of Southern California, 1942, 47.

21. Pitt and Pitt, *Los Angeles A to Z,* 41–42; beach attendance figure from *Annual Report of the Department of Playground and Recreation,* City of Los Angeles, 1928, 15, "Old Department History" file, Los Angeles Department of Recreation and Parks.

22. Flamming interview.

23. "Resort Was an Oasis for Blacks until Racism Drove Them Out," *Los Angeles Times,* July 21, 2002.

24. Flamming interview.

25. "Pershing Square Park," Histories—P, Los Angeles Department of Recreation and Parks Archives. See also William McClung, *Landscapes of Desire: Anglo Mythologies of Los Angeles* (Berkeley, 2000), 142–53. The definitive history of the Los Angeles Plaza is William David Estrada's "Sacred and Contested Space: The Los Angeles Plaza" (Ph.D. diss., UCLA, 2003).

26. Editorial staff of *Sunset* magazine and Cliff May, *Sunset Western Ranch House* (San Francisco, 1946), 84.

27. Keil, "Swimming at the Park Pool," 32. For a history of swimming pools, see Thomas A. P. van Leeuwen, *The Springboard in the Pond: An Intimate History of the Swimming Pool* (Cambridge, 1998).

28. Nugent, *Into the West,* 94–95; 274–79.

Part III

The Function of Nature in the City

Nature, Sport, and the European City

London and Helsinki, 1880–2005

Peter Clark, Salla Jokela, and Jarmo Saarikivi

Across most of Europe, from the harvested forests of Finland to the shepherded uplands of the French Pyrenees, the natural landscape is a social construct, the outcome of man's ongoing, increasingly pervasive interaction with the ecological world. No more so than in European cities, where green spaces—from parks and villa estates to cemeteries, playing fields, hospital grounds, allotment gardens, wasteland, and brownfield sites—are the product of a matrix of factors including economic development; municipal policy; cultural, ecological, and aesthetic discourses and strategies; and changing leisure fashions. In this last connection, one of the most important developments transforming nature in the modern and contemporary city has been the growth of organized and more informal sports, creating an extensive new landscape of outdoor playing fields, often in established parks and specialist sports grounds. This development began in European cities toward the end of the nineteenth century, and took off in the interwar period, often promoted by clubs as well as municipalities. After the Second World War, the provision of grounds for organized sports became an important component of urban planning and social welfare policies in European cities, and was seen as contributing to health, social cohesion, and education. This movement reached its peak in the 1970s and 1980s, when a variety of factors, including the new popularity of more individualistic or informal sports, began to have an effect on sports spaces in cities.

The impact of sporting activity on the natural landscape in cities has not been uncontroversial. If initial opposition from the respectable middle classes and some conservationists in the late nineteenth century to the creation of new sports areas, particularly in parks, was soon overcome, in the late twentieth century there was growing criticism of the way that heavily mowed sports fields (pitches), treated golf fairways, and the intensity of sporting use were affecting biodiversity—the incidence of flora and fauna. More recently, research by urban ecologists has led to a more positive view of outdoor sports areas, particularly golf courses, and their contribution to the natural environment of the city, providing habitats for insects, animals, birds, and wildflowers.

This essay investigates the role of nature in the city in its distinct historical and geographical contexts from two perspectives: first, it examines the development of green space for sport in European cities from the late nineteenth century to the present time, looking at some of the key variables—discourses, politics, governance, management, and demand—shaping the landscape of sport; second, it tries to assess how such changes in sports areas have impacted on urban ecology and biodiversity. These issues are considered from a comparative perspective, looking at the northern European cities of London and Helsinki. Both are capitals and metropolitan centers, but they are cities of different orders of demographic and economic magnitude and with different climates. Both cities have experienced a major expansion of sports sites but with a different chronology and important divergences in the interplay of key variables.

Sports, particularly commercial and organized sports, have attracted extensive attention from historians and social scientists, but so far there has been much less work done on the major urban spaces allocated for sports, with the notable exception of sports stadia.[1] There is an enormous variety of recognized sports—more than a hundred, according to one British study in 1997. Henning Eichberg has argued that sports can be categorized either as an achievement, to secure records; as a strategy for health, lengthening the life span of an individual; or as a folk activity, manifested in traditional games or in contemporary popular, experiential sports in which the physical benefits and achievements are of less concern.[2] It is difficult to make distinctions, but an important one is between organized competitive sports such as soccer, cricket, or golf (with a further division between commercial/professional activity and amateur games); and individual, informal sports such as jogging, rock climbing, and skateboarding. As well as outdoor activity, recent years have seen the growing popularity of indoor sports. This is changing the balance between the provision of outdoor green space and indoor, artificially enclosed space.

Sport and Sports Spaces before the Second World War

London has hosted organized sports activity since the early eighteenth century. At Blackheath in South London in the 1730s, cricket teams played matches, often before large crowds of spectators, and by the last years of that century, club cricket was increasingly well established under the leadership of the Marylebone Cricket Club. Other types of sports also developed in this period, including horseracing, archery, rowing, and golf, on an associational basis. Such activities began to develop their own specialist spaces, or used public commons. However, most sports into the early nineteenth century appear to have been essentially elite activities with the lower classes present as spectators rather than participants. Lower-class involvement was largely confined to street sports like football (soccer) or bull running, though these suffered increasing social criticism and police control by the early Victorian era.[3]

The main breakthrough in organized sporting activity came in Britain during the last half of the nineteenth century, especially the final decades. Traditional football was transformed though the medium of the public schools into two organized games—football and rugby: the Football Association was formed in 1863 and the Rugby Football Union in 1871. Hockey spread quickly in the 1870s as a middle-class game, and the Hockey Association was established in 1886. Athletics developed from the 1860s with the Amateur Athletic Club founded in 1866. There was only one English golf club in the 1850s (in London at Blackheath), but a dozen existed by the 1870s, and London had about one hundred before the First World War. Lawn tennis was invented in the 1870s.[4] Older sports like cricket also expanded, developing a wider base; cricket became a more middle-class game, with at least 1,100 cricket clubs in London by 1914.[5]

How do we explain this tremendous efflorescence of sports? Urbanization was clearly an important factor: London's population rose from 2.7 million in 1851 to 7.3 million by 1911, as the metropolis expanded as a great imperial port and commercial and manufacturing center. From the mid-nineteenth century, ordinary people had more leisure time—due to the spread of half-day working on Saturdays and recognized holidays after the Bank Holiday Act of 1871. Rising living standards also began to have an effect by the 1890s, stimulating consumer demand for a wide range of leisure activities.[6] There was a strong middle-class dimension to the new wave of sporting activities. The middle classes increasingly incorporated outdoor sports and related fitness into the emerging cult of moral masculinity, as imperial Britain struggled to keep pace with American and German economic and military success.[7] Sport was promoted by the well-to-do as a way of weaning the working classes from traditional pastimes such as street games and boozing, and educating them in a middle-class sense of order and discipline. Many football clubs were established by churches and employers.

No less significant, commercial and media interests increasingly promoted sports, particularly football.[8]

The new organized sports of late Victorian Britain quickly spread to overseas metropoles. Paris had athletics clubs by the 1880s, and football clubs the following decade; by 1900, St. Petersburg had acquired a variety of mainly elite clubs for horseback riding, tennis, rowing, and skating, mostly using public parks. Barcelona had its first football club in 1899.[9] There was a similar trend in the case of Helsinki, which by the late nineteenth century was growing quickly as the capital of Finland, a semi-autonomous area of the Russian Empire. Helsinki's population rose from only 26,000 in 1871 to 62,000 in 1891 and 147,000 twenty years later as manufacturing and port activity fuelled economic growth. Bicycling, rowing, swimming, and winter sports such as skating were well established before the end of the nineteenth century.[10]

The impact of organized sports on urban space was considerable, marked by a proliferation of more or less standardized, rectilinear sports fields in existing parks, as well as the growth of specialist sports spaces such as lawn tennis courts and golf courses. It was not unproblematic. All urban space is contested and green space equally so. Attempts by sportsmen to have areas of parks set aside for them ran into opposition from those who saw the traditional civilized world of the park with its formal gardens and tranquil promenades, with its educational, aesthetic, and horticultural functions, being disrupted by noisy teams of sportsmen and their standardized fields. At Helsinki, controversy erupted over the creation of playing fields in city parks like Kaisaniemi. Specialist sports areas also provoked opposition, as when a plan to make a golf course at One Tree Hill in South London led to a crowd of fifteen thousand people, anxious about customary rights and nature conservation, pulling down the fences and stopping the development.[11]

Yet opposition to the growth of urban sports grounds was soon overcome, not least because of the high level of middle-class participation and support. In London, the main increase of specialist recreation grounds and playgrounds came in the 1890s, and there was also a strong growth of sports fields in public parks about the same time. In the 1880s, London parks had only a hundred or more cricket and football fields and tennis courts, but within a few years of the creation (1888) of the London County Council (LCC) it had more than four hundred cricket fields, more than three hundred tennis courts, and a hundred or so football fields.[12] A new vision of urban parks was emerging, one with less emphasis on formality, carpet bedding, and exotic trees and flowers and a greater stress on a diversity of uses, informality, and recreational activity including sport: nature in the park was not just there to be observed and admired but to be actively pursued.

These developments can be illustrated by the example of Battersea Park, which was opened in South London in the 1840s. Though the original plan was for an ornamental, essentially bourgeois park with a lake and exotic gardens, from the start there were limited facilities for sport, a cricket club playing there from 1856. The main expansion of sports activity came later, however. Football was played in the park from 1888, and tennis courts arrived in 1891. Tennis, essentially a middle-class activity, became the most played game in the park, with 70,000 participants in 1904–5; English bowls also grew quickly, with 17,000 players that year. Cricket was popular, with 22,000 players, well ahead of football, with 16,000. But sports were not a priority for the park authorities before the First World War. In 1907, many games were banned to preserve the sports grounds, and there was a general prohibition on Sunday sports until the 1920s.[13]

In Helsinki, the advance of sports grounds was more modest before 1917. The first skating rinks were opened at Hietalahti, Kaisaniemi, and Töölön-lahti as a result of private initiative, but by the start of the twentieth century, the city council had opened two rinks for working-class people. There was also municipal provision of outdoor swimming pools for men by the shore at Kaivopuisto Park. Sports grounds were established in Kaisaniemi Park, but prior to the First World War, the city had only four public playgrounds and one bigger sports ground. In the years before and after the First World War, the council began to develop the Eläintarha District as a recreation area, with 3.7 acres (1.5 hectares) set aside for sports.[14]

The First World War, which mobilized large armies of young men, played an important part in the mass popularization of organized sports. By the 1930s, competitive sports had become a mainstream physical activity involving all social classes. In interwar Britain, there was growing government and municipal support for the development of sports facilities, support that was fuelled by the wartime experience of unhealthy working-class recruits and the growing influence of the eugenics movement. Pressure came from educationalists and elite figures like the imperialist Earl of Meath (1841–1929), who called for better sports facilities and compulsory physical exercise to improve the fitness of children. The London Playing Fields Association, founded in 1891, was increasingly influential, promoting "the value of organized games in the elementary and central schools."[15] Exposure to nature, fresh air, and outdoor recreation was more and more regarded as a precondition for a healthy population. In 1937, the Physical Training and Recreation

Act encouraged outdoor sports through the provision of government grants to local councils and clubs for playing fields and other sports facilities. Sport was increasingly associated with national identity and international competitions (London hosted the Olympic Games in 1908 and 1948 and the Empire Games in 1934). However, popular demand also played its part in the metropolitan expansion of sports and sports grounds, as a result of improvements in living standards and more popular leisure time.[16]

Broadly similar developments occurred in Helsinki after Finland secured independence from Russia in 1917. Politicians saw sporting activity as a way of improving public health and binding up the wounds from the ferocious civil war that had followed independence. Competitive sports were important for nation building. Moreover, intellectuals, artists, and architects were influenced by the German *Licht und Luft* (light and air) movement, with its stress on outdoor activities. As Katri Lento has shown, publications by elite circles supported healthy living habits and athletics. Increased consumption of sports—both participation and spectatorship—was further encouraged by the introduction of the eight-hour workday in 1918. Improvements in public transport, as in London, also contributed to the growing use of sports facilities.[17]

In London, a major expansion of municipal provision was undertaken by the London County Council. In the 1930s, a growing number of LCC schools had their own sports grounds. The number of outdoor swimming pools (lidos), either set in parks or with green areas, rose sharply from a handful before 1914 to several dozen by 1939, with admission open to women and with a range of facilities. At Battersea Park, the number of cricket and football fields and tennis courts soared. In 1939, London's parks boasted "fine new lidos and athletics tracks; more and better playing fields and bowling greens; municipal golf courses."[18] As well as municipal provision, private sports areas multiplied. Golf courses, run mainly by private, sometimes exclusive, clubs, continued to spread, though those in the inner suburbs (as at Neasden and Harrow) were overrun by housing development and replaced by others on cheaper land in the outer suburbs. Private tennis clubs and courts were likewise widespread in the respectable new suburbs on the edge of the capital, where they attracted a large female clientele, reflecting the increasing female participation in sports. In addition, private companies developed extensive sports grounds as a way of improving the health and productivity of their workers. In 1929, the Oxo Company, a food-processing firm in Southwark, owned a 22-acre sports ground in the suburbs with twelve tennis courts, football and cricket fields and other facilities.[19]

In Helsinki, most of the expansion of sports areas came as the result of municipal action. In 1919, a special Sports Committee was established by the city to supervise developments. In 1920, the city had forty-one outdoor sports grounds, and by the Second World War this had grown to eighty-six. Growing opportunities for more informal sporting activity were to be found in the people's parks that the city established on the islands around the city. Frequently there was a public-private partnership arrangement, with the city constructing sports spaces but maintenance being left to sports clubs or workers' associations. The number of sports clubs subsidized by the city rose tenfold between 1920 and 1944. At the school level, a growing number of new schools had nearby sports tracks. Particularly important for the city was the creation of an extensive sports complex with attendant green areas in north Helsinki (along with an Olympic Village) for the abortive 1940 Olympic Games.[20]

Developments after the Second World War

Provision for organized sports accelerated in the postwar era, particularly in the suburbs. A variety of factors played a part. Demographic trends were less dynamic than earlier. Metropolitan populations continued to grow for a while after the war, but then turned down (in London before Helsinki) as a result of demographic decentralization, only reviving with reurbanization in the last decade or so.

TABLE 1 Population estimates (in thousands) for London and Helsinki

	1931	1951	1971	1991	2001
London	8,216	8,348	7,452	6,803	7,172
Helsinki	369	524	524	491	556

At the same time, there was a strong boost in living standards and leisure time in the postwar decades. A growing mass interest in sport for personal health and fitness emerged, as social participation widened and more women became involved. In the late 1960s, a London survey of leisure activity suggested that 11 percent of men (and up to 17 percent of teenage boys) were engaged in organized sports in parks. More than 33 percent of men (and 16 percent of women) said they played sports regularly or occasionally, and a half of men (and a third of women) watched sports in parks; at Helsinki in 1977, about half the residents were actively engaged in outdoor sports.[21] Growing personal mobility with the spread of car ownership may have encouraged the rising participation rate in sports. Also significant in Britain was the greater democratization of sports as middle-class ones like golf, rugby, and cricket became less exclusive by the 1960s and 1970s following official pressure—with government grants for facilities tied to public access. In 1980, a new Sport Act in Finland provided for a sports committee in every community to take care of the planning and development of sporting activity; representatives of sports clubs shared in the planning of sports sites.[22]

Public expenditure on sports facilities experienced strong growth, partly reflecting demand but also as a result of social welfare policies that envisaged sports and recreation, along with health and housing provision, as vital for social cohesion and advancement. In the case of Helsinki, the city council spent about 15 Finnish marks (2 euros) per inhabitant on sports and recreation in the interwar era; in the years 1945–63, this jumped to 67 marks (11 euros) per annum, and in the following decades averaged 160 marks (23 euros), reaching a peak of 298 marks (nearly 50 euros) in 1991, before slipping back. City planning departments, growing rapidly in powers and personnel in this period, privileged sports areas in urban master plans through ratios of sports space to population. Already in the 1940s, Patrick Abercrombie's *County of London Plan* proposed four acres of green space per one thousand inhabitants, with a high emphasis on recreation grounds and playing fields. The Helsinki master plan of 1972 proposed 90 square meters (969 square feet) of recreation area per inhabitant in outer urban areas and 25 square meters (260 square feet) in districts with apartment blocks. In Britain, the Greater London Council, which replaced the LCC in 1965, probably continued earlier policies with regard to sports and recreation, but parks became much lower-profile than previously. In Britain, private support for sports continued unabated, with private companies after the war maintaining or expanding sports grounds for workers and the private clubs for golf and tennis in particular continuing to play an important role.[23]

The impact of the growth of organized sports on urban space was clear. In Helsinki, a network of multifunctional sports parks was planned in the 1950s and 1960s that catered to professional sportsmen as well as ordinary exercisers. In the city, the area for sports roughly doubled between 1965 and 1987, and the number of sports parks went up from 207 to 556 over the same period. Planned sports complexes were created in suburban forest areas like Pirkkola in 1968. There was a parallel expansion of school playing fields as population growth and suburbanization led to a multiplication of new schools. Compared to the nine school sports grounds created in the decades prior to 1950, thirty-six were completed in the next twenty years. Exercise tracks trebled in number. In new suburban areas such as the garden suburb of Tapiola, British visitors praised the way that "residents are provided with every opportunity . . . for physical exercise." Although there is little information available for this period for London, the trends there were probably broadly similar, if less dynamic, due to the onset of funding problems in the 1970s. Sports grounds seem to have encroached on the (more expensive to maintain) traditional garden environment of urban parks.[24]

Recent Trends in Sports and Sports Areas

By the 1980s, the dynamic growth of sports grounds in European cities was starting to run out of steam. Finance was an important factor. Urban economies were in growing difficulty as manufacturing collapsed and unemployment rose. Municipal budgets faced many demands, and there was a growing trend for retrenchment and privatization of services. In Britain, municipal difficulties were aggravated by the Thatcher government's attack on local government autonomy, culminating in the abolition of the Greater London Council in 1985 and the transfer of many of its responsibilities to local boroughs and a mishmash of other bodies. A related assault on local planning departments occurred with the drive toward planning deregulation.[25] Controls on municipal budgets in Britain contributed to a 20 percent decline in overall expenditure on parks, including sports areas, between 1990–91 and 1999. In London, competitive tendering led to park management being transferred to private contractors and a consequent decline in staffing, maintenance, and the quality of green areas.[26] In Finland, the major economic crisis came in the early 1990s with the collapse of Soviet trade, which led to cutbacks in municipal expenditure on sports and sports spaces.[27] On the other hand, Helsinki City retained considerable political and financial autonomy and benefited from economic recovery during the late 1990s; at the same time, there was a move toward the contracting out of some leisure services. While municipal support for the sports areas of cities came under pressure, commercial developers exerted mounting pressure on green spaces, including sports grounds, to build private housing, particularly as reurbanization reversed the earlier tide of suburbanization and decentralization.

No less significant was the changing pattern of demand, increasingly evident from the 1970s and 1980s. There was a growing trend away from organized competitive sports on an amateur basis toward more informal, individualistic, and experiential sports, such as jogging, boating, cycling, horseback riding, and fishing. Here personal health and lifestyle concerns were influential, as well perhaps as greater car use, making access to the countrified edges of cities easier and quicker. How far these developments were driven by a new vision of nature is problematic, given the growing environmental anxiety from this time about the de-greening of the countryside. Jogging was probably the first of the new sports of this type, imported from the United States and quickly spreading to European cities. Jogging tracks or circuits began to be laid out in Helsinki and London parks during the 1970s. By the 1990s, however, jogging was being overshadowed by event running (such as marathons). Orienteering, rock climbing, and skateboarding became popular. One consequence has been a move away from traditional parks and sports spaces to all kinds of open and peri-urban sites. Another trend has been the growth of indoor sports and ball games, including aerobics and circuit training but also outdoor pursuits such as tennis. In both cities, this often takes place in private health clubs.[28]

A further development of recent decades has been the expansion of the commercial and professional sector in sports. League football in London, strongly commercial from the late nineteenth century, has become dominated by a few highly successful clubs playing in increasingly elaborate or new stadia, often on artificial turf, before large crowds that pay highly for the privilege. Here, sports space has turned from being public space to a restricted, unnatural environment. Other sports have followed suit. In Helsinki, one finds a similar development in the case of ice hockey, with stadia and organization on the American model. Boosted by the media, the growth of professional spectator sports has had a negative impact on amateur organized sports.[29]

In London, all this has had important implications for green spaces devoted to sports. Already in 1983 an official report suggested that sports activity in parks had been on the decline since the 1970s. In 1993, 80 percent of London councils were planning cuts in park expenditure, and many small parks had no park keeper. About this time, it was suggested that the thirty thousand or so amateur footballers in the capital were experiencing growing difficulty finding places to play because of the neglect of parks and fields. Due to falling budgets for maintenance, there have been moves toward the greater provision of artificial all-weather and floodlit fields for football and cricket, posing a clear threat to natural habitats.[30] In the late 1990s, 16 percent of London football fields were earmarked for development. Another casualty of financial retrenchment and changing demand have been outdoor swimming lidos often with areas of greenery: their number has fallen sharply since the 1980s, with many closed or mothballed and others under threat of closure.[31]

The changes were not limited to municipal parks. School playing fields, established in the interwar and postwar years, were frequently sold off in the 1980s and later by councils short of cash and needing to take advantage of development demand. Likewise, company sports grounds suffered. Public utilities privatized by conservative governments were quick to sell their staff sports grounds to private developers. In other cases, privately owned playing fields have been deliberately neglected and shut up "in the hope that their poor condition will allow planning approval" for housing developments.[32] One of the few sports areas to have held their own are golf courses. Often run by private clubs and packed with wealthy members, these have been able to ward off the blandishments of developers. Currently there are eighty-nine private golf clubs and courses in the metropolitan area, together with an unknown number of municipal courses.[33]

In Helsinki, the changes in terms of green space for sports have been less dramatic, partly because the financial problems of municipal authorities have been less severe and partly because interest and participation in sporting activity have remained stronger. In terms of municipal provision, there has been some overall stagnation or decline in older sports spaces such as tennis courts, outdoor swimming areas, athletic fields, and basketball and volleyball courts. On the other hand, one sees a steady growth in ball-game fields related to the expansion of the urban area (see below).

When new residential areas and schools have been built, new ball-game fields have been constructed in their vicinity. Ball-game fields have the ad-

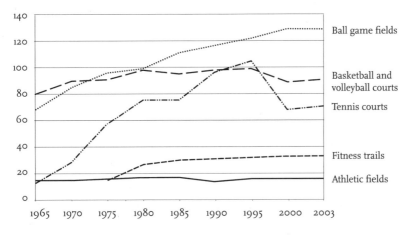

Outdoor sports sites managed by the Sports Department, Helsinki, 1965–2003

vantage that they can be used for many sports and informal games. It is also likely that traditional sports sites are being used in new ways for informal, unorganized games and experiential sports.

In the private sector, there has been an important growth of golf courses, with fifteen at present in the Helsinki metropolitan area (Helsinki, Vantaa, and Espoo). Of those whose dates of origin are known, only one was founded in the pre–Second World War era (Tali); most have been established since the 1970s. Demand has been buoyant, many women taking up the sport. In Helsinki, golf-club membership rose from 529 in 1982 to more than 1,000 in 2005.[34]

Sport, Nature, and the City

So far we have examined the main phases in the growth of sports areas in European cities from the late nineteenth century. In this last section, we sketch out the significance of these developments for the natural environment. Generally the last half century has seen mounting concern about the magnitude of the global loss of biodiversity. Cities were initially seen as hostile to nature, with the assumption that few plants, insects, or animals could survive there. But current research by ecologists suggests that urban areas embrace a wide variety of habitats, organisms, and communities: indeed, initial evidence from a number of European cities indicates a tendency for greater species richness—for instance, in birds and ground beetles—in urban areas than in their rural hinterland. Though more research is needed, this may be true of a wide range of open spaces in cities, including sports parks.[35]

Recreation and sports activities clearly have environmental impacts, with some disturbance to wildlife and habitats. As we noted earlier, the initial creation of sports grounds attracted some opposition, partly on aesthetic grounds but also from those concerned with nature conservation. In the interwar period, however, as organized outdoor sports became a fashionable motif in the green-space discourse, environmental criticism seems to have faded. In part this may have been because the management and maintenance of sports areas was less intensive and standardized, less mechanized and drastic than it became after the Second World War. Thus golf courses in the early twentieth century were often muddy wildernesses, with one writer describing the West Drayton course as having "streamlets, willow trees, and more unctuous mud." Scattered reports and photographic images of sports grounds likewise indicate rough-and-ready fields.[36] Photographic images of athletic fields and football grounds in London and Helsinki from the 1920s suggest that the grass was not heavily mowed and that the area around the competitive areas was not well cultivated.

In the postwar era, more intensive preparation and treatment of sports areas (as well as parks in general) were facilitated by bigger budgets, the greater availability of chemical products like fertilizers and weed killers, and more mechanization. The Sports Department of Helsinki shifted to mechanized lawn mowing for its sports fields in the 1940s. Chemical fertilizers were used from the 1970s, though at that time it was still common to supplement chemical fertilizers with natural fertilizers, such as chicken manure. After World War II, the golf course of the Helsinki Golf Club was managed with one horse, while the greens were mowed by hand. In 1947, a new mower was bought; it was pulled by a truck. The first motor vehicle for the management of the course came in 1954.

Heavy mechanized management led to growing criticism that parks in general and sports grounds in particular were "green deserts" with "their extensive sheets of severely mown rye grass." Reports from the London Ecology Unit on different areas in the 1980s and 1990s suggest that the practice was widespread, particularly in less wealthy inner-city boroughs. Golf course fairways have also been condemned for their heavy mowing and treatment, as well as intensive use of chemical products. Habitat modification, chemical contamination, and water management have all been seen as problems by critics claiming that golf courses are, in ecological terms, a poor use of land. The public perception of golf remains that it is bad for the environment. In a survey in southeast England in 2002, only 36 percent of respondents (nonplayers) felt the game had a beneficial environmental effect (though the figure was much higher among players!). Sports in general have been criticized because of the disturbance caused by intensive movement in the playing areas. They have also been seen contributing to the wider destruction of nature in the city by generating traffic and parking problems, and through construction work.[37]

In recent years, however, this generally negative view of sports and sports grounds as being bad for nature in the city is being revised as a result of detailed work by ecologists. Formal parks (and amenity open space) tend to support a wider range of biodiversity because they have a greater degree of structural diversity (that is, trees and shrubbery are scattered throughout the mowed grassland), and many contain a variety of habitats including ponds, lakes, and copses. Some parks (particularly in Helsinki) have been created in areas of open space that once supported a semi-natural habitat that may still survive in certain areas. These relic features provide the resource from which more extensive areas of grassland or woodland can be restored or created. Also important may be the size of a green-space area. It seems likely that in bigger, multifunctional parks the space used for sports activity is often relatively limited and so considerable areas of greenery are not disrupted by human activity. While the London Ecology Unit noted the low levels of biodiversity in parts of London parks, particularly those used for sports, its reports also drew attention to other, often peripheral spaces in parks with a prevalence of birds and other wildlife. Here wildlife was not so much eliminated as displaced by intensive sporting use. In the same way, research has shown that, in Helsinki, designated sports trails in nature parks such as Uutela concentrated use and disturbance in a very restricted area, with a large part of the park hardly visited at all. In some cases, declining municipal budgets (and the resulting decrease in heavy mowing of sports grounds) can be seen as having a positive ecological effect, while abandoned sports areas may turn into refugees for wildlife. More ecologically sensitive park management, including the provision of wilderness areas in parks near sports areas, may also have an effect.[38]

Few detailed scientific studies of the ecology of European golf courses have appeared so far, and clearly there are differences between courses and their management. Early research suggests, however, that in general they are not significant sources of water pollution and they may contain as much animal and plant diversity as many natural habitats. Frequently offsetting the intensively managed fairways are large areas of streams and wilderness, which can serve as a major refuge for biodiversity. Comparing golf courses not to a pristine natural habitat but to agricultural land (on which most golf courses have been constructed), a recent study has concluded that golf courses of any age enhance local biodiversity, providing a greater variety of habitats than intensively cultivated farmland. In London, golf courses offer home to "a remarkable diversity of flora and fauna." The nearly ninety golf courses in the London area include many with over 100 acres (40 hectares) of land, and are more extensive than the capital's nature reserves. Detailed surveys in the 1990s highlighted the importance of golf courses for wetlands, for birdlife (because of low levels of disturbance), and for plant species. New golf courses have increasingly retained ecologically important features, and the opportunities for ecological enhancement are considerable. Golf courses can participate in environmental-management programs, and their efforts are recognized through a national awards program in Britain.[39]

Conclusion

The relationship between nature and the European city is a complex one. As we have seen in the case of the evolution of outdoor sports areas—one of the major components of socially constructed landscape in the city—such green spaces have been influenced by a kaleidoscope of factors, among them sports fashions, ideas about planning, public health and social well-being, political and governmental changes, greenery management, and consumer demand. If the spread of sports grounds up to the Second World War owed much to a mixture of public and private sponsors, the postwar expansion was heavily associated with state and municipal agendas regarding social welfare and urban planning. Urban parks became large-scale, heavily managed arenas for organized and competitive sports at the amateur level. The natural world was subject to mechanization and the heavy use of fertilizers. By the 1980s, however, the organized sports movement and the dedicated sports grounds that it generated were starting to falter, linked to the spread of more informal individual sports, the dynamic rise of commercial sports, and increasing public financial constraints. Important losses of sports grounds have recently occurred, notably in London, but the period has also seen, in some measure, a more pluralist regime emerge in terms of the running of sports areas, offering greater opportunities for protecting and enhancing biodiversity.

Notes

This essay is derived from research for an international and interdisciplinary project entitled "Green Space and Sport since the First World War," which was funded in 2005–7 by the University of Helsinki European Networks Program and was led by Professor Peter Clark (History Department), Professor Jari Niemelä (Department of Biological and Environmental Sciences), and Dr. Ossi Rahkonen (Public Health Department). The project researchers in 2005 were Salla Jokela and Jarmo Saarikivi, and the project had British, German, Dutch, and Austrian partners. The project continued work from an earlier international project entitled "Space, Nature and Culture in the City, 1850–2000," funded by the Finnish Academy in 2001–4. The general results from the earlier project were published in Peter Clark, ed., *The European City and Green Space: London, Stockholm, Helsinki and St Petersburg 1850–2000* (Aldershot, 2006). Findings from the "Green Space and Sport" project were published in P. Clark, M. Niemi, and J. Niemelä, eds., *Green Space, Sport and Recreation in the European City* (Helsinki, 2009).

1. See, for instance, John Lowerson, *Sport and the English Middle-Classes 1870–1914* (Manchester, 1993); and Wray Vamplew, *Pay up and Play the Game: Professional Sport in Britain 1875–1914* (Cambridge, 1988). See also the studies of individual sports: e.g., football (soccer),

Tony Mason, *Association Football and English Society 1863–1915* (Brighton, 1980). One of the few writers on the sports landscape is John Bale; see, for instance, his excellent *Landscapes of Modern Sport* (London, 1994).

2. John Kremer et al., eds., *Young People's Involvement in Sport* (London, 1997), 11; Hennig Eichberg, "Popular Identity in Sport and Culture: About Living Democracy," www.ifo-forsk.dk/qHE2004_5.doc.

3. Peter Borsay, *The English Urban Renaissance: Culture and Society in the Provincial Town* (Oxford, 1989), chap. 7; Peter Clark, *British Clubs and Societies 1580–1800* (Oxford, 2000), 123–26.

4. Lowerson, *Sport*, 85 et seq.; Vamplew, *Pay Up*, 61–64, 187.

5. Hugh Cunningham, *Leisure in the Industrial Revolution* (London, 1980), 114 et seq.; Lowerson, *Sport*, 73, 79, 81.

6. On London, see Richard Dennis, "Modern London," in *The Cambridge Urban History of Britain: III,* ed. Martin Daunton (Cambridge, 2000), chap. 3; Douglas A. Reid, "Playing and Praying," in *Cambridge Urban History,* ed. Daunton, 746, 747; and Hugh Cunningham, *Leisure,* 142 et seq.

7. John Nauright and Timothy J. L. Chandler, eds., *Making Men: Rugby and Masculine Identity* (London, 1996). See also, generally, John Tosh, *A Man's Place: Masculinity and the Middle-Class Home in Victorian England* (London, 1999).

8. Mason, *Association Football,* 21–49, 195.

9. Richard Holt, *Sport and Society in Modern France* (London, 1981), 64 et seq.; Konstantin Semenov, "St Petersburg's Parks and Gardens," in *The European City and Green Space,* ed. Clark, 283–84; Helen Meller, *European Cities 1890–1930s* (Chichester, 2001), 72.

10. Peter Clark and Marjatta Hietala, "Helsinki," in *European City,* ed. Clark, 178.

11. Clark, ed., *European City,* 178; John Archer et al., *Nature Conservation in Southwark* (London Ecology Unit, 1989), 31.

12. Clark, ed., *European City,* 32; Matti Hannikainen, "Park Life: An Urban Environmental History of Battersea Park, 1846–1951" (master's thesis, History Department, University of Helsinki, 2005), 67. (I am indebted to Mr. Hannikainen for allowing me to refer to his thesis.)

13. Hannikainen, "Park Life," chaps. 4 and 5.

14. Clark, ed., *European City,* 178.

15. F. H. A. Aalen, "Lord Meath, City Improvement and Social Imperialism," *Planning Perspectives* 4 (1989): 137 et seq.; *London Society Journal,* no. 148 (June 1930): 109; Mason, *Association Football,* 87.

16. 1 George 6, c. 46.

17. Katri Lento, "The Role of Nature in the City: Green Space in Helsinki, 1917–60," in *European City,* ed. Clark, 189 passim.

18. David Reeder, "The Social Construction of Green Space in London," in *European City,* ed. Clark, 46; Alan Powers, ed., *Farewell My Lido* (London, 1991), 2 et seq.; Hannikainen, "Park Life," 67; *Open-Air London* (London County Council and London Transport, 1939), vii, 25.

19. D. Steel, "London's Vanished [Golf] Courses Recalled," *Country Life,* November 10, 1983, 1366; Richard Holt, *Sport and the British; London Society Journal* 138 (August 1929): 12.

20. Clark, ed., *European City,* 180–81, 200.

21. *Surveys of the Use of Open Spaces,* 2 vols. (Greater London Council, 1968–72), 1: tables 20, 29; Clark, ed., *European City,* 184.

22. Neil Wigglesworth, *The Evolution of English Sport* (London, 1966), 132 et seq.; Richard Holt and Tony Mason, *Sport in Britain 1945–2000* (Oxford, 2000), 5 et seq.; Anna-Katariina

Salmikangas, "Haasteena osallistuva liikuntasuunnittelu," in *Pelit ja kentät: Kirjoituksia liikunnasta ja urheilusta,* ed. Kalervo Ilmanen, Jyväskylän yliopiston liikunnan sosiaaliti-eteiden laitoksen tutkimuksia (Jyväskylä, 2004), 276.

23. Kalervo Ilmanen, *Ensimmäisensä Liikkeellä: Helsingin kaupungin liikuntatoimi 1919–1994* (Helsinki, 1994), 199; Patricia L. Garside, "Politics, Ideology and the Issue of Open Space in London 1939–2000," in *European City,* ed. Clark, 71.

24. Ilmanen, *Ensimmäisenä Liikkeellä,* 121, 137–41, and in the following report: *Helsingin yleis-kaavaehdotus: Helsingin kaupungin julkaisuja,* no. 9 (1960): 65–67; LIPAS, a national data-base on sports sites in Finland; Clark, ed., *European City,* 184; Royal Institute of British Architects, London, Library, X (079)H: M. Welbank, "Report." Statistical publications by the Greater London Council from the late 1960s contain very little on parks and gardens in general, and sports grounds in particular.

25. Cf. Poul Erik Mouritzen, ed., *Managing Cities in Austerity: Urban Fiscal Stress in Ten Western Countries* (London, 1992); and Clark, ed., *European City,* 94 et seq.

26. *Green Spaces Investigative Committee: Scrutiny of Green Spaces in London, November 2001* (London, 2001), 37–38.

27. Ilmanen, *Ensimmäisenä Liikkeellä,* 192.

28. *Toward a Green Strategy for London* (London, 1991), 15; Bale, *Landscapes,* 114 passim. An article in *Helsingin Sanomat,* 27 April 1973 ("Purupolku huippuhalpa liikuntalaitos") re-ported that approximately twenty new jogging tracks had been built in Helsinki from the start of the 1970s to cater to the growing popularity of the sport. In London, for instance, a jogging track was added at Crystal Palace Park in 1976 (London Development Agency Web site). Yrjö Määttä, *Nuorten liikuntaharrastukset ja vapaa-aika: Helsingin kaupungin tietokeskus, 379/8* (Helsinki, 1998). The listing of public sports facilities in *National Statis-tics: Focus 2000 on London* (London, 2000), 175, concentrates on indoor facilities including sports halls, indoor tennis centers, and indoor bowling centers.

29. Bale, *Landscapes,* 49 et seq., 84.

30. *Urban Parks and Urban Spaces: A Review* (Edinburgh, 1983), 59; J. Kossoff and K. McVeigh, "Green, Unpleasant Lands," *Time Out,* 28 September–5 October 1994, 12; *Green Spaces In-vestigative Committee,* 46.

31. Charlie Connelly, *London Fields: A Journey through Football's Metroland* (Edinburgh, 1999), 59–60; Powers, *Farewell My Lido,* 16 passim; Janet Smith, *Tooting Bec Lido* (London, 1996), 35–38.

32. Garside, "Politics, Ideology and the Issue of Open Space in London," 3; Kossoff and McVeigh, "Green, Unpleasant Lands," 12; *Green Spaces Investigative Committee,* 2 passim.

33. For a list of private clubs in the London area, see the Web site golfeurope.com/clubs/greater_london.

34. Local agenda 21 in Helsinki, Web site: www.hel2.fi/ymk/agenda/paikallisagenda21.html; *Suuri kansallinen liikuntatutkimus 2001–2002: Lapset ja nuoret.* Nuori Suomi ry, Suomen Lii-kunta ja Urheilu (SLU), Kunto ry, Suomen Olympiakomitea & Helsingin kaupunki, *Suuri kansallinen liikuntatutkimus 2001–2002. Aikuisliikunta.* Nuori Suomi ry, Suomen Liikunta ja Urheilu (SLU), Kunto ry, Suomen Olympiakomitea & Helsingin kaupunki; S. Tiitola, Sel-vitys golfharjoitteluradan sijoittamisesta Helsinkiin. Helsingin yleiskaava 2002, selvitys, 11.6.2001. *Helsingin kaupunkisuunnitteluviraston kaavoitusosaston selvityksiä 2001:2.* See also the official Web site of the Finnish Golf Association (Suomengolfliitto): www.golf.fi/. L. Kal-liala, *HGK 1932–82* (Helsinki, 1982), 114.

35. Kevin J. Gaston, *Biodiversity: A Biology of Numbers and Differences* (London, 1996); Jari

Niemelä, "Is There a Need for a Theory of Urban Ecology?" *Urban Ecosystems* 3 (1999): 57–65; Jari Niemelä, "Ecology and Urban Planning," *Biodiversity and Conservation* 8 (1999): 119–31; H. Sukopp, "Urban Ecology—Scientific and Practical Aspects," in *Urban Ecology*, ed. Jürgen Breuste et al. (Berlin, 1998), 3–16; A. Kurtto and L. Helynranta, "Helsingin kasveja 2: Erään 'kansallisnäkymän' kasvisto" (English abstract: "Plants of Helsinki 2. Flora of a 'National Scene'"), *Lutukka* 13 (1997): 56.

36. Steel, "London's Vanished Courses Recalled," 1366. See also Mason, *Association Football*, 88; photographic material collected for Helsinki by Niko Lipsanen for a Helsinki City–funded project entitled "Images of Sports Spaces."

37. Information from Sports Dept., Helsinki City; Kalliala, *HGK 1932–82*, 56, 72. Views citied in Archer et al., *Nature Conservation in Southwark*, 18; Meg Game and John Whitfield, *Nature Conservation in Tower Hamlets* (London Ecology Unit, 1996), 15–16; Jan Hewlett et al., *Nature Conservation in Barnet* (London Ecology Unit, 1997), 72, 79; M. R. Terman, "Natural Links: Naturalistic Golf Courses as Wildlife Habitat," *Landscape and Urban Planning* 38 (1997): 183–97; E. A. Murphy and M. Aucott, "An Assessment of the Amounts of Arsenical Pesticides Used Historically in a Geographical Area," *Science of the Total Environment* 218 (1998), 89–101; S. Cohen et al., "Groundwater and Surface-Water Risk Assessments for Proposed Golf Courses," *ACS Symposium Series* 522 (1993): 214–27; A. C. Gange et al., "The Ecology of Golf Courses," *Biologist* 50 (2003): 63–68; Bale, *Landscapes*, 11 passim.

38. Stuart Carruthers et al., *Open Space in London: Habitat handbook 2* (London, 1986); Hewlett et al., *Nature Conservation in Barnet*, 94–95; Niko Lipsanen, "The Seasonality of Green Space: The Case of Uutela, Helsinki," in *European City*, ed. Clark, 238 et seq.; Meg Game et al., *Nature Conservation in Ealing* (London, 1991), 63.

39. B. H. Green and I. C. Marshall, "An Assessment of the Role of Golf Courses in Kent, England, in Protecting Wildlife," *Landscape and Urban Planning* 14 (1987): 143–54; S. Cohen et al., "Water Quality Impacts on Golf Courses," *Journal of Environmental Quality* 28 (1999): 798–809; M. R. Terman, "Natural Links: Naturalistic Golf Courses as Wildlife Habitat," *Landscape and Urban Planning* 38 (1997): 183–97; A. C. Gange and D. E. Lindsay, "Can Golf Courses Enhance Local Biodiversity?" in *Science and Golf: 4*, ed. Eric Thain (London, 2002), 721–36; Gange et al., "The Ecology of Golf Courses," 63–68; D. Stubbs and T. Hare, "Wildlife Links: Flora and Fauna of London's Golf Courses," *Country Life*, November 14, 1985, 1513–14; Game et al., *Nature Conservation in Ealing*, 14, 35, 62; Hewlett et al., *Nature Conservation in Barnet*, 64.

From the "Functional City" to the "Heart of the City"

Green Space and Public Space in the CIAM Debates of 1942–1952

Konstanze Sylva Domhardt

In 1952, the Congrès Internationaux d'Architecture Moderne (CIAM) published a book entitled *The Heart of the City: Towards the Humanisation of Urban Life*.[1] As the principal publication of the eighth congress of the organization in 1951 and bearing the same name, the book acknowledged "a civic landscape of enjoyment of the interplay of emotion and intelligence," and furthered the claim that "CIAM does not ignore the great movement of social renewal that, under different aspects, occupies all the peoples of the world."[2] This publication advocated a city space with new qualities that the urbanite would experience spontaneously, creatively, and comprehensively; a city space that would reflect the social composition and intellectual heft of the people who used it. The graphic layout of the book, sketches by Saul Steinberg, and countless photographs of everyday scenes suggested "as much popular appeal as possible"[3] and illustrated vividly the central metaphor of the title: heart. It unequivocally outlined the strategy for analyzing a city: focus on its social and cultural functions.

This essay examines how green space contributed to CIAM's idea of the city as an integrated entity that embraces the relationship between the individual and the community, the structural and spatial interaction of the center of the city and its periphery, and the interdependence of the two poles of "city" and "region." On the one hand, the conceptual definition and the spatial articulation of green space became an important feature of CIAM's urban planning projects. Along with advocating the recentralization of the city, CIAM argued that landscape elements should reshape the city's contours and guide the future development of its spaces. On the other hand, a fixation on the natural components of the city determined a crucial social point in CIAM's debates—namely, the design of a public realm. The follow-

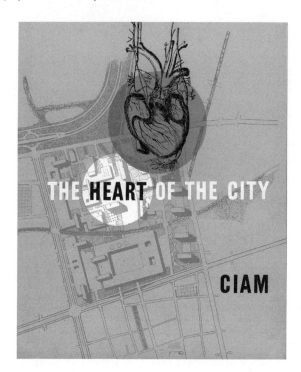

Cover of the CIAM publication *The Heart of the City: Towards the Humanisation of Urban Life*, by Jaqueline Tyrwhitt, José Luis Sert, and Ernesto Nathan Rogers (Lund Humphries, 1952). (© Ashgate Publishing Limited)

ing analysis, therefore, not only provides evidence that CIAM conceived of green space as a mediator of the various parts of the city and its surroundings, but it also shows how architectural elements were to be augmented by natural elements to support the function of green space as a "civic landscape."[4]

The contents and appearance of the CIAM book *The Heart of the City* demonstrated, at the beginning of the 1950s, that simultaneous with the development of the urban planning concept of the "functional city"—the central idea of CIAM in the prewar era—a view developed within the organization that clearly opposed a purely rational understanding of the city. The intellectual focal point of urban planning became the desire for new means of architectural expression for the public within the urban space. The discussion of concepts for the city center became its primary architectural task. Thus, a reform of the structure of the city at all scale-levels was propagated. The idea that an integrated city model had to be created that addressed social issues and weighed them against the backdrop of a rapidly changing society was the sole point of consensus within CIAM's debates. However, CIAM 8—the third postwar congress—was not the first manifestation of this new orientation within the organization. Indeed, hidden beneath the demands of this congress lay a continuous development whose roots reached back to the late 1930s—a period when most of CIAM's members had experienced cultural and geographical displacement through emigration.[5]

Whereas CIAM's conference reports, press releases, and publications, which were already the subject of various studies,[6] provide a coherent picture of the official activities of the organization, the correspondence of CIAM's leading figures and the memos from informal meetings reveal that the development of CIAM's postwar urban planning theory was influenced more by a constant transatlantic exchange of ideas than by the periodic meetings of the organization held in Europe. Broader research on CIAM makes evident that the American planning debate supplied essential guidelines for CIAM's work. Eric Mumford stated that the experiences of the CIAM protagonists in the United States altered the organization's postwar direction, and Jos Bosman spotted, in the CIAM idea of the city center, the result of a "transition experience" of the CIAM emigrants in America.[7] Nevertheless, there are only a few examples of systematic research on the perception of American planning theories within the congresses.[8] In retrospect, José Luis Sert (1902–1983)—who served as CIAM's president in the postwar era, arrived in the United States in 1939, and immediately established an architectural business in New York—characterized the impact of emigration on the work of CIAM as follows: "As a consequence of this dispersion CIAM has broadened its scope, and its views had to be broadened accordingly."[9] Walter Gropius (1883–1969), the former director of the Bauhaus and an influential member of CIAM from 1930 on, became a professor of architecture at the Graduate School of Design at Harvard University in 1937.[10] Other important figures, such as Jaqueline Tyrwhitt (1905–1983),[11] a member of the Modern Architectural Research Group (MARS), the English branch of CIAM,[12] remained in Europe during the war, but acted as mediators in a transatlantic dialogue.

In general, in the 1940s CIAM members oriented their work toward new concepts in the development of the city. They were deeply shocked by the brazen restructuring of American cities into massive suburban complexes. Descriptions of this trend, employing expressions like "neither-city-nor-country complex,"[13] attempted to explain the phenomenon of loss of identity and the process of civic disintegration in cities. As a result, CIAM members discussed urban planning solutions that enabled urban functions to penetrate each other, to be expanded, and to be spontaneously rebuilt. The goal was not to separate residential areas, business areas, community and cultural centers, sports grounds, and parks in isolated zones, but to combine these forms of land use within one continuous city space and, furthermore, to relate them to the context of its surroundings. For CIAM's intention to understand urban planning in the future as "community planning," and to divide the city hierarchically by a network of main and subsidiary centers, two planning concepts served as leading models: First, the CIAM emigrants were interested in the idea that a general plan should control all major changes in the urban physical environment—within the city and its suburban areas—a concept that had been introduced in the American urban planning debates with the designation "comprehensive planning" by the leading figures of the City Beautiful movement around the turn of the twentieth century.[14] The second concept was that of the "neighborhood unit," which had been articulated in the 1920s and had already been employed repeatedly in various planning projects in the United States.[15] CIAM 8 marked the climax of the congress's attempts to align the social and cultural dimensions of the city and of its debates that pictured the city as an integrated entity in which a system of cores fosters a process of recentralization. Therefore, CIAM provided the European postwar urban planning scenario—which, on the one hand, was characterized by a focus on the reconstruction of city centers, but, on the other, was often advocating a zoning system with lower building densities and a decentralization of the city—with a broad catalogue of alternative strategies.

The Heart of the City

In 1942 in the CIAM publication *Can Our Cities Survive?* Sert put forward a new formulation of the resolutions—"Feststellungen"—that had been decided upon at CIAM 4 held in 1933 with the theme "The Functional City."[16] In the chapter entitled "The Civic Centre, the Nucleus of Urban Culture," Sert explains his criticism of the inadequacy of the prewar conception of the city: "To many, the 'functional city' would therefore have a purely material meaning. To us, however, a city would not be functional unless it satisfied and stimulated the more noble aspirations of its people as well—aspirations which strive towards a better life and which have always impelled men to seek a community existence."[17]

Sert's argument in this chapter concluded with the decisive statement that the "human scale" no longer sufficed, and that the "human scale of values" needed to inform every basic planning decision. With that, Sert expanded the concept of the functional city with an interpretation that Le Corbusier (1887–1965) did not even consider in his publication of the "Feststellungen" in *La Charte d'Athènes* (Athens Charter) one year later. MARS, in its quest for functional structures that were also socially motivated, chose an approach similar to Sert's by presenting the following definition in their explanation of the *MARS Plan*—a proposition for restructuring London— in 1942: "Culture means education, training, development of mental and bodily faculties, intellect and judgment" and should be understood as an "amenity for the population" and as the "final aim of all town planning."[18] From today's perspective, MARS can be recognized as the most active and influential of all the CIAM groups in the postwar era. Because MARS was crucial in preparing the organizational structure and the content of CIAM 6 and CIAM 8, it had a great impact on CIAM's postwar work. At the end of the 1940s, MARS came to the following landmark conclusion: "CIAM 7 in its analysis of Community Life distinguished four Functions (*a*) Dwelling (*b*) Work (*c*) Cultivation of Mind and Body (*d*) Circulation. But there is another function of Community Life, in fact the function which makes it a Community life and distinguishes the community from a mere aggregation of individuals or families. . . . Somewhere there is a physical setting for the expression of collective emotion, the heart of the organism."[19]

In particular, the work of Sert and MARS promulgated new principles for urban planning and for the definition of green spaces: CIAM now conceived of places for social interaction as essential, the "heart" of the body of the city. These were understood as neurological points around which the cities of the future would develop. CIAM's prewar concept of the city therefore had to be revised. If the functional city of the 1930s had ordered the functions of dwelling, working, recreation, and circulation as autonomous features without a hierarchy, in the 1940s these functions would be dependent on a social understanding that was internally weighted and spatially centralized. Essentially, CIAM now argued that socially and culturally determined city centers should define the structure of the city. On the one hand, these city centers would help further the process of recentralization that would bring the city back into defined borders. On the other hand, they were expected to serve as a link that permeated all the social and spatial areas of community life within a city.

How did CIAM's new urban planning focus and their now broader interests translate into urban-design projects? With few exceptions, almost all of CIAM's members were active practitioners or people with a background in practical experience. Understandably, they were greatly interested in the development of concrete design principles. Thus, CIAM's postwar activities swung between the two poles of theory and practice, which strongly influenced each other. In all of their debates, CIAM members attempted to build a bridge between these two poles of urban planning. In these circumstances, the idea of the "humanization of urban life" became an important guideline for many of their designs. This desire for architecture to work toward a more human urban life was expressed in the minutes of countless official and unofficial meetings. In 1951, the term "humanization" became part of the subtitle of CIAM 8's official report and of the subsequent publication. Yet, this term and the claims associated with it exposed much broader concerns: Could social interaction be functionally categorized? Which architectural methods promote urban vitality? Should city centers be developed in a specific spatial constellation so that they radiate over the entire city?

On the one hand, CIAM members tried to illuminate the many aspects of a humanized urban life by considering the latest findings of urban sociological studies. For example, the assignments of tasks in Walter Gropius's seminars on urban planning at Harvard and the descriptions of the student projects include various references to the writings of Louis Wirth, one of the most influential figures of the Chicago School of Urban Sociology, who in 1938, in his pioneering text "Urbanism as a Way of Life," characterized the urban milieu as "a distinctive mode of human group life."[20] In addition, Gropius's book *Rebuilding Our Communities* (1945), his first comprehensive comment on "community planning," was based on the outcome of the social experiments of the British biologists George Scott Williamson and Innes Hope Pearse at the Peckham Health Centre in London.[21]

On the other hand, CIAM members tried to incorporate an abstract understanding of nature into their ideas. CIAM statements referred to descriptions of natural processes of growth and to the composition of the human organism in order to create a construct for city planning. Analogies with nature were used to open up a new perspective on the humanization of the urban environment. Nevertheless, as far as the definition of a city model was concerned, the discussions remained somewhat inconclusive. They fell short of clearly stating whether the term "organic" was put forward to support a process of decentralization or, rather, to foster a model for recentralization.

The Humanization of Urban Life

At the beginning of the 1940s, the designation "organic" in the American planning debate had already become associated with manifold meanings: "organic life," "organic thinking," "organic order," and so forth. Different biological metaphors are included in the theoretical contributions of the Chicago School of Urban Sociology and were employed to describe the interdependency between the city space and the social relationships of its inhabitants.[22] In general, planners understood urban projects labeled "organic" as directly representing the trends of social development. In contrast, "inorganic" projects were viewed as those characterized by a design strategy that subordinated human needs to economic interests; the term "inorganic" denoted a failure in planning. The notion that "organic planning" should be based on social thought—as Frank Lloyd Wright suggested with his concept of an "organic architecture"—and not on a figurative idea as opposed to the rational and geometric, was widespread. The consensus among planners was that an urban project was "organic" as long as it proposed an urban space that was responsive to nature and the needs of the people, and its parts added up to a harmonious greater whole.[23]

The definition of the term "organic" in the writings of CIAM's leading figures is similarly imprecise. In CIAM discussions during the 1940s, "inorganic" had been considered synonymous with "unorganized," "inhuman," and "without scale." In contrast, "organic growth" promised a process of organized city planning and a new legibility in city structures. In CIAM's debates, this notion of "organic growth" shed light on the relationship between city and nature from a regional-planning perspective. The construct "city-region" was pictured within a framework that directly related the expansion of cities to natural growth. Walter Gropius's argument, in the early 1940s, for the establishment of a system of satellite "townships" around existing cities expresses this new point of view: "Nature shows different kinds of growth. Plants, for instance, may grow in a more or less concentric or linear pattern; but they cease growing at any rate when they have reached their inherent optimum of growth; then they 'grow' by throwing off fruits, that is to say, by 'colonization.'" The township should guarantee "a true organic growth for a city."[24] A decade later at CIAM 8, the term "organic" was used in another way. It was used in collocations such as "organic life," and the term was understood to be synonymous with expressions like "a greater whole" or "cultural entity." The analogy between the city and the human body that Sert employed in his 1944 article "The Human Scale in City Planning" provided the basis for this interpretation: "The organic city will thus be composed, as its name implies, of different parts or organs. Each organ or unit having a specific function to perform, and being so composed that each can fulfill this function to the greater efficiency of the city as a whole."[25] Here, Sert proposed dividing the city into discrete units, with every unit grouped around a social center that made available all the functions necessary to community life. In this system, every unit would be part of a larger subordinate unit that in turn cultivated a social center. In this way, a unified system—"a city as a whole"—would be formed. A city structured according to this model would no longer build on determined constellations of functional zones. Rather, the city would be compartmentalized in terms of the social-spatial interaction of flexible living groups within an "organic social structure."

Besides these spatial and structural implications, the humanization of urban life also referred to a social concept that had been intensively debated within CIAM since its foundation in the late 1920s. At CIAM 4, the organization had articulated as a goal of its urban planning activities the development of a harmonious relationship between the individual and society: "In its intellectual and material bases, the functional city should create a harmonious relationship between individual and community life."[26] With these comments, CIAM's members expressed a desire that has since characterized city planning: the hope for a balance between individual freedom and social cohesion. In the 1930s, however, they did not pose the question of how the new organization of life—one of the most important points in the Athens Charter—would be coupled within a comprehensive reorganization of society. Defined as "function," human activities were only partly considered as socially relevant performance, and the theory of the functional city did not include any definition of the function of social centers. Rather, in the "Feststellungen," "dwelling" was considered the true center of all urban planning approaches—despite the fact that, in both Europe and America, influential voices had advised against equating housing with urban planning. For example, the pioneer of British town planning, Patrick Abercrombie (1879–1957), declared, in his well-known book *Town and Country Planning* (1933): "Nevertheless, housing, however important an aspect, is not town planning."[27] At the end of the 1940s, Lewis Mumford expressed a similar view even more forcefully in a letter to Sert: "But what of the political, educational, and cultural functions of the city: what of the part played by the disposition and plan of the buildings concerned with these functions in the whole evolution of the city design. . . . I regard their omission as the chief defect of routine city planning; and their absence from the program of the C.I.A.M. I find almost inexplicable."[28]

In the prewar period, the original starting point of CIAM's urban planning remained the "dwelling cell," that is, the home. According to the "Feststellungen," social life should wholly exist within the family circle, and the family should create a "social cell."[29] All extended functions were placed close to, and in immediate relation to, the home. In addition, social arrangements were not supposed to offer opportunities for social interactions that reached beyond the uses associated with home. For the most part, therefore, open spaces in CIAM's prewar theoretical models were simply conceived of as intervals between buildings. Their major functional purpose was, on the one hand, to create spaces for circulation within the living quarters, and on the other, to fill a very generally formulated need, "relaxation during free time."[30] For this reason, open spaces were usually pictured as green areas without precise spatial qualities. Furthermore, they were not conceptualized as specific places that citizens might fashion according to their interests.

Compared to this view, in which the social relationship of the unit to the whole—of the individual to the community—found very little expression in CIAM's urban planning approaches, most of CIAM's statements from the 1940s onward sounded a decidedly different note: "A community of people is a self-conscious organism: that is to say, each member is aware of the interdependence of all the members. And this awareness, or sense of community, is expressed with varying degrees of intensity at different scale-levels."[31] A necessary conclusion of this thinking was the idea that the home as an isolated cell should no longer constitute the smallest unit in the body of the city. In its place a new urban pattern must come into being, one that was ready to undertake a mediating role and also include social centers as integrated elements. To achieve this, in discussions as early as the beginning of the 1940s, CIAM members revived the concept of the neighborhood unit. This concept had been widely propagated by the members of the Regional Planning Association of America (RPAA) since the 1920s to support their idea of "community planning," which was based on the assumption that "a good house can not exist in a city by itself; it can come only as part of a community plan, and until we learn to design our communities and our houses cooperatively, treating each separate unit as a part of the whole, we shall not succeed much better than the jerry-builder does today."[32] Since his first visit to the United States in 1928, Gropius was in contact not only with Lewis Mumford, the leading figure of the RPAA, but also with Clarence Samuel Stein. As soon as Gropius arrived in America, he met with Stein in his office in New York. In the 1940s, Stein's interpretation of the neighborhood unit, above all his principles of the "superblock" and the "cul-de-sac," became an important reference for Gropius's work.[33]

In 1929, in his contribution to the *Regional Plan of New York and Its Environs*, Clarence Arthur Perry (1872–1944) introduced the term "neighborhood unit" to the American urban planning debate to identify a concept that incorporated a wide range of impulses from the social sciences around the turn of the century—above all, the theory of Charles Horton Cooley delineated in his most influential book, *Social Organization: A Study of the Larger Mind* (1909)—and directed the attention to them from an urban planning point of view.[34] With the project for Radburn (1928–33), Clarence S. Stein suggested a physical interpretation of Perry's theory and created a structural system that was thereafter adopted as the "Radburn Principle."[35] In 1951, Jaqueline Tyrwhitt revised Perry's definition of the neighborhood unit as follows: "1. Make the elementary school the focus of the neighborhood. 2. Eliminate through traffic from the neighborhood and reform local streets to serve the residents. 3. Localize and segregate the shopping at the corners of the neighborhood. 4. Provide minimum standards for open space and neighborhood parks."[36]

But the defining intellectual grounding for the integration of the neighborhood unit in the city planning theory of CIAM was presented by Sert: "Open space distributed to each family in a group is not as valuable nor as useful as the same amount of open space planned and arranged to serve the same families as a unified group. This is the outstanding lesson of today: people will get more out of life by living interdependently with each other rather than independently of one another."[37]

The CIAM protagonists perceived the neighborhood unit as an important element of urban design that reflected the social structure of the people, and that could be used to support the idea of an integrated city that fosters the social intercourse and the multifaceted social activities of its inhabitants. This idea had significant influence on the functional and formal interpretation of the spaces between buildings. These were no longer regarded as gaps serving only some recreational or traffic needs. Now they were regarded as places for activity on the part of the inhabitants in which the life of a neighborhood unit could be constituted. Green space is now referred to as a public realm within the city pattern that incorporates a wide range of social and cultural facilities, including community centers, shopping centers, museums, galleries, theaters, churches, and schools, and that connects them to residential areas.

Toward a Gradual Layout of the City

After its first postwar congress in 1947, CIAM continued to explore how to organize city life into neighborhood units.[38] In the run-up to CIAM 8, the question of whether this concept offered assumptions for the design of community centers on the scale of the whole city began to be discussed. Additionally, no answer had emerged to the question of how the concept of neighborhood units could help to unite these centers—and thereby the open space within a city—into one public network. How could individual neighborhood units—in themselves well-functioning entities—be integrated within the whole body of a city and, at the same time, establish a city center? For CIAM's response to these questions, Stein's project for Radburn formed an important point of reference. It is worth looking at two of its components in more detail: On the one hand, in each neighborhood unit of Stein's project, a so-called shopping center serves as a meeting point along with the school, combining social interaction with commercial usage. On the other hand, a continuous park, accessible only to pedestrians, mediates the

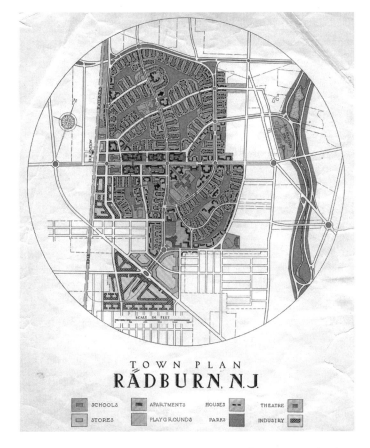

Extract from Clarence S. Stein's master plan for Radburn, N.J. (undated). (Courtesy of the Frances Loeb Library, Harvard Graduate School of Design)

different neighborhood units. It gives space to a variety of public buildings such as a high school, a recreational field, and, in particular, the town community building. By acting as an ensemble in the geographical focal point of the whole layout, "occupying a beautiful hill," they form a civic center and facilitate the interaction of the neighborhood units.[39]

In the run-up to CIAM 8, it became obvious that to produce a cohesive city structure rather than an abstract constellation of urban functions, a focus on the various scale-levels of the city was of the utmost importance. To achieve a more gradual layout of the city, MARS suggested a very pragmatic task: for CIAM 8, case studies should be examined from at least two perspectives—that of a city for 1,500 inhabitants (the size of a neighborhood unit), and of one for 25,000 inhabitants (the size of a conglomerate of neighborhood units). At the same time, Tyrwhitt and Sert tried to turn their extensive theoretical research to this end and to define criteria for a differentiated partitioning of a city according to different scale-levels. Inasmuch as they thereby established important guidelines, this essay examines their findings more closely.

In a series of lectures delivered in 1951 at the University of Toronto, Tyrwhitt expanded on Perry's definition of a neighborhood unit and introduced a complex classification schema. In one of her first lectures with respect to the differing levels of social interaction, she spoke about neighborhoods in which face-to-face contact was possible (the "residential unit" of 500 to 1,500 people); and about an area within which the members of the family group could find all their needs (the "urban unit" of 15,000 to 70,000 people). Furthermore, she mentioned the "roving neighborhood" of every inhabitant (the "urban constellation" of 250,000 to 2 million people).[40] Later, she expanded this classification and defined a system of four scale-levels: "village or housing unit" (500 people); "market center or residential unit" (15,000 people); "town or urban unit" (50,000 people); and "city" (250,000 people). Taken together, all of these levels created the "urban constellation."[41] On the other hand, by 1944 Sert had already defined five basic planning units that ranged from the "neighborhood unit" to the "economic region."[42] Both Tyrwhitt and Sert explored the question of what should connect the different levels of the urban constellation. For example, one finds in Tyrwhitt's attempt to classify the different types of community centers, which is documented in the congress publication, the very interesting comment: "The possibilities are different at each 'scale-level' of community, and the need is for a hierarchy of Cores that punctuate the 'Urban Constellation'—city plus countryside."[43] In contrast to the functional city, in which the movement of traffic eliminated the space between functions such as working and dwelling with the strictest economy of time, in this system, city space would be conceived in a "hierarchy of Cores." The neighborhood units of different scale-levels would be linked by means of a network of urban centers. In this way, public space would be composed of multiple individual city centers spatially connected "by elements of the urban landscape."[44] But Tyrwhitt added yet another interesting aspect: concerning the definition of city centers, the relationship between the city and its environs should be reformulated, for she suggested, with the coupling of the two terms "city" and "countryside," an openness of the physical boundaries of the city. The urban constellation described in her theory would ideally intertwine with the surrounding landscape, and in this respect Tyrwhitt directly referred to the demand that MARS had formulated in 1944: "There might be at least some green arteries not of just promenade width but representing rally [sic] wide strips, of park land or open country penetrating deep into the heart of the town."[45]

Against the backdrop of this theory, the major themes of all of CIAM 8's case studies were marked by the spatial connections among the diverse social centers within the body of the city and by the relationship between public space and surrounding countryside. This is amazing considering that the various projects had vastly different planning backgrounds. Among the drafts could be found examples ranging from reconstruction plans for bombed-out city centers (such as Coventry and Hiroshima); alterations of existing city centers (like New Haven and Lausanne); the planning of new city centers (including Chimbote and Bogotá); and the total restructuring of cities (Paris) to the reconstruction (Saint-Dié) or new planning of entire cities (Stevenage and Nagele). Even if the wide range of stories of the evolution of these projects does not permit us to make a generally systematic comparison, two important observations can still be made: (1) almost all of the projects chose the concept of the neighborhood unit as the guiding theme of their urban structure; and (2) it was green space that penetrated the spatial borders of these neighborhood units and placed their centers within the whole urban system. I examine below two CIAM 8 case studies that illustrate this very clearly: "Chimbote" (presented by Sert) and "Stevenage" (presented by Gordon Stephenson).

In 1948, Sert and his colleague Paul Lester Wiener sketched out the first draft for the city of Chimbote.[46] At that time, this industrial city on the Pacific coast of Peru had approximately four thousand inhabitants. The two architects proposed a reorganization of the city based on the four functions of the Athens Charter, but they buttressed the entire concept with the use of

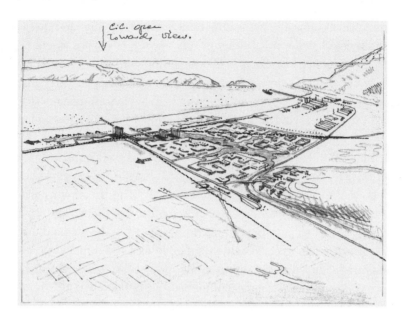

José Luis Sert, first scheme of the Chimbote Pilot Plan, perspective (undated). (Courtesy of the Frances Loeb Library, Harvard Graduate School of Design)

neighborhood units. These neighborhood units were ordered along a linear park—"a green pedestrian way"[47]—that wound through the entire city. This park ran from the open countryside to the city center, thereby forming the spine of the city. Several linear green veins connected it to the social centers of each neighborhood unit. In this way, green space penetrated the different levels of the city and created a spatial continuum that connected all its public spaces not only with the main city center but also with the surrounding countryside.

These principles, which had already been formulated in Sert's *Can Our Cities Survive?* (1942), found wide practical application in the plans for the New Towns of the first generation around London.[48] The first of these plans was for Stevenage, a small city of six thousand inhabitants that would be expanded to create a city of sixty thousand inhabitants. In the master plan designed by Gordon Stephenson in 1946, neighborhood units were grouped around the city center in a star-shaped constellation.[49] Each of these units would consist of approximately ten thousand residents organized around a community center, restaurants, a post office, and medical facilities. The neighborhood units would be separated from each other by greenbelts intended to "bring the country into the heart of the town."[50] These green spaces were to be shaped in order to create several paths and vistas between the individual neighborhood units and the city center. This would serve both to accentuate the structure of the city and to support the identification of specific places that would, in turn, permit better orientation within the spaces of the city.

"To Create the Shell"

While the papers and case studies presented at CIAM 8 focused more heavily on the relationship of spaces within the city, the congress publication the following year presented the projects in a typological system that concentrated solely on the task of designing a city center.[51] On the basis of Tyrwhitt's systematization, the publication defined categories such as the *core of the village,* the *core of a New Town,* or the *core of the city.* This frame of reference gave the theme of the congress a new focus. The core—no longer the urban constellation—was now considered the decisive planning instrument for the reorganization of the city, and, according to the authors, the task of designing it could be concretely defined. They argued that once the principles for the design of a core were outlined, they could be applied to every urban context: "These places and buildings, equipped with those elements that are necessary and sufficient, should be distributed in town and country wherever a centre of vitality occurs."[52]

However, achieving this goal was fraught with difficulties. For example, the terms of reference for this debate had not been established. Before the beginning of the congress, it had been hotly debated how the new focus of interest—locations for social interactions—could be designated by a specific term. This was not only a linguistic issue but, more importantly, one about content. Consequently, the diverse points of departure for definitions at the congress clearly illustrated the differing perspectives that had been put forth in considering the idea of city centers. The breadth of the statements encompassed terms such as "civic centre," "nucleus," "coeur," "pedestrian realm," "rendezvous," "organic synthesis of modern technology and the plastic arts," and "urban center."[53] Later, in the official compilation of the conference proceedings and in the texts of papers included in the congress publication, the term already suggested by MARS—"core"—emerged as the preferred designation. By 1952, another term had gained favor, as reflected in the title *The Heart of the City.* This ambivalence about terminology resulted in many important definitions being left open to interpretation in the work that followed. Even so, all the statements exposed an important common theme: within the core, a new breadth of functions should flourish. This public space should become a place of synthesis of the most diverse components and influences and serve as the main support for urban life. In this way, the claim expressed went much further than a simple improvement in the general quality of life—one of CIAM's prewar goals. The city center now became associated with spontaneity, creativity, and temporality, and the inhabitant became a "type of man who will take part in activities and be himself both spectator and actor."[54] Even in the text of the invitation to CIAM 8 that MARS had formulated in 1949, effusive mention was made of the activities as "just plain gregariousness without specialized motives," further noting: "but its demands on planning and architecture are as real and as important as any others."[55] This served to present the city space as the platform for a host of activities that would be initially achieved by the direct appropriation of the space by its inhabitants. Above all, therefore, an overarching goal of planning was to be the creation of public spaces that afforded a flexible and complex cultural program and also allowed for multifaceted interpretation. In this connection, CIAM acknowledged that one of the most important requirements was that "the Core should be a place secure from traffic—where

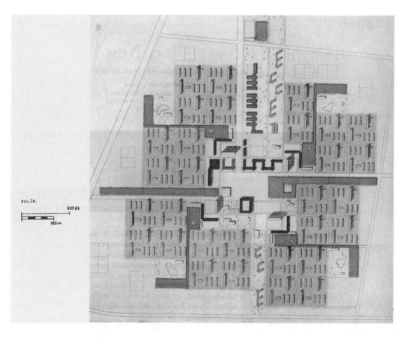

The case study "Rotterdam" presented by the Dutch CIAM Group at CIAM 8 (1951), from *The Heart of the City: Towards the Humanisation of Urban Life*, by Jaqueline Tyrwhitt, José Luis Sert, and Ernesto Nathan Rogers (Lund Humphries, 1952). (© Ashgate Publishing Limited)

the pedestrian can move about freely," "a royauté du pieton."[56] Thus, the inhabitants would be offered choices for every possible type of use of the spaces. Many congress delegates shared the conviction that the variable uses of public spaces and their specific design could and should be determined beforehand. They contended that human activities could be purposefully steered by the design of a city's spatial milieu.

Both aspects—the definition of uses as well as the design of their spatial frame—were discussed in connection with the design potential of landscape elements to create points of visual reference. Among others, the case study for CIAM 8 by the Dutch CIAM Group OPBOUW illustrates this very precisely. The project's alignment of the development was essentially composed of two urban planning entities. On the one hand, four tall slab buildings were proposed, each placed at the interface of the neighborhood units and the city center. In this way, they emphasized the relationship between different functions and the city space on a three-dimensional plane. In addition, they visually framed the central plaza while simultaneously marking its position in the city space. On the other hand, these dominant altitudes were bound by green spaces that served as orientation points for the pedestrians on the ground level. Intended, above all, to provide a visually diverse experience, the two components—the slab buildings and their related green spaces—molded a spatial ensemble.

"A Meeting Place of the People and the Enclosed Stage for Their Manifestations"

In the European postwar period, in the process of reconstruction of cities the tenets of the functional city were promoted and applied widely, even though, by the 1940s, CIAM had already begun to criticize this model and to present an alternative: the "heart of the city" concept.[57] As CIAM's urban planning debate has demonstrated, the search for the "heart of the city," beginning in 1942 with Sert's book Can Our Cities Survive? and concluding with the report of CIAM 8 in 1952, produced a wide spectrum of results. CIAM's members allowed themselves to be guided by the idea that human activities could be directly determined by the design of city space. Many CIAM protagonists disseminated the belief that through the concept of the core, places would be created in which the greatest possible individual freedom and interactive community life could be imagined: "a meeting place of the people and the enclosed stage for their manifestations." Accordingly, the debate achieved a structural complexity and thematic openness that prewar discussions had not known. The functional city lent to this debate a number of thought-provoking stimuli, and yet, its critical revision redirected the various views in multiple respects: as a result, the idea of the humanization of urban life directly addressed community and social questions. The proposal of a more gradual layout of the city was meant to link public spaces within the city structure and with its surrounding landscape. And, finally, the view that "the task of the architect is merely to create the shell"[58] was expected to concretely structure a setting for the activities of civic life. These different attempts served a single goal, to create a core as a physical framework for human intercourse that must be flexible enough to accommodate changing social needs and varying activities, and yet always be sufficiently articulated—in itself and in its approaches—to remain part of the city's spatial continuity.

The CIAM analysis was aimed at the city as a whole for the purposes of comprehensive planning, while at the same time it did not regard urban space as a static system. The development of urban space was to be subject to a dynamism that would produce informality, growth, and transformation and would be linked to the interplay between constant and variable elements—a concept that was to have a decisive influence on urban planning theories in the 1950s and 1960s. For example, the city that Alison and Peter Smithson described in their essay entitled "Cluster City: A New Shape for the Community" had a polycentric structure, like the urban constellation. Its structure was guided by the community's localities and was organized through "population pressure points" intended to promote "the change, the growth, the flow, the vitality of the community."[59] In the mid-1960s, Aldo Rossi presented his view of the city as a human artifact and as a continuous process of construction. In contrast to the CIAM, he focused on the question of the identity of the city, and his analysis differentiated between the "primary elements" and the "urban area" of a city. Nevertheless, there are clear conceptual parallels between his theory and the system of cores in the CIAM's urban planning. For example, in his treatise *L'architettura della città* (1966), Rossi argues that there are always "fixed activities" with a public and collective quality that are attached to the "primary elements" as the catalysts of a city.[60] An environment favoring community life was to be produced through the definition of a constant urban infrastructure and by designing focal points in the body of the city.

With their conception of a humanized environment, the representatives of CIAM were evidently attempting to set modernism on new foundations during the 1940s. CIAM had developed a decisive basis for discussions on the structural design of the modernized city and for views on the formation of urban identity. The term "core" became the theoretical code for the definition of public space; above all, green space became the instrument of its physical formulation and its integration into the city pattern. With these developments, landscape architecture played an essential role from two perspectives. On the one hand, it was expected to create legible public spaces within the city: green space contained the city and established connections. It created overarching visual and spatial references, and defined the internal and external form of the city. On the other hand, landscape was a decisive architectural element differentiating the public space for multiple uses. As CIAM moved from the concept of the functional city to the idea of the heart of the city, green space again morphed into a socially defined space and thereby became the essential element in the design of urban spaces.

Nevertheless, the CIAM debates on urban planning left numerous questions open. Although in terms of the history of ideas, there is surprising continuity between the works produced by CIAM in the 1940s and those of subsequent movements, there were many leaks in CIAM's theoretical edifice that were never sealed. Social interaction in the urban space continued to be a topic reserved more for pictorial or film presentation and was rarely a subject of urban planning. The analyses of architectural types and of structures of social relationships were not correlated with one another. The idea of integrative comprehensive planning remained fragmentary and in practice continued to give way to the autarchic project. Often conceptual links to the work of the congresses were deliberately not sought out. In the second half of the twentieth century, numerous programmatic texts were produced whose authors attempted to legitimize their own views of the city through a critique of CIAM. Without exception, their statements focused on the organization's activities during the 1920s and early 1930s. Subsequent debates on urban planning theory among the major figures in CIAM—whether in exile in America or on the periphery of the continental avant-garde in Britain—were categorically ignored. If this deliberate rupture was intended to create space for new, radical points of view, it nevertheless left much unexplored. This rendered important CIAM insights inaccessible, and they have remained so to the present day.

Notes

1. Jaqueline Tyrwhitt et al., eds., *The Heart of the City: Towards the Humanisation of Urban Life* (New York, 1952). With its eleven congresses and numerous unofficial meetings between

1928 and 1959, CIAM provided one of the most important discussion forums for the modernist movement, and assembled not only architects and planners but also historians and sociologists. For a detailed description of CIAM's activities during the prewar era, see Martin Steinmann, ed., *CIAM: Dokumente 1928–1939* (Basel and Stuttgart, 1979); for the postwar era, see Eric Mumford, *The CIAM Discourse on Urbanism, 1928–1960* (Cambridge, Mass., 2000).

2. Quoted from "A Short Outline of the Core," in *The Heart of the City*, ed. Tyrwhitt et al., 168. CIAM 8 ("The Heart of the City") took place July 7–14, 1951, in Hoddesdon, England. It was the third congress of the postwar period. The preceding congresses of this period were CIAM 6 ("Reunion Congress"), September 7–14, 1947, in Bridgewater, England; and CIAM 7, July 22–31, 1949, in Bergamo, Italy.

3. Quoted from the letter of José Luis Sert to Jaqueline Tyrwhitt, August 8, 1951, CIAM-Archive, Institute for the History and Theory of Architecture, ETH Zurich (CIAM-Archive) [CIAM 42-JT-9–281].

4. The expression "civic landscape" is used in the conclusions of CIAM 8, summarized in "A Short Outline of the Core," in *The Heart of the City*, ed. Tyrwhitt at al., 165.

5. For the emigration of German architects and planners to America, see Bernd Nicolai, ed., *Architektur und Exil: Kulturtransfer und architektonische Emigration von 1930 bis 1950* (Trier, 2003). The most comprehensive insight into the emigration of former Bauhaus members to the United States is found in Gabriele Diana Grawe, *Call for Action: Mitglieder des Bauhauses in Nordamerika* (Weimar, 2002).

6. See, among others, Jos Bosman, "CIAM 1947–1956," in *Fünf Punkte in der Architekturgeschichte*, ed. Katharina Medici-Mall, (Basel, Boston, and Stuttgart, 1985), 196–211; Jos Bosman, "Jenseits des Textes: Die Charta von Athen im Lichte der Projekte der Nachkriegszeit," *Werk, Bauen + Wohnen* 80 (1993–94): 8–17; John R. Gold, "In Search of Modernity: The Urban Project of the Modern Movement, 1929–39," in *Modern Britain 1929–1939*, ed. James Peto et al. (London, 1999), 40–51; Volker M. Welter, "Post-War CIAM, Team X, and the Influence of Patrick Geddes," in *CIAM—TEAM 10: The English Context: A Report on the Expert Meeting, Held at the Faculty of Architecture, TU Delft, on November 5th 2001*, ed. Kenneth Frampton (Delft, 2002), 87–112; and Annie Pedret, "CIAM and the Emergence of Team 10 Thinking, 1945–1959" (Ph.D. diss., MIT, 2001).

7. See Eric Mumford, "CIAM Urbanism after the Athens Charter," *Planning Perspectives* 7, no. (1992): 413; and Jos Bosman, "CIAM after the War: A Balance of the Modern Movement," *Rassegna* 14, no. 52 (1992): 8.

8. A discussion of potential sources of CIAM's intellectual reorientation in the 1940s is included in Volker M. Welter, "From Locus Genii to Heart of the City: Embracing the Spirit of the City," in *Modernism and the Spirit of the City*, ed. Iain Boyd Whyte (London and New York, 2003), 35–56; and Eric Mumford, *Defining Urban Design: CIAM Architects and the Formation of a Discipline, 1937–1969* (New Haven, 2009), 20–61. The transatlantic exchange of ideas within CIAM, and above all, the adaption and interpretation of the concept of the neighborhood unit, is analyzed in detail in Konstanze Sylva Domhardt, "Die CIAM-Debatten zum Stadtzentrum und die amerikanische Nachbarschaftstheorie: Ein transatlantischer Ideenaustausch, 1937–1951" (Ph.D. diss., ETH Zürich, 2008).

9. Quoted from José Luis Sert, "Centres of Community Life," in *The Heart of the City*, ed. Tyrwhitt et al., 4. For the work of José Luis Sert in America, see Xavier Costa et al., eds., *Sert: Arquitecto en Nueva York* (Barcelona, 1997); Josep M. Rovira, *José Luis Sert, 1901–1983* (Milano, 2000), 289–363; Josep M. Rovira, *Sert, 1928–1979, Complete Work: Half a Century*

of Architecture (Barcelona, 2005), 108–227; and Jaume Freixa, *Josep Lluís Sert* (Barcelona, 2005).

10. For Gropius's teaching activities in the United States, see Reginald R. Isaacs, *Walter Gropius: Der Mensch und sein Werk*, vol. 2 (Berlin, 1983–84), 845–995; Anthony Alofsin, *The Struggle for Modernism: Architecture, Landscape Architecture, and City Planning at Harvard* (New York and London, 2002); and Jill Pearlman, *Inventing American Modernism: Joseph Hudnut, Walter Gropius, and the Bauhaus Legacy at Harvard* (Charlottesville, 2007).

11. Immediately after the war, Tyrwhitt explored new transatlantic challenges, beginning with her 1945 lecture tour of Canada and the United States, and pursuing her career at the University of Toronto (1951–55) and Harvard University (1955–69). For the beginning of the relationship between Tyrwhitt and Gropius, see her letter to Gropius from 17 January 1948, in Walter Gropius Papers, Houghton Library, Harvard University, Cambridge, Mass. [bMS Ger 208 (1645)]. *Ekistics* 52, no. 314–15 (1985) sheds light on Tyrwhitt's contribution through a chronological narrative. It includes a collection of essays that interweaves the biographical facts of Tyrwhitt's career with the larger themes of her work. The only attempts to evaluate Jaqueline Tyrwhitt's impact on the discourse on urbanism in the postwar era are found in Ellen Shoshkes, "Jaqueline Tyrwhitt: A Founding Mother of Modern Urban Design," *Planning Perspectives* 21, no. 4 (2006): 179–97; and Ellen Shoshkes, "Jaqueline Tyrwhitt and Transnational Discourse on Modern Urban Planning and Design, 1941–1951," *Urban History* 36, no. 2 (2009): 263–83.

12. For a detailed description of the activities of MARS, see Farouk Hafiz Elgohary, "Wells Coates: Beginning of the Modern Movement in England" (Ph.D. diss., Bartlett School of Architecture, 1966); Beata Keller-Kerchner, *Modern Architectural Research Group: Die englische Gruppe der CIAM, 1933–57*, research report, ETH Zürich, 1994; John R. Gold, "Towards the Functional City? MARS, CIAM and the London Plans, 1933–42," in *The Modern City Revisited*, ed. Thomas Deckker (London and New York, 2000), 80–99.

13. In 1940, the influential MARS Group member Thomas Sharp introduced this expression into the English urban planning debate (see Thomas Sharp, *Town Planning* [Harmondsworth and Middlesex, 1940], 45).

14. For a study of an overall idea history of the concept of "comprehensive planning" in the United States, see Jon A. Peterson, "The Origins of the Comprehensive City Planning Ideal in the United States, 1840–1911" (Ph.D. diss., Harvard University, 1967); and Konstanze Sylva Domhardt, "Der ganzheitliche Planungsansatz im amerikanischen Städtebau: Von der City Beautiful zum Regional Planning," in *Anthologie zum Städtebau*, ed. Vittorio Magnago Lampugnani et al., vol. 2: *Von den Anfängen des theoretischen Urbanismus zur Stadt der Moderne* (Berlin, forthcoming).

15. The concept of the "neighborhood unit" itself was the product of a transatlantic exchange of ideas. From a European point of view, the concept was exported to the United States in the first decades of the twentieth century along with the American perception of Ebenezer Howard's model of a garden city (Howard used the term "ward") and reimported in the early 1940s. For a study of the origins of the concept, see James Dahir, *The Neighborhood Unit Plan: Its Spread and Acceptance: A Selected Bibliography with Interpretative Comments* (New York, 1947); and Donald Leslie Johnson, "Origin of the Neighbourhood Unit," *Planning Perspectives* 17, no. 3 (2002): 227–45. The adoption of the concept on both sides of the Atlantic is analyzed in Kermit C. Parsons, "British and American Community Design: Clarence Stein's Manhattan Transfer, 1924–74," *Planning Perspectives* 7, no. 2 (1992): 181–210; Dirk Schubert, "'Heil aus Ziegelsteinen'—Aufstieg und Fall der Nachbarschaftsidee:

Eine deutsch-anglo-amerikanische Dreiecks-Planungsgeschichte," *Alte Stadt* 25, no. 2 (1998): 141–73; Edward K. Spann, "The Regional Planning Association of America: British-American Planning Culture at Work, 1923–1938," in *The City after Patrick Geddes,* ed. Volker M. Welter et al. (Bern, 2000), 149–69; and Dirk Schubert, "The Neighbourhood Paradigm: From Garden Cities to Gated Communities," in *Urban Planning in a Changing World: The Twentieth Century Experience,* ed. Robert Freestone (London, 2000), 118–38.

16. CIAM 4 took place from July 29 to August 13, 1933. It was the most influential congress of CIAM's prewar period. Its "Feststellungen" formulated basic premises for the idea of the functional city. For an introduction to this concept, see Thilo Hilpert, *Die funktionelle Stadt: Le Corbusiers Stadtvisionen—Bedingungen, Motive, Hintergründe* (Braunschweig, 1978); and John R. Gold, "Creating the Charter of Athens: CIAM and the Functional City, 1933–43," *Town Planning Review* 69, no. 3 (1998): 225–47.

17. José Luis Sert, *Can Our Cities Survive? An ABC of Urban Problems, Their Analysis, Their Solutions Based on the Proposals Formulated by the C.I.A.M.* (Cambridge, Mass., 1942), 228.

18. The MARS Plan was first published in "A Master Plan for London: Based on Research Carried out by the Town Planning Committee of the M.A.R.S. Group," *Architectural Review* 91, no. 546 (1942): 143–50.

19. Quoted from "MARS Group Proposals for CIAM 8. November 1949," CIAM-Archive [CIAM 42-GS-1-38/39].

20. Quoted from Louis Wirth, "Urbanism as a Way of Life," *American Journal of Sociology* 44, no. 1 (1938): 4. See also Louis Wirth, "The Urban Mode of Life," *American Society of Planning Officials* (1937): 23–30.

21. In *Rebuilding Our Communities* (Chicago, 1945), 53, Gropius describes Williamson's and Pearse's experiments in detail. The Peckham Experiment took place between 1926 and 1950, initially generated by rising public concern over the health of the working class and an increasing interest in preventative social medicine. For an overview of the history of the Peckham Health Centre, see Elizabeth Darling, *Re-forming Britain: Narratives of Modernity before Reconstruction* (London and New York, 2007), 54–71.

22. For example, see Robert Ezra Park et al., eds., *The City* (Chicago and London, 1925).

23. For the application of the term "organic" by Frank Lloyd Wright, see Anja Nadine Klopfer, "'The only possible city looking toward the future': Individualität und organische Gesellschaft bei Frank Lloyd Wright," in *Stadtformen: Die Architektur der Stadt zwischen Imagination und Konstruktion,* ed. Vittorio Magnago Lampugnani et al. (Zürich, 2005), 266–80. There is also a strong relationship to the organicism and morphology in the theories of Patrick Geddes, who identified the city as the "specialized organ of social transmission." For Geddes's city-organ analogy, see Volker M. Welter, *Biopolis: Patrick Geddes and the City of Life* (Cambridge, Mass., and London, 2002), 92–99.

24. Quoted from "Housing as a Townbuilding Problem: A Post-War Housing Problem for the Students of the Graduate School of Design, Harvard University, February–March, 1942," Special Collections in the Frances Loeb Library, Harvard University (SC) [Rare NA2300. H37G76x].

25. José Luis Sert, "The Human Scale in City Planning," in *New Architecture and City Planning,* ed. Paul Zucker (New York, 1944), 398.

26. "Die funktionale Stadt soll auf geistiger und materieller Basis das individuelle und das gemeinschaftliche Leben in harmonische Beziehung bringen." Quoted from "Die Feststellungen des 4. Kongresses," in *Internationale Kongresse für Neues Bauen,* ed. Steinmann, 163 (English translation by the author).

27. Quoted from Patrick Abercrombie, *Town and Country Planning* (London, 1933), 157.

28. Lewis Mumford to José Luis Sert, December 28, 1940, Sert Collection, Special Collections in the Frances Loeb Library, Harvard University (SC/JLS Collection) [JLS/folder E1].

29. See "Feststellungen: Definitive Fassung," in Internationale Kongresse für Neues Bauen, ed. Steinmann, 157; and postulation (79) in ASCORAL, *La Charte d'Athènes: Urbanisme des C.I.A.M.* (Paris, 1943).

30. See postulations (37) and (79) in Le Corbusier, *Charte d'Athènes.*

31. "Proposals submitted to the council of CIAM by the MARS Group: April 1950," CIAM-Archive [CIAM 42-JT-7–52/61].

32. Quoted from Lewis Mumford, "American Architecture," *American Federationist* 34 (December 1927): 1484. For the RPAA discussion of "community planning," see Henry Wright, "Shall We Community Plan?" *Journal of the American Institute of Architects* 9, no. 10 (1921): 320–30; and Roy Lubove, *Community Planning in the 1920s: The Contribution of the Regional Planning Association of America* (Pittsburgh, 1963).

33. For his visit at Stein's office in New York, see Walter Gropius to Lewis Mumford, February 26, 1938, Houghton Library [WG/bMS Ger 208–1248]. References to Stein's planning principles are included, for example, in Gropius, *Rebuilding Our Communities* (Chicago, 1945), 19–21; and in his assignment of tasks in "Housing Problem (Problem V for the 2c classes and the 2d class)," p. 10, April 7, 1941 [SC/Rare NA2300.H37W343x].

34. See Clarence Arthur Perry, "The Neighborhood Unit: A Scheme of Arrangement for the Family-Life Community," in *Regional Survey*, vol. 7: *Neighborhood and Community Planning*, ed. Committee on Regional Plan of New York and Its Environs (New York, 1929), 22–140. This contribution was based on a speech entitled "A Community Unit in City Planning and Development," which Perry delivered at a conference organized in 1923 in Washington by the National Community Center Association and the American Sociological Society, and on his article "The Relation of Neighborhood Forces to the Larger Community: Planning a City Neighborhood from the Social Point of View," *Proceedings of the National Conference of Social Work*, Toronto, 25 June–2 July 1924 (Chicago 1924), 415–21.

35. See Eugene Ladner Birch, "Radburn and the American Planning Movement: The Persistence of an Idea," *Journal of the American Planning Association* 46, no. 4 (1980): 424–39.

36. Jaqueline Tyrwhitt, "The Neighbourhood Unit Idea," in "Programme of Lectures on Principles of Town Planning, University of Toronto, Fall Term 1951," typescript, CIAM Collection, Special Collections in the Frances Loeb Library, Harvard University (SC/CIAM Collection) [CIAM/folder E5].

37. José Luis Sert, "The Neighbourhood Unit—Its Creation, Improvement, and Conservation," typescript, SC/CIAM Collection [CIAM/folder C12].

38. See the proposal of the American CIAM Group for the topic of CIAM 6, entitled "Community Development: Proposal for the 6th Congress Theme Submitted by CIAM Chapter for Relief and Postwar Planning. December 1945," SC/CIAM Collection [CIAM/folder B4].

39. See Clarence S. Stein, "Toward New Towns for America," *Town Planning Review* 20, no. 3 (1949): 203–51.

40. See Jaqueline Tyrwhitt, "Lecture 8: The Neighbourhood Unit"; and Jaqueline Tyrwhitt, "Lecture 9: The Neighbourhood Unit in Practice," both in *Programme of Lectures on Principles of Town Planning, 1951.*

41. See "Lecture 10: The Urban Constellation and the Core of the City," ibid.

42. *"(a) The neighbourhood unit, (b) The sub-city or township, (c) The city proper, (d) The metropolitan area, (e) The economic region"* (quoted from Sert, "The Human Scale in City Plan-

ning," 398). A similar classification is also included in Sert's unpublished text "Unguided and Misguided Growth of Communities," SC/CIAM Collection [CIAM/folder C12].

43. Jaqueline Tyrwhitt, "Cores within the Urban Constellation," in *The Heart of the City*, ed. Tyrwhitt et al., 104.

44. See "A Short Outline of the Core," 165.

45. Quoted from "Observations on the County of London Plan, edited by Ernö Goldfinger, London, December 1944," in *MARS News* 2 (February 1945), RIBA [MARS/1].

46. For a detailed description of the project for Chimbote, see Josep M. Rovira, *José Luis Sert: 1901–1983* (Milan, 2000), 113–61; Patricia Schnitter Castellanos, "José Luis Sert y Colombia: De la Carta de Atenas a una Carta del Hábitat" (Ph.D. diss., Universitat Politècnica de Catalunya, Barcelona, 2002). Schnitter Castellanos gives an introduction to the planning context.

47. See the paragraph "Chimbote" in the descriptions of the individual *MARS GRID*, CIAM-Archive [CIAM 42-JT-6–31].

48. See Sert, *Can Our Cities Survive?* 232. For the history of the development of New Towns, see J. Frederic Osborn and Arnold Whittick, *The New Towns: The Answer to Megalopolis* (London, 1963).

49. See the illustration entitled *Original Neighbourhood Concept* in Jack Balchin, *First New Town: An Autobiography of the Stevenage Development Corporation 1946–1980* (Stevenage, 1980), 69.

50. Quoted from the clipping "Stevenage: The Text Case for Town and Country Planning," CIAM-Archive [CIAM 42-JT-8–660].

51. Giedion used the expression in his article "The Heart of the City: A Summing-Up," in *The Heart of the City*, ed. Tyrwhitt et al., 161: "The task of the architect is merely to create the shell."

52. Quoted from "A Short Outline of the Core," 166.

53. All terms, except "coeur," are included in "A Short Outline of the Core." For the term "coeur," see "La Séance du Dimanche 8/7/51: Urbanisme du Noyau," CIAM-Archive [CIAM 42-JLS-17–52/59].

54. Quoted from "A Short Outline of the Core," 165.

55. Quoted from "MARS Group Proposals for CIAM 8. November 1949," CIAM-Archive [CIAM 42-GS-1–38/39].

56. Quoted from "A Short Outline of the Core," 164, 168.

57. Ibid., 167.

58. Quoted from "The Heart of the City: A Summing-Up," 161.

59. Quoted from Alison and Peter Smithson, "Cluster City: A New Shape for the Community," *Architectural Review* 122, no. 730 (1957): 333.

60. See Aldo Rossi, *L'architettura della città* (Padua, 1966), 91.

Part IV

Ecology and the Urban Environment

Property Rights, Popular Ecology, and Problems with Wild Plants in Twentieth-Century American Cities

Zachary J. S. Falck

For more than a decade, cities in the United States have been making new places for their old flora. At Tifft Nature Preserve in Buffalo, New York, botanists mapped "native" plants and protected their habitat.[1] The Chicago Park District established neighborhood "nature and wildlife gardens" where milkweed, goldenrod, dock, and other wildflowers were cultivated in patterns appropriate for home gardens.[2] In Lincoln, Nebraska's Pioneers Park, the Prairie Legacy Garden featured scores of the region's shrubs, grasses, and herbs.[3] In St. Louis, Missouri, revitalizing the 1,293-acre Forest Park included creating small savannas and prairies with "natural vegetation" and a "diversity of native species" to enhance "nature in the city."[4] These cities employed indigenous species to improve environmental quality, to beautify the urban landscape, and to provide their inhabitants with connections to nature.[5] Landscapers and park stewards stated that native plants consumed less water and required fewer chemicals to maintain than plants conventionally placed in parks and urban landscapes. They also worked to recover forms of life that had disappeared from the land when it was settled and urbanized by peoples from Europe, Africa, and Asia. Within the bounds of these gardens, parks, and preserves, distinctions between indigenous, native, natural, and wild plants blurred and disappeared.[6] To cultivators, the plants' biological attributes, ecological qualities, and historical legacies made them desirable species to grow in these spaces. These plants were the "nature" that belonged in cities. Yet, at different times throughout the twentieth century, municipal officials in all four cities penalized and prosecuted landowners for neglecting to remove or nurturing the same plants, as well as a host of others from around the globe.

In twentieth-century American cities, the urban landscape changed year after year as structures and systems appeared and disappeared as well as plants pullulated, were placed in, and were pulled out of the land.[7] Plants that grew or seemed to grow wildly caused conflict among urban Americans who were concerned about nature in the city. During periods of urban growth and decline, municipalities and many of their residents disparaged these plants and attempted to destroy them, whether the plants grew on private property or public land.[8] Yet, some city people found the same plants beautiful, interesting, or useful. Wild plants were both resented and admired; their control was desired and disputed. Urban Americans typically denigrated wild plants as weeds. In historical perspective, however, weeds were perplexing plants that reveal the complicated place of nature in city life.

Historians of urban environments examine nature in the city as the material world with which cities were built and interacted, and, more recently, as the mastery and manipulation of the natural world to order city people's social worlds.[9] Most broadly, nature in the city, sometimes referred to as urban nature or rendered tangible as the urban landscape, includes the organisms inhabiting and the ecological processes sustaining cities.[10] The relationships of urban people, their cities, and the natural world are studied at scales ranging from the reliance of a metropolis on water and air to the microscopic particles and pathogens circulating through people and places.[11] The plants coloring cities are also useful for understanding urban environmental change and the problems with nature in American cities.[12]

Investigating the disputes over wild plants provides a basis to assess how and to what extent the place of nature changed in twentieth-century American cities. Conflicts over what plants belonged and which plants did not belong in the urban landscape recurred periodically as urban Americans cultivated and maintained nature in the city.[13] Urban environmental change, property laws, and ecological ideas influenced what plants grew in cities and how people dealt with them. Over the course of the century, cities expanded, and urban environments changed continuously. Building, abandoning, and remaking cities continually altered the populations of plants occupying urban land. Laws detailed city dwellers' responsibilities for their properties and the plants on them. During this time, rigid regulations regarding plants on private property persisted. Urban Americans developed concerns about, practical uses for, and hopes tied to the plants around them. This essay investigates controversies over wild plants in St. Louis, Lincoln, Buffalo, and Chicago at different points of time in the twentieth century. Urban Americans' problems with and the promises of urban vegetation changed as cities evolved. Nuisance law and popular ecology influenced how urban Americans related to wild plants. Twentieth-century urban Americans' struggles with and disputes over wild plants indicated the troubled place of nature in the city.

Regulating and Appreciating Urban Plants

Exercising property rights and meeting property-ownership responsibilities influenced how Americans created and maintained environments in cities. Property rights isolated a piece of land from the environment and allowed the owner to rework nature for profit or pleasure. Property-ownership responsibilities recognized the interconnections among land parcels and bounded how owners used nature. Acting with the power or neglecting the responsibilities of ownership could create conflict between landowners who utilized nature and property differently.[14] These tensions between rights and responsibilities were most evident in environmental transformations such as dam building, but also surfaced in the relationships between people and plants on city land.

Nineteenth-century urban growth increased concerns over environmental nuisances in cities. Municipal officials and courts established and enforced nuisance laws to protect public health and safety from dangerous activities on and conditions of private property. Cities' efforts to differentiate nuisances that caused physical injury from conditions that offended olfactory or visual senses, often of the middle class, were imperfect and often contested, but courts defended their police power. Commercial and industrial enterprises such as slaughterhouses were common nuisances. The ordinary vegetation that flourished on open spaces where new homes were being built outside the dense urban core created environmental problems as well. In the late nineteenth and early twentieth centuries, city officials believed these plants were nuisances that endangered public health by spreading disease. Legislation varied from city to city, but the plants and vegetation were variously described as injurious, noxious, rank, and unwholesome. For example, in 1892, officials in Indianapolis, Indiana, prohibited the growth of "weeds or noxious plants" because they were "injurious to public health."[15] Cities exercised their authority to decide what plants belonged on urban properties and in urban landscapes.[16]

Banning nuisance plants emphasized the responsibilities of city property owners. Urban weed laws required landowners to control plants growing on their land and suspended the property right to ignore vegetation change. These laws held residents responsible for growing weeds. Owners had to prevent plants from reaching a certain height or had to clear their land in the spring, summer, and fall. Cities attributed the existence of wild vegetation to human dereliction. As one leading legal commentator wrote, only nuisances resulted from landowners' actions—not from what occurred due to "purely natural causes."[17] As nuisances, the plants were viewed not as organisms born of ecological processes but as messes produced by irresponsible property owners. By neglecting their land and allowing the vegetation to thrive there, property owners made weeds. As nuisances, weeds legally resembled pollution such as tannery by-products and smoke. By making weeds unlawful, city officials made the plants unnatural. While local ordinances might identify some plants by common name such as thistles or burdock, the laws banned plants over a certain height—only "4 inches" in Washington, D.C.— or vegetation that was vigorous and dense, called "rank growth" in Columbus, Ohio.[18] The nature that belonged in cities was, almost exclusively, nature that human hands had put into place.

Weeds laws established municipal control over plants in the city, but compliance with the laws was erratic. In order to combat this nuisance, cities deployed health inspectors to identify weed-covered land. They also relied on police and residents to report violations. In practice, cities struggled to enforce the provisions. Officials posted notices on signs or mailed notices to property owners residing in other cities. They prosecuted landowners in courts. When owners did not comply, cities expended additional funds to do the work and attempted to recoup the costs by placing liens on the properties.

The limited effectiveness of nuisance law to rectify urban environmental problems compelled introduction of additional regulatory frameworks. Between 1910 and 1929, municipal officials implemented zoning laws to protect environmental quality and property in better residential areas as well as to legitimate industrialists' property rights to engage in unrestricted enterprises. In effect, zoning reduced public-nuisance liability and expectations of responsible property use. In addition, environmental problems could also still be treated as private nuisances for which adjacent property owners received compensation for damages. In the 1960s, environmental lawyers and activist citizens revived public-nuisance law to settle conflicts ranging from the siting of helicopter pads to wetland destruction.[19] Despite these developments, the regulation of urban vegetation remained unchanged. Cities retained police power over plants causing public nuisances. Residents concerned about weeds often registered complaints with sympathetic or dutiful public officials, although municipal bureaucracies proved unable to eradicate plants.

Although the law guided how Americans managed wild plants, writings about nature, ecology, and the environment also influenced how Americans thought of, felt about, and handled urban vegetation. The historian Samuel Hays used the term "popular ecology" to describe the citizens' political efforts of the 1960s and 1970s to respond to environmental degradation.[20] This term is also applicable to the tradition of writing about the relationships of people and the natural world traced by the historian Donald Worster. Other scholars might categorize this work as nature writing.[21] Popular ecology works were based on scientific knowledge explaining the relationships of organisms with their environment. These popular writings were efforts to shape perceptions and understandings of nature by translating scientific ideas for wider audiences. Authors could conduct or borrow empirical scientific studies to support their ideas. They often moved beyond the material and statistical to the moral and practical as they addressed ambivalence about, alienation from, and dependence on nature.

Popular ecological writings were not produced primarily for scientific communities. Scientists, magazine readers, nature lovers, and children were audiences for and could be proponents of popular ecology. The authors were conservationists, preservationists, environmentalists, or they were unaffiliated with any political or social organization attempting to influence policies of resource development, use, appreciation, or disposal. Conversely, there were likely Americans who were involved in environmental politics but not intellectually engaged with nature. Popular ecology could, but did not necessarily, become more sophisticated with the advancement of ecological science over time. This writing spans the works of John Muir and John Burroughs to John Kieran and Rachel Carson to Sarah Stein and Robert Sullivan.[22]

Throughout the twentieth century, popular ecology writers nurtured Americans' appreciation of urban nature. One popular ecology topic was plants in urban life. Writers suggested that there were relationships other than enmity between people and the vegetation commonly dismissed as weeds. They explained how to inspire children's awareness and to increase their knowledge of plants. These works also suggested that appreciating urban plants might improve urban environmental quality. In addition, some of these writers thought that the study of wild urban plants could possibly ease the pressure of cities on surrounding areas.

In the early twentieth century, nature-study proponents advocated teaching children about biology and the natural world by bringing them outdoors to interact with plants.[23] Nature study was not necessarily an urban or rural pursuit, although many nature-study teachers believed it was less practi-

Although this field full of plants in an Indianapolis neighborhood might have been deemed a nuisance by municipal officials, in the eyes of the nature-study advocate David Dennis, such plants presented opportunities to observe nature. (David Worth Dennis, *Nature Study: One Hundred Lessons about Plants* [Marion, Ind.: O. W. Ford, 1903], 85)

cal inside urban cores than outside of cities, where a more diverse array of plants furnished more and richer possible lessons. But nature study advocates were pragmatists, too. David Dennis argued that bringing children into the outdoors was pedagogically superior to book learning about nature. To study the seed dispersal of plants, David Dennis recommended the ubiquitous dandelion, noting, "We need not go away from home for wonders; there is not in all the earth a creature more wisely cared for than the dandelion that grows at every door."[24]

Nature study could encourage moral behavior and responsibility. Clifton Hodge, a Clark University biologist, believed that all children needed to plant seeds and to rear plants in order to develop patience, carefulness, and faithfulness. According to Hodge, failing to provide this experience was "a crime against civilized society" that had produced "hoodlums." Hodge also claimed that nature study provided a knowledge of right and wrong necessary to support fights against disease, insects, weeds, and forest fires.[25] In an extensive compendium of nature-study lessons, Anna Comstock, who worked with preeminent horticulturist Liberty Hyde Bailey at Cornell University, remarked that goldenrod abounding in cities and towns went unnoticed because urban people were "so stupid that they hardly [knew] a flower when they [saw] it."[26] Despite preferences for particular plants to teach particular lessons, these authors all believed that Americans, including and perhaps especially city dwellers, needed more regular contact with nature. Although reformers worked to sharpen the consciousness of nature among city dwellers and used city landscapes for this purpose, elite Americans who frequently traveled to natural places well outside the limits of their cities had limited need for such exercises.[27]

Although nature study faded from school curricula, botanists in universities attempted to advance Americans' understanding of nature in the city. For example, in post–World War I Philadelphia, John Harshberger proposed that students practice ecological research in local fields, parks, and gardens. During and after World War II, Edgar Anderson encouraged awareness of urban vegetation. He tried to reintroduce his automobile-enthralled students to their surroundings by leading them into St. Louis's dump heaps and alleys in search of sunflowers and wild lettuce. Anderson also wrote short essays for botanical garden publications and *Landscape* magazine. He challenged his readers to search for nature not only in distant national parks but also inside their cities. He believed that appreciating the diversity of life, including wild plants, was necessary to the cultivatation of livable urban environments.[28]

In Cold War America, urban reformers and environmentalists alike considered weed-covered urban land to be evidence of the deterioration of and the impoverished nature in squalid cities. However, in the 1970s, popular ecology works appeared that featured wild plants as sources of inspiration. Anne Ophelia Dowden painted weeds as beautiful and tenacious green life in cities that were overwhelmed with brown, black, and grey structures and surfaces.[29] Maida Silverman, a native city dweller, "came to love" the plants growing "wild in cities" that saved cities from becoming "hideous, barren places."[30] The botanist Richard Weaver produced a guide to the plants that thrived in the urban environments. Although he conceded that plants that inhabited neglected land exacerbated its "untidyness," Weaver believed that the "delightful" plants created "an intriguing sense of life."[31] These writers recognized the relative paucity of nature in the city, but they admired the plants that endured and sometimes even flourished in harsh urban environments.

While animosity toward weeds and respect of wild plants were among the ways urban Americans expressed their understanding of nature, they also developed relationships with the natural world in their home gardens. Horticultural catalogues, gardening books, and businesses selling seeds and plants helped city people transform and enliven urban landscapes. Women and men graded land and nurtured plants that changed seasonally and annually in size, color, and smell. They simultaneously exercised their property rights and fulfilled their property-ownership responsibilities. In these spaces, city dwellers maintained regular contact with the natural world, but they also bounded it. Garden tastemakers and landscape architects empha-

Richard Weaver thought that nature-admiring city dwellers could be fascinated by a seemingly derelict 1970s Boston streetscape. ("Along Washington Street," *Arnoldia* 34, no. 4 [July–August 1974], 146. © President and Fellows of Harvard College, Arnold Arboretum Archives)

sized controlling plants. For example, one garden writer remarked, "even the smallest city garden should be kept orderly."[32] Another landscape expert recommended deciding on precise locations for shrubs and bushes before they were purchased to create the "picture" and the "frame."[33] Gardens were places where civilized minds produced artful land with nature as a medium. This property was not a space to admire unencumbered ecological processes. Control of plants remained necessary in "natural gardens" and "natural landscapes" later in the century. Even as urban Americans reintroduced plants to the city that had disappeared from the city, they excluded longtime city plants. Gardens that tested the boundaries of taste did not necessarily expand the boundaries of what was considered "natural." The manipulation of plants and plastic consumer goods was often seen as a more acceptable use of property than allowing nature to do too much work. Plants that were grown, but that appeared to go unmanaged, by property owners could irritate neighbors and be dismissed as unseemly. When conflicts between cities and landowners over what plants belonged in the urban environment occurred, the species involved were not seen merely as objects or consumer goods; these plants expressed the relationship between people and ecological processes.[34]

As cities became more populated in the first half of the twentieth century and began emptying in the second half of the century, ecologically informed Americans became aware that protecting the countryside and lands beyond depended in part upon improving environmental quality where most Americans lived. Refined parks, residential and botanical gardens, and ornamental displays sprinkled plants throughout cities. However, wild plants connected the city to ecological processes and changes. Unlike city officials who detested the weeds that landowners failed to eliminate, ecologically motivated city dwellers believed that many of these same plants promised to ameliorate their urban environments. The respect for wild urban plants that emerged sharply diverged from the animosity toward weeds established in municipal ordinances. The gap between law and ecological sensibility generated disputes between cities and property owners in St. Louis, Lincoln, Buffalo, and Chicago.

Propagating and Policing Wild Urban Plants

The City of St. Louis's 1896 law banning weeds was among the first such laws in American cities. Even as new streets and houses became part of the urban landscape, clover, dog fennel, horseweed, milkweed, mullein, and thistles flowered around and in between them. In the summer, vegetation grew thick and provoked weed-fearing St. Louisans to complain to the health department. City officials responded with an ordinance that stated weeds released "unpleasant and noxious odors" and hid "filthy deposits" on subdivided blocks. A newspaper warned that weeds infected schoolchildren with typhoid, scarlet fever, and diphtheria as well as exposed pedestrians and streetcar passengers to malaria.[35] Some St. Louisans worried that criminals hid in the weeds. One strategy to eliminate weeds was to impose fines to compel property owners to clear the plants from their land. In 1900, the city notified Smith Galt, a powerful corporate lawyer, that he had violated the ordinance by "unlawfully allow[ing] and maintain[ing] . . . a growth of weeds to a height of over one foot" on a vacant lot about a half mile away from his home.[36] The outraged Galt challenged the city in court. He argued that the city's vague weed definition did not apply to his vegetation. The city's victory in the Missouri Supreme Court reinforced that there was no place for weeds in St. Louis's changing urban environment.

The tension between property rights and property responsibility generated Galt's resistance to the city's power to regulate nature as a nuisance. Galt claimed that the city violated his Fifth Amendment property rights by requiring him to destroy his plants without compensation. The city, however, insisted that Galt's property responsibilities outweighed his rights as a landowner. The court's decision secured the city's power to protect public health and acknowledged the landowners' contribution to it. *St. Louis v. Galt* showed that the city exercised substantial authority over the cultivation and neglect of nature throughout the urban landscape.

Whether Galt's vegetation belonged in the city hinged on the arguments that both sides made about the city's ecology. The city argued that Galt's lack of evidence that weeds were "indisputably and universally . . . unobnoxious and harmless" necessitated that the city exercise police power over his property.[37] The common perception that weeds were dangers required limiting the interaction of people and these plants. Galt countered that his "uncultivated" plants were part of the "economy of nature" and produced oxygen that city people needed.[38] He offered a layman's interpretation of mutual and beneficial ecological relationships between people and plants. This disagreement over the possible dangers and benefits of plants in the changing urban landscape left room for some uncertainty over which plants belonged. After the trial, editors of the *St. Louis Post-Dispatch* expressed contradictory opinions on the sunflowers and goldenrods flourishing all around the city. One editorial denounced a patch of sunflowers as "a forest of weeds" that had to be "cut down," while another deemed goldenrod an "innocent and beautiful" plant rather than one of the "outcasts of the vegetable kingdom."[39] The newspaper did not see these two different plants as part of the same ecological process. Officials' beliefs that weeds had nothing to contribute to the modern city's ecology and the city's broad law obviated the need to attempt distinguishing innocents and outcasts.[40]

This dispute over wild plants indicated that nature ideally would be easily controlled but actually was diversely and only partially understood. Nevertheless, *St. Louis v. Galt* established that property-ownership responsibilities included subjugating ecological processes in urban environments. The case reinforced the legal status of wild plants as public nuisances, and it was cited throughout the twentieth century to uphold the power of cities to control vegetation. Urban Americans had the opportunity to admire plants that they had put into place, but they had little need for plants perpetuating natural processes. Cities across the country adopted antiweed laws, and at least eighty-three cities were working to control weeds by 1940.[41]

In mid-twentieth-century Lincoln, Nebraska, putting plants into the urban landscape proceeded along with eliminating vegetation that no longer belonged. Thickets of sunflowers, ragweed, and butterweed as well as patches of pigweed, sorrels, and dock disappeared as city officials buried the prairie under broad streets lined with elms, maples, and oaks.[42] Yet, prairie remnants and unkempt yards interfered with the city's well-planned nature. In 1950, city officials found "various tall weeds, six to eight feet in height" on land belonging to Ben Greenwood, a truck driver, and his wife, Ruby.[43] Unsatisfied with the Greenwoods' effort to remove "all weeds and worthless vegetation," the city cleared the land with a tractor and destroyed the couple's raspberry bushes in the process.[44] Although a jury awarded the couple $1,250 in damages, the city triumphed in the Nebraska Supreme Court, which ruled "the power and duty of the city to require the destruction and removal of weeds . . . could not be" questioned.[45]

To maintain an orderly urban landscape, Lincoln controlled landowners' relationships with nature around their homes. The city expected the Greenwoods to manage their vegetation responsibly, not to expect a right to neglect it. The Greenwoods' raspberry bushes and other vegetation did not belong in a neighborhood distinguished by "nice homes, attractively kept yards, strong churches, [and] good schools."[46] The case also emphasized the value of plants rather than their place in nature. The Greenwoods sold their raspberries to supplement their income. They challenged the damage to their property—not the city's control over weeds. Both parties cultivated nature for the value it returned or added, whether as a crop to sell or as labor invested in maintaining neatness. Plants that people did not place in the land did not enhance the land's value, although the Greenwoods did not appear worried that wild vegetation detracted from it.

Lincoln's destruction of the Greenwoods' plants occurred as understandings of the natural world in the city were changing. The city found "considerable natural growth on the premises of wild grass, sunflowers, rag weed, and all kinds of wild vegetation that is included in natural growth."[47] The city distinguished the widely recognized sunflower and the widely disdained ragweed from the dozens of other grasses and "natural weeds" that constituted the "natural growth" on the Greenwoods' land, but they were all weeds in terms of the ordinance. Although all plants grow naturally with water and sunshine, vegetation naturally became unacceptable over time. The type of nature that the city appreciated and encouraged was not the nature that resulted from "natural growth." Yet, Americans with ecological consciousness began to sense that wild plants were desirable in cities. They appreciated the vegetation that defied the control that people exercised over modern land-scapes. When the University of Pennsylvania anthropologist Loren Eiseley reminisced about his boyhood in Lincoln, he wrote fondly of the plants that city officials had destroyed on the Greenwoods' land. Eiseley treasured a sunflower thicket southwest of downtown where he and his friends romped during the 1910s.[48] The University of Wisconsin ecologist Aldo Leopold questioned the ecological costs of the impulse of urban efficiency that eliminated both "native flora" and "interesting stowaways" from "the normal environment of every citizen."[49] Eiseley and Leopold articulated places in urban life for plants that city laws prohibited and landowners typically destroyed. Like nature-study proponents, they thought that urban Americans should experience unplanned nature; like later urban-nature enthusiasts, they recognized the need for diverse types of and places for nature in the city.

By the mid-twentieth century, nature in American cities had become increasingly controlled but not necessarily better understood as cities continued to make intensely developed urban environments even more efficient. In Lincoln, city leaders celebrated the nature that they put into place for the city's future and disdained the plants lingering from the past. *Greenwood v. Lincoln* indicated that property-ownership responsibilities included eliminating semblances of the wild in orderly urban environments. *Greenwood* sustained *Galt* as precedent and reinforced the legal and cultural consensus that weeds did not belong in cities. The municipal goal of controlling vegetation remained more influential than emerging ecological ideas regarding the place of wild plants in the urban landscape.

In the final decades of the century, controlling plants in cities remained important as urban landscapes continued to change. In sections of the northeastern and midwestern United States, industrial cities seemed to decay as housing deteriorated, factories shut down, commercial blight expanded, and demographics shifted. Fire-ravaged structures surrounded by fields of grasses and herbs intensified some Americans' fears of urban environments. At the same time, the popularity of lawns made uncultivated vegetation appear even more out of place and reduced space for other landscapes in the city. Despite the range of attitudes toward wild plants at the end of the twentieth century, weeds remained nature out of place because urban Americans intended to remain in control of rather than simply impressed by environmental change.[50]

City officials and ordinary city dwellers were reluctant simply to observe ecological processes in the urban landscape. Appreciation of wild plants and their transformation of urban space—whether private or public, vacant or designed—was not widespread. For example, in 1978, on a city lot in New York City's Greenwich Village, the landscape artist Alan Sonfist completed a space planted with native trees that would mature and simulate the forest that predated European colonization of the island. The garden writer Michael Pollan called it an "impenetrable tangle" that risked becoming indistinguishable from "an everyday vacant lot."[51] Pollan thought that land worked by uninterrupted ecological processes served no purpose and provided little appreciation of nature in urban life. However, Sonfist did not isolate the land from city dwellers. A city worker occasionally raked leaves; older New Yorkers fed birds there; and a dedicated volunteer gardener removed invasive plants. Just as in gardens, in this urban open space, human hands had to keep nature from becoming repulsive. To the extent that some reliance on and appreciation of ecological processes seemed more acceptable and more efficient in larger open spaces by the end of the twentieth century, urban nature as an ecological process had been zoned into parks. Nature as the undirected and unregulated dynamics of an urban environment was not desirable throughout the city.[52]

Although ecologically inspired urban Americans attempted to diversify nature in their cities, municipalities small and large maintained their authority over vegetation on private property. For example, in the 1980s, the hardships and anxieties of deindustrialization that pervaded Buffalo also reached its neighbors, including Kenmore, a village bordering Buffalo on the north. Many Kenmore wage earners worked at nearby airplane and automobile factories and lived with their families in modest homes with trim lawns. Kenmore's residential tranquility, jeopardized by the region's struggling economy, was further threatened when SUNY-Buffalo graduate student Stephen Kenney created a wildflower yard in front of his rented home. Kenmore officials warned him to tame the vegetation. They also won court rulings that the wildflowers had to be eliminated and that the municipality could regulate the aesthetics of citizens to sustain the community's character, health, and welfare. Keeping order in Kenmore required asserting municipal power over how its residents related to nature.[53]

In *People v. Kenney*, the responsibilities rather than the rights of the resident determined why a field of wildflowers could not be a front yard. Kenney's neighbors saw urban dereliction that imperiled their property values. Kenmore Judge H. Walker Hawthorne stated that Kenney's yard did not fit "the nature of the community."[54] The rights of surrounding property owners whose welfare was attached to that of the community were more important than Kenney's desire to let plants grow freely on the land. It was Kenney's responsibility to contribute to the community's health and wealth; it was not his right to undermine them with weeds. When two vigilante neighbors destroyed the wildflowers, Hawthorn dismissed Kenney's attempt to file vandalism charges because the judge did not consider the plants to be property.[55]

Conflicting understandings of ecology divided Kenney and his neighbors. To Kenney, the forty-one species of plants in his flower patch, which included dandelions, goldenrods, ox-eye daisies, black-eyed Susans, poppies, and asters, demonstrated ecologically sensitive property ownership. Kenney had spent twenty-five dollars on wildflower seeds; he did not believe these plants were weeds. The pesticide-free patch of land prevented the contamination of the environment. Kenney, who was inspired partly by Henry David Thoreau's quest "to wonder" as "a sunflower welcomes the light," considered the space a truly "natural yard."[56] He advocated a relationship between people and plants that improved urban environmental quality and reduced risks to people posed by chemicals. In the ecological perspective of Kenney's critics, people coexisted and prospered with particular types of vegetation in urban landscapes. Some neighbors disliked particular plants; others disliked how the plants grew. Whether ugly plants or a densely growing, poorly tended variety of species, the effect was the same. Such vegetation repelled good neighbors and perhaps attracted bad ones. Plants had the potential to destabilize a community and subject it to the prospects and vagaries of unwanted change. Kenney's antagonists believed that weed-covered land risked decline. They believed that people had to keep plants under control and their environment pleasant to keep the human urban community peaceful.[57]

As in Kenmore, vegetation-covered vacant land in Chicago elicited similar concerns over danger and decline. Despite the city's tremendous growth, in the early 1950s, some patches of the city remained undeveloped and covered with vegetation.[58] Plants also proliferated in the city's built-up sections. One city task force observed, "where once there had been homes and retail stores . . . there were yawning gaps . . . [of] abandoned cars, refuse, and overgrown weeds."[59] City officials employed their authority over property and nature to limit the spread of weed-covered urban landscapes. Asserting this power forced the city to confront residents whose ecologically inspired natural landscapes, which often featured prairie plants native to the region, seemed to resemble vacant lots in troubled city neighborhoods. The courts protected Chicago's power to control weeds by finding that the city's law was neither "unconstitutionally vague nor irrational."[60] The city retained its power over vacant private property as well as private property inhabited and maintained by its owner.

Chicago officials insisted that its citizens manage property responsibly by keeping vegetation on their land orderly rather than exercise their property rights irresponsibly by allowing vegetation on their land to become disorderly. From 1989 to 1994, the city tangled with Marie Wojciechowski, who had converted her vacant parcel next to her house into a natural landscape. The city acknowledged her right to cultivate native prairie plants but seized on the existence of dandelions, lambsquarters, and sunflowers on her grounds as evidence that she lacked full control of the plants and had neglected her land. Although the city and Wojciechowski disagreed over how well she managed the vegetation, they shared a common vocabulary of cultivation that emphasized the landowner's power to control nature.

Chicago's conflicts with natural landscapers reflected the spread of the ecological ideal that property owners had the responsibility to work with and rework nature in ways that seemed unconventional or contradictory to weed laws. Wojciechowski argued that the charges against her were unreasonable because the city cultivated the same species in parks. In an ecologically planned landscape, whether on private or public property, nature was being employed in new ways to benefit the urban and regional environments by reducing soil erosion, improving water quality, enhancing their beauty and providing wildlife habitat. Natural gardeners and landscapers were partly inspired by popular ecology's enthusiasm for wild plants. However, they did not embrace weeds or plants that were from another region or continent. In attempting to secure their property rights in courts, they often bounded what arrays of vegetation might be considered "natural." They adopted botanic and geographic knowledge of plants' origins; they tended their plants with a sense of property responsibility. They were committed to re-creating or restoring old patches of landscape, but they were not interested in how ecological processes and vegetation continually changed a garden area or a vacant lot. Like city officials and city dwellers who believed that wild plants did not belong in urban space, natural landscapers similarly agreed that not all nature belonged in the city. The tensions in their views resulted from the ecological question of what plants most belonged and best benefited people in urban environments.[61]

The disputes in Kenmore and Chicago demonstrated that conflicts between property ethics and ecological values persisted at the end of the twentieth century. Kenney and Wojciechowski saw themselves as stewards of nature, not of neighborhoods. Their neighbors saw their natural landscapes as irresponsibly maintained property. Harmonizing the responsibility to nature and responsibility to neighbors proved difficult. The turn-of-the-century attitudes toward weeds expressed in *Galt* were deeply rooted in Americans' minds, even as ecological sensibilities emerged. Whether weeds or wildflowers; whether alien plants or native plants; whether on vacant neglected lots or in yards, some plants remained unwelcome, perceived as antithetical to the built environment, and needed to be controlled. Streets where homes were close together, as the *Ken-Ton Bee* opined about Kenney's yard, typically lacked a "proper place to convert into a wildflower preserve."[62] Many residential landscapes, like conventional gardens, were places where landowners arranged plants and followed the seasonal changes; they were spaces to protect from weeds. A natural landscape did not secure a new place for nature as the ecological processes occurring in the city. Although these gardeners cultivated land in ways that other city dwellers might perceive as lacking order—distasteful displays of nature—these gardeners did not relinquish control of their land to the larger ecosystem.

Conclusion

As urban environments in the United States changed throughout the twentieth century, wild plants remained common and weeds remained troublesome. Cities grew denser with people and buildings and dispersed over greater territory. All the while, ecological processes shaped the plant life growing on urban land. In most parts of most cities, vacant land covered with wild plants appeared to be derelict land that contributed to urban disorder. Vegetation-covered vacant land remained a widely perceived problem. The problems with these plants revealed the difficulties of conceiving too narrowly of what organisms belonged and what ecological processes should occur in cities. The natural world in American cities of gardens, lawns, parks, and street trees could not eliminate and in some instances sustained and intensified dissatisfaction with urban landscapes of wild plants or semblances of them.

Establishing and controlling plants in cities concerned Americans who wanted to create livable urban environments. Cities never relinquished the power to prohibit weeds from their urban environments; and municipal officials and courts remained authorities of what constituted legitimate and desirable plant life. Ecologically conscious Americans suggested that vibrant wild plants resisted the lifelessness of cities and possibly helped counter environmental degradation. However, the view that unregulated plants—uncontrolled nature—more often degraded rather than ameliorated urban land predominated. In the tidy ecology of modern urban life, Americans maximized their role in environmental dynamics and minimized the influence of other organisms. The duties of property owners and the prerogatives of municipal governments bounded landowners' rights to and the places for freely flourishing plants.

The animosity toward weeds inhibited city officials and city dwellers from discovering ways to make the plants useful in urban environments. The responsibility to put and to keep plants in place and municipal power to maintain this order limited urban Americans' ability to rethink their relationships with the natural world as cities continued to change. Efforts to rid cities of weeds initiated at the turn of the century made it difficult to find a place for wild plants in cities at the end of the century. Urban Americans did not attempt to protect wild plants for scientific and cultural study as did ecologists in Berlin.[63] These constraints minimized the variety of ordinary city landscapes and possibly the diversity found there. Despite the ecological values and the visual aesthetics that distinguished urban Americans who insisted on simple, orderly environments from those who advocated reestablishing habitats and plants indigenous to their regions, both groups were wary of vegetation consisting of plants from around the world. The former worried about how weeds jeopardized health and social order. The latter, which included gardeners, natural landscapers, and environmental scientists, believed that weeds proliferated, homogenized flora across the globe, and accelerated biotic impoverishment. In this dichotomy, there was the "nature" that people put into place and kept in order as well the "nature" that people thought might have been in place before people built cities. In both cases, people defined nature in terms of time and types of species to prevent unexpected and unplanned historical and ecological changes. If cities were the gardens that many Americans inhabited, these urban spaces needed people to nurture the nature there toward perfectibility. There was no place for nature like wild plants that endangered cities or urban life.[64]

Notes

1. Karen E. Geiger, *Tifft Farm's Botanical Heritage* (Buffalo, 1980).
2. See www.chicagoparkdistrict.com/index.cfm/fuseaction/custom.natureOasis07.
3. Becky Seth and Kay Young, *Prairie Legacy Garden* (Lincoln, 1998).
4. *Restoring the Glory of Forest Park* (St. Louis, n.d.); www.treeswallow.com/fp/savanna/index .html.
5. One recent guide to incorporating plants into these spaces is: Ann Forsyth and Laura R. Musacchio, *Designing Small Parks: A Manual for Addressing Social and Ecological Concerns* (Hoboken, 2005).

6. Botanists, ecologists, gardeners, and landscapers often classify plants on the land as alien, exotic, indigenous, introduced, invasive, and native species. Some of these terms are synonymous, and some of them are sometimes defined by their opposites. For example, a native plant is an indigenous plant. An exotic plant is a non-native or nonindigenous plant. The distinction between native and non-native plants is typically based on the continents or regions in which they were believed to originate or to settle without human introduction, especially prior to the age of European colonization. A plant native to Europe is non-native in Australia. In carefully researched instances, and in the language of the 1999 Invasive Species Executive Order in the United States, the distinction is made on an ecosystem basis. A plant native to a southern California beach might be an alien plant in a northern California forest. An alien plant becomes an invasive plant if it causes economic or environmental damage (see www.epa.gov/owow/invasive_species/EO13112.pdf; U.S. Congress, Office of Technology Assessment, *Harmful Non-Indigenous Species in the United States*, OTA-F-565 [Washington, D.C., September 1993], 51–54; and "Green Landscaping with Native Plants," www.epa.gov/greenacres/faq.html). A sophisticated study of the cultural and political dimensions of these distinctions is: Philip J. Pauly, "The Beauty and Menace of the Japanese Cherry Trees: Conflicting Visions of American Ecological Independence," *Isis* 87 (1996): 51–73. Two important recent works include: Philip J. Pauly, *Fruits and Plains: The Horticultural Transformation of America* (Cambridge, 2007); and Peter Coates, *American Perceptions of Immigrant and Invasive Species: Strangers on the Land* (Berkeley, 2006).

7. The ecology of urban land is the subject of: J. Bastow Wilson and Warren McG. King, "Human-Mediated Vegetation Switches as Processes in Landscape Ecology," *Landscape Ecology* 10 (1995): 191–96; Herbert Sukopp and Slavomil Hejný, eds., *Urban Ecology: Plants and Plant Communities in Urban Environments* (The Hague, Netherlands, 1990); Matthew Vessel and Herbert Wong, *Natural History of Vacant Lots* (Berkeley, 1987), 1–29; and T. M. Crowe, "Lots of Weeds: Insular Phytogeography of Vacant Urban Lots," *Journal of Biogeography* 6 (1979): 169–81.

8. This essay focuses on wild plants found on private property. Whether on vacant land or in front yards, these plants' visibility made them publicly controversial, and they were regulated for the public good. Municipal government efforts to control weeds in public spaces and on public land reinforced the distinction between acceptable and unwanted urban vegetation.

9. Andrew C. Isenberg, ed., *The Nature of Cities: Culture, Landscape, and Urban Space* (Rochester, 2006); Jennifer Price, "Thirteen Ways of Seeing Nature in LA," in *Land of Sunshine: An Environmental History of Metropolitan Los Angeles*, ed. William Deverell and Greg Hise (Pittsburgh, 2005), 220–44.

10. Anne Whiston Spirn, "The City as a Garden: Urban Nature and City Design," *Illume* (Summer 2002): 3, http://web.mit.edu/spirn/www/newfront/2005/IllumeforPDF.pdf.

11. Recent works include: Martin V. Melosi and Joseph A. Pratt, eds., *Energy Metropolis: An Environmental History of Houston and the Gulf Coast* (Pittsburgh, 2007); Michael F. Logan, *Desert Cities: The Environmental History of Phoenix and Tucson* (Pittsburgh, 2006); Harold L. Platt, *Shock Cities: The Environmental Transformation and Reform of Manchester and Chicago* (Chicago, 2005); Ari Kelman, *A River and Its City: The Nature of Landscape in New Orleans* (Berkeley and Los Angeles, 2003); and Joel A. Tarr, ed., *Devastation and Renewal: An Environmental History of Pittsburgh and Its Region* (Pittsburgh, 2003).

12. For an insightful study of trees and the passage of time in the urban landscape, see Thomas J. Campanella, *Republic of Shade: New England and the American Elm* (New Haven, 2003).

13. In cities, almost any vegetation that urban Americans disliked could be referred to as "weeds." In this essay, the word "weeds" is limited primarily to clusters of plants that people at a particular time in a particular place despised. "Weeds" are not specific plants; the word is entirely contextual. In sections of the text in which plants are not being denigrated, the terms "wild plants" and "vegetation" are used interchangeably. Wild plants, regardless of their origins, grow or seem to grow in ways that indicate no urban American is cultivating or maintaining them. These wild plants in some instances likely resemble what Jens Lachmund, in his essay in this volume, identifies as "spontaneous vegetation."

14. Eric T. Freyfogle, *The Land We Share: Private Property and the Common Good* (Washington, 2003), 15–16, 229; Adam Rome, *The Bulldozer in the Countryside: Suburban Sprawl and the Rise of American Environmentalism* (New York: 2001), 119–52; Theodore Steinberg, *Slide Mountain, or, The Folly of Owning Nature* (Berkeley, 1995), 17–18.

15. *The General Ordinances of the City of Indianapolis* (Indianapolis, 1904), 1202–4.

16. Among the best analyses of these environments are: Martin V. Melosi, *The Sanitary City: Urban Infrastructure in America from Colonial Times to the Present* (Baltimore, 2000); and Adam Rome, "Coming to Terms with Pollution: The Language of Environmental Reform, 1865–1915," *Environmental History* 1 (1996): 6–28. On these weed laws, see Zachary J. S. Falck, "Controlling the Weed Nuisance in Turn-of-the-Century American Cities," *Environmental History* 8 (2002): 611–31.

17. Horace G. Wood, *A Practical Treatise on the Law of Nuisances in Their Various Forms; Including Remedies There for at Law and in Equity*, 3rd ed. (San Francisco, 1893), 148–49.

18. 30 Stat. at L. 959, chapter 326; *Ordinances of the City of Columbus, Ohio, Revised, Codified, and Consolidated* (Columbus: 1896), Section 149.

19. Andrew Hurley, "Busby's Stink Boat and the Regulation of Nuisance Trades, 1865–1918," in *Common Fields: An Environmental History of St. Louis*, ed. Hurley (St. Louis, 1997), 159–62; Louise Halper, "Untangling the Nuisance Knot," *Boston College Environmental Affairs Law Review* 26 (1998): 115–30; Denise E. Antolini, "Modernizing Public Nuisance: Solving the Paradox of the Special Injury Rule," *Ecology Law Quarterly* 28 (2001): 821–55; William H. Rodgers Jr., *Environmental Law* (St. Paul, Minn., 1986), 33.

20. Samuel Hays, *Beauty, Health, and Permanence: Environmental Politics in the United States, 1955–1985* (New York, 1987), 26–27.

21. Daniel J. Philippon, *Conserving Words: How American Nature Writers Shaped the Environmental Movement* (Athens, Ga., 2004); Ralph H. Lutts, *The Nature Fakers: Wildlife, Science & Sentiment* (Charlottesville, 2001), 69–100; Frank Stewart, *A Natural History of Nature Writing* (Washington, 1995); Donald Worster, *Nature's Economy: A History of Ecological Ideas* (Cambridge, 1977).

22. John Burroughs, *Pepacton* (Boston, 1893); John Muir, *A Thousand-Mile Walk to the Gulf* (Boston, 1916); John Kieran, *A Natural History of New York City* (Boston, 1959); Rachel Carson, *Silent Spring* (Boston, 1962); Sara Stein, *Noah's Garden: Restoring the Ecology of Our Own Back Yards* (Boston, 1993); Robert Sullivan, *The Meadowlands: Wilderness Adventures at the Edge of a City* (New York, 1998). For other writers' and city-dwellers' perceptions of nature in the city, see Michael G. Kammen, *A Time to Every Purpose: The Four Seasons in American Culture* (Chapel Hill, 2004), 199–204.

23. Kevin C. Armitage, *The Nature Study Movement: The Forgotten Popularizer of America's Conservation Ethic* (Lawrence, 2009); Sally Gregory Kohlstedt, "Nature, Not Books: Scientists and the Origins of the Nature-Study Movement in the 1890s," *Isis* 96 (2005): 324–52; Elizabeth B. Keeney, *The Botanizers: Amateur Scientists in Nineteenth-Century America* (Chapel

Hill, 1992), 132–45; Peter J. Schmitt, *Back to Nature: The Arcadian Myth in Urban America* (New York, 1969), 189.

24. David Worth Dennis, *Nature Study: One Hundred Lessons about Plants* (Marion, Ind., 1903), 84–85.

25. C. F. Hodge, *Nature Study and Life* (Boston, 1902), 10–11.

26. Anna Comstock, *Handbook of Nature-Study for Teachers and Parents* (Ithaca, 1911), 555.

27. Schmitt, xvii, 189; Thomas Bassett, "Vacant Lot Cultivation: Community Gardening in America, 1893–1978" (master's thesis, University of California at Berkeley, 1979), 1–49; Kevin Dann, *Across the Great Border Fault: The Naturalist Myth in America* (New Brunswick, N.J., 2000), 19–51.

28. John W. Harshberger, "Hemerecology: The Ecology of Cultivated Fields, Parks, and Gardens," *Ecology* 4 (1923): 297, 306; Edgar Anderson, "The Country in the City," *Landscape* 5 (Spring 1956): 32–35; Edgar Anderson, "The City Is a Garden," *Landscape* 7 (Winter 1957–58): 3–5. On cars and environmental consciousness in the United States, see Paul S. Sutter, *Driven Wild: How the Fight against Automobiles Launched the Modern Wilderness Movement* (Seattle, 2002), 19–53.

29. Anne Ophelia Dowden, *Wild Green Things in the City: A Book of Weeds* (New York, 1972).

30. Maida Silverman, *A City Herbal: A Guide the Lore, Legend, and Usefulness of 34 Plants That Grow Wild in the City* (New York, 1977), 3–4.

31. Nancy M. Page and Richard E. Weaver Jr., *Wild Plants in the City* (New York, 1975), 4.

32. Minga Pope Duryea, *Gardens in and about Town* (New York, 1923), 174.

33. M. E. Bottomley, *The Design of Small Properties: A Book for the Home Owner in City and Country* (New York, 1926), 156, 162.

34. Phyllis Andersen, "The City and the Garden," in *Keeping Eden: A History of Gardening in America,* ed. Walter T. Punch (Boston, 1992), 162–65. The gardening guides that emerged with the modern environmental movement eschewed formalism and embraced naturalistic landscapes. However, they also emphasized control of space and nature (see, for example, William Flemer III, *Nature's Guide to Successful Gardening and Landscaping* [New York, 1972]; Laura C. Martin, *The Wildflower Meadow Book: A Gardener's Guide* [Charlotte, 1986]; Stevie Daniels, *The Wild Lawn Handbook: Alternatives to the Traditional Front Lawn* [New York, 1995]).

35. *St. Louis Post-Dispatch,* 10 August 1905, 11 (hereafter *SLPD*); St. Louis City Ordinance 18,415; *SLPD,* 30 August 1900, 11; *SLPD,* 7 August 1905, 3; *SLPD,* 30 August 1900, 4.

36. Weed Statement, 29 August 1900, in *City of St. Louis vs. Smith P. Galt,* Case File No. 10769, Judicial Case Files; Missouri Supreme Court, Record Group 600; Missouri State Archives, Jefferson City (hereafter MSC-10769).

37. *City of St. Louis v. Galt,* 179 Mo. 11.

38. Appellant's Brief, 2, in MSC-10769.

39. "Weeds Are Being Cut," *SLPD,* 10 August 1905, 12; "Goldenrod Not a Weed," *SLPD,* 12 August 1905, 4.

40. Recent analyses of the relationship of environment and health include: Conevery Bolton Valencius, *The Health of the Country: How American Settlers Understood Themselves and Their Land* (New York, 2002); and Gregg Mitman, "In Search of Health: Landscape and Disease in American Environmental History," *Environmental History* 10 (2005) 184–210.

41. "Health and Weeds," *American City* 54 (January 1939): 15; Charles S. Rhyne, *Municipal Law* (Washington, D.C., 1957), 548, 582.

42. Roscoe Pound and Frederic E. Clements, *The Phytogeography of Nebraska,* 2nd ed. (Lincoln:

1900), 400–415; Neale Copple, *Tower on the Plains: Lincoln's Centennial History, 1859–1959* (Lincoln, 1959), 103–5. On tree planting and spatial beautification, see Campanella, *Republic of Shade*, 99–102.

43. Defendant's Answer, 13, in *Ben A. Greenwood vs. City of Lincoln*, Case File No. 33175, Records of Nebraska Supreme Court, Record Group 069; Nebraska State Historical Society, Lincoln (hereafter NSC-33175).

44. "Exhibit B," 16, NSC-33175.

45. *Greenwood et al. v. City of Lincoln*, 55 N.W. 2d 346.

46. *Lincoln Sunday Journal and Star*, 28 February 1937, 3D.

47. *Greenwood*, 345.

48. Gale E. Christianson, *Fox at the Wood's Edge: A Biography of Loren Eiseley* (New York, 1990), 28–31.

49. Aldo Leopold, *A Sand County Almanac and Sketches Here and There* (1949; New York, 1987), 48.

50. Jon C. Teaford, *Rough Road to Renaissance: Urban Revitalization in America, 1940–1985* (Baltimore, 1986), 206–7; Michael H. Ebner, "Re-Reading Suburban America: Urban Population Deconcentration, 1810–1980," *American Quarterly* 37 (1985): 366–81; Virginia Jenkins, *The Lawn: A History of an American Obsession* (Washington, D.C., 1994), 91–115. See also Ted Steinberg, *American Green: The Obsessive Quest for the Perfect Lawn* (New York, 2006).

51. Michael Pollan, *Second Nature: A Gardener's Education* (New York, 1991), 133–37.

52. Paul Kelsch, "Constructions of American Forest: Four Landscapes, Four Readings," in *Environmentalism in Landscape Architecture*, ed. Michel Conan (Washington, D.C., 2000): 163–85.

53. Mark Goldman, *High Hopes: The Rise and Decline of Buffalo, New York* (Albany, 1983), 267–95; David Halle, *America's Working Man: Work, Home, and Politics among Blue-Collar Property Owners* (Chicago, 1984), 11–12; John W. Percy, *Pioneer Suburb: A Comprehensive History of Kenmore, New York, 1899–1974* (Kenmore, N.Y., 1974), 117–19; "Not Everyone Is Wild about Wildflowers," *Christian Science Monitor*, 1 July 1985, Home sec., 29; Matt Gryta, "Convictions Upheld, Lawn-Case Fines Cut," *Buffalo News*, 14 November 1985, sec. C, 11.

54. Hawthorne quoted in "Vegetation Litigation," *National Law Journal*, 8 October 1984, 43.

55. David Robinson, "Kenmore Lawn-Mowing Charges Dismissed," *Buffalo News*, 13 November 1985, sec. C, 5.

56. Stephen Kenney, "Home Grown: The Native American Spirituality of Henry David Thoreau" (Ph.D. diss., SUNY-Buffalo, 1989), epigraph.

57. Bob Dearing, "'Wild' Lawn a Fertile Area for Dispute," *Buffalo News*, 13 September 1984, sec. C, 11; Richard Haitch, "Freedom of Lawn," *New York Times*, 14 October 1984, sec. 1, 49.

58. On the transformation of Chicago, see William Cronon, *Nature's Metropolis: Chicago and the Great West* (New York, 1991); and Larry Bennett, *Fragments of Cities: The New American Downtowns and Neighborhoods* (Columbus, 1990).

59. Mayor's Task Force on Neighborhood Land Use, *Vacant Land* (Chicago, 1987), 1, 21.

60. Federal judges dismissed a lawsuit initiated by a group of natural landscapers that claimed that the prosecution of Marie Wojciechowski caused them to fear future prosecution. These Chicagoans, some of whom the city had previously notified of the need to control their plants, claimed the city's weed ordinance and its penalties filled them with fear and compelled them to build fences to hide their vegetation. The court decided that, as in *Galt*, the ambiguities involving particular plants as weeds did not compromise the law's power to include the broad array of vegetation in weed laws. These disputes prompted city offi-

cials to consider issuing permits to raise "native lawns" without violating the city weed law that required controlling weeds "so that the average height of such weeds does not exceed 10 inches" (*Schmidling et al. v. Chicago* [1993], 1 F.3d 501–2; Alf Siewers, "Judge Won't Mow Down City's Weed Ordinance," *Chicago Sun-Times*, 10 March 1992, 16; Municipal Code of Chicago Section 99–9, *Journal of the Proceedings of the City Council of the City of Chicago* [Chicago, 1989], 10124).

61. Bret Rappaport, "As Natural Landscaping Takes Root We Must Weed Out the Bad Laws— How Natural Landscaping and Leopold's Land Ethic Collide with Unenlightened Weed Laws and What Must Be Done About It," *John Marshall Law Review* 26 (1993): 867–913. Rappaport served as counsel for both Wojciechowski and Schmidling.

62. "Pursuit of Happiness," *Ken-Ton Bee*, 19 September 1984, 6.

63. See Jens Lachmund's essay in this volume.

64. Reed F. Noss, "Some Principles of Conservation Biology, as They Apply to Environmental Law," *Chicago-Kent Law Review* 69 (1994): 902; Randy G. Westbrooks, *Invasive Plants: Changing the Landscape of America* (Washington, D.C., 1998), 1–6.

Building an "Urban Homestead"

Survival, Self-Sufficiency, and Nature in Seattle, 1970–1980

Jeffrey Craig Sanders

Amidst the 1970s energy crisis, Jody Aliesan, a seasoned political activist, converted the private realm of her Seattle home to public display. As a participant in the U.S. Department of Energy's Appropriate Technology Small Grants Program, Aliesan dubbed her home the "Urban Homestead." Over 4,500 strangers milled around her kitchen, examined her furniture, and marveled at her vegetable gardens. In her open houses and in subsequent weekend columns she wrote for the *Seattle Times*, Aliesan illustrated how urbanites could live more self-sufficiently by reconnecting the city to nature. *Times* photographs featured her in a beekeeper suit gathering honey from rooftop hives or spreading compost in her backyard garden. Her weekly columns were a catalog of how-to's: how to insulate a water heater and weatherstrip a house, make homemade tofu, live without a car, recycle cans and bottles, even how to save urine for the compost pile. Her home modeled efficiency and conservation.[1]

Visitors to the homestead responded with hundreds of reply cards and thank-you letters that expressed an overwhelmingly positive response to the spectacle of Aliesan's work. Many wrote of being "inspired" and "amazed" that an "ordinary-looking household could conserve energy." Most pledged to improve their own homes. Wrote one visitor, "We are going total compost/recycling . . . [and] we're going to build a retrofit passive solar system this spring." Another said that Aliesan lived "in about as much harmony with the Earth as is possible in an urban setting." Aliesan launched her homestead experiment at a moment when Americans were forced to seriously contemplate scarcity for the first time since the Great Depression. Aliesan's Seattle neighbors welcomed the idea of exposing connections between personal

domestic consumption and the seemingly distant hinterland of natural resources. In the process, she popularized counterculture ideas of "whole-
earth ecology" for everyday urbanites. Indeed, her home appeared to perfectly harmonize the challenge of city living with nature. Her columns and
the example of her model home combined a potent American mythology—a
resonant image of frontier living and self-sufficiency—with a radically new
version of what home could mean in the evolving postindustrial city.[2]

I open with this brief story of Aliesan because I think her example crys-
tallized an emerging urban environmental ethos in the late 1960s in places
like Seattle. Despite our long-standing romance with wild places and the association of wilderness with environmental activism, the modern environmental movement in the United States was very much an urban-focused
phenomenon. Many activists, like Aliesan, self-consciously linked their concerns about the city's social conditions to their emerging understanding of
the idea of ecology, hoping to bring nature into the city in less obvious ways.
Despite the dominant image of 1970s "white flight" from cities, or even the
narrative of counterculture retreat to communes, many politically engaged
and environmentally active Americans by the 1970s committed themselves
to remaking urban spaces, and in the process they laid the foundation for
contemporary movements such as new urbanism and the green building
movement. Places like Seattle were early hothouses for such activity.[3]

The urban home stood at the center of this new political ethos, and domestic urban space in the 1970s was the place where activists connected
political concerns as seemingly discrete as gender, the environment, and
poverty. Urban consumption served as a fulcrum for these concerns, and
the urban house as artifact, as well as a set of daily practices, played an important but ambivalent role in social change. As private lives and public politics merged, many Americans began to stretch and reimagine the idea, and
even the physical shape and boundaries, of home. Aliesan for example, a
committed feminist and antipoverty activist, struggled to transform and
model a domestic realm that encompassed her ideas of personal liberation,
social justice, and environmental balance.[4] These new politics could be unstable at the same time. Urban environmental activists often walked a per-
ilous line between advocating a radical reconception of society and a more
conservative and libertarian conception of social and environmental change.
This essay describes the national and local contexts that converged in Seattle
during the late 1960s and early 1970s, and shows, with the example of one
neighborhood, how counterculture Seattleites attempted to connect their city
and their politics with nature, sometimes with unintended consequences.

Origins of the Middle City

Seattle was ideal habitat for urban environmental activists at the end of the 1960s, but people in Seattle also acted within a much broader and decentralized context of counterculture environmentalism. By the late 1970s, many young people saw in urban landscapes like Seattle and Portland the promise of a more malleable urbanism, a place where the architecture and city functions could work *with* natural systems. Ernest Callenbach's popular 1975 cult book *Ecotopia* popularized one image of this reconstructed urban utopia. Callenbach described the area that stretches northward from northern California along the Cascade Mountains into Canada. His postindustrial fantasy conjured a northwestern place where people planted flowers in the cracks of sidewalks and where streams gurgled through downtown streets reclaimed from the automobile.[5] Few people moving to Seattle during the 1970s had likely read *Ecotopia*, but such notions of recycling, reusing, and redeeming the city were common among a restless youth culture in search of home during the early 1970s.[6]

Salvaging the city for new uses required more than fantasy, however. The job of reclaiming neglected neighborhoods and reinventing urban domesticity required good tools, ideas, and cooperation. Seattle's green counterculture of the 1970s found common cause and practical inspiration in the *Whole Earth Catalog* (*WEC*). Described as a Sears Catalog for the counterculture,[7] the *WEC* provided the American counterculture with the inspiration to claim what the editors called a new "realm of intimate, personal power."[8] Like many other American cities, between 1970 and 1980 Seattle saw a burst of this decentralized "green" counterculture activity inspired in part by the *WEC* and by the new interest in ecology. One historian of the movement described it as a "politicized counterculture environmental movement."[9] The *WEC* was their informal manual. Each subsequent edition exposed readers to a do-it-yourself "ecology" linking personal choices to a broader movement for social change. In featured advertisements and lengthy lists of recommended reading, the catalog connected its readers to the flood of Earth Day–inspired "ecology" paperbacks with titles such as *Earth Tool Kit/Environmental Action* (1970), *The Environmental Handbook* (1970), and *Ecotactics* (1970). In addition, the *WEC* published manifestos of various organizations that promoted everything from recycling to alternative technology. These ideas floated from coast to coast—and especially up and down the west coast—helping to shape a highly decentralized movement that would take root in Seattle neighborhoods.

The *WEC* encouraged readers to transform their homes and neighbor-hoods in the city, sometimes in fairly radical, if personal, ways. Always a compendium of tips about off-the-grid-living, the WEC offered one 1968 essay, "The Recovery of Cities," by the group Berkeley People's Architec-ture (PA) that notably drew a connection between "ecology" and proposed changes to urban living.[10] Five years before Ernest Callenbach popularized the idea of ecotopia, the PA group had begun to map out a counterculture environmentalist vision for the city of the future; one that sounded fantastic, but ultimately resembled the ideas that many mainstream activists in Seattle would embrace by the late 1970s. The group suggested a wholesale redesign of cities and the decentralization of power into neighborhood groups. PA blamed the imperial control of the old downtown power structure of finan-ciers and law firms for laying waste to older neighborhoods, spreading sub-urbs into farmland, and building ever-taller office buildings. By attempting to merge "ecology" with a concern for the built environment, PA took this vision a step further to suggest dismantling existing high-rises and reusing their materials; they advocated closure of downtown streets "for orchards, vegetable gardens, [and] parks"; and they advocated elimination of private automobiles. The group even suggested taking advantage of southern expo-sures in office buildings for "hydroponic gardens."[11]

People's Architecture cared most about what they referred to as the "middle city," arguing that "the downtown environment will be reclaimed when the middle city defeats the bid of downtown for its territory and when suburbia becomes self-supporting communities." By "middle city," these activists meant neighborhoods with older housing stock and ghettoes ("in many ways . . . the most together communities," they argued). Here coun-terculture environmentalist rhetoric echoed the concerns of Jane Jacobs and other critics of mid-1960s urban renewal: "Paradoxically, the oldest and poorest sections of the city have a head start," PA argued, and such neigh-borhoods "will be the first areas to show the rest of the urban population the way to an ecologically sane environment."[12] In their Jane Jacobs–meets–Rachel Carson vision, PA urged a program for community self-sufficiency that would become the "bridge to people's understanding of whole earth ecology."[13] Along with dismantling downtown and closing streets, the pro-gram included neighborhood drives to separate organic and inorganic wastes, creation of community-development corporations and master plans, and new businesses based on recycling automobile parts and garbage col-lection.[14] Counterculture environmentalists in Seattle may not have drawn their ideas directly from PA's "program for self-sufficiency," but the diverse strands that each edition of *WEC* brought together provided counterculture environmentalists a range of possibilities and "access" to the "tools" with which they would try to balance home in the city with nature.

If the *WEC* transmitted broad counterculture messages and formed an inspirational context, Seattleites developed their own experiments and local networks. The Puget Consumers Co-operative (PCC)—"the food co-op," as it was called in the 1970s—served as an important magnet, drawing together a growing group of counterculture environmentalists and concerned Seattle consumers in search of health, organic foods, and a sense of self-sufficiency. By 1967, the co-op had delivery and pickup points in most of Seattle's middle-city neighborhoods, such as Madrona, Montlake, Capitol Hill, Northlake near Fremont, and Ravenna in the North End. The co-op newsletter was the main link for consumers and provided prices and availability for wheat germ, carob, honey, and other bulk staples. By the time the PCC opened its first storefront in north Seattle's middle-city Ravenna district, it was one of a growing number of newer co-ops near the centers of youth culture (such as the neighborhoods around the University of Washington and Capitol Hill).[15] While the cooperative brought awareness of the food chain to consumers, it also nurtured local producers in their backyard vegetable gardens. Seattleites who wanted to grow their own food in the 1970s found guidance and inspiration through the PCC. More than a store, the cooperative funded local food projects that explored techniques for growing winter vegetables in the northwestern climate.[16] In 1974, the PCC even helped to finance a large-scale community organic garden near its store, and eventually the co-op convinced the city to set up the city's enduring community garden program (later named the P-Patch). According to the newsletter, the garden was a "space for people to grow their own food and get in touch with the earth, experiences that are not usually possible in an urban environment."[17] The P-Patch was also another forum around which middle-city residents could rethink the meaning of making a home in the city, a place where people shared gardening methods, traded seeds and cuttings, and learned about composting.

The co-op store helped to bring once fringe ideas into the mainstream of urban consciousness. Throughout the 1970s at the PCC, Seattleites learned to place consumption in their private lives and homes into a larger picture of a more humane and ecologically healthy urban and rural landscape; a landscape achieved through everyday choices about what one ate, bought, grew, composted, and recycled.

In addition to co-ops and community gardens, Seattle activists explored ways to remake the home itself into a site of production and more thought-ful consumption. Alternative-technology groups in Seattle created "Eco-tope," an "energy resource center" along the lines advocated by the PA and chronicled in the *WEC*. Ecotope (echoing the title of Callenbach's utopian novel) defined its name and mission: "(Gr: oikos = habitat + topos = place)," or "a specialized habitat within a larger region" and "a non-profit research and demonstration corporation working in Seattle, WA since 1974 for dem-onstration and development of renewable energy and conservation technolo-gies."[18] The group encouraged residents in the Capitol Hill area to use solar power, conserve energy, recycle, and redesign buildings, and their efforts added to the citywide set of resources available to urban homesteaders. They taught the general public to pay attention to how dwellings and the climate of Seattle and the Northwest could function in concert for increased energy efficiency. Ecotope explained its mission: "Ecotope Group maintains a spe-cialized resource library featuring conservation and appropriate technology publications and up-to-date technical information on renewable resource technologies."[19] Ecotope also published how-to pamphlets, such as *A Solar Greenhouse for the Northwest*, that taught Seattleites how to create solar green-house extensions to be "used for heat in conjunction with a house."[20] These tips and events emphasized Ecotope's roots in a specific community in ac-cordance with the local, middle-city orientation of counterculture environ-mental groups in the 1970s.[21] But after the mid-1970s, with the energy crisis in full swing, the longtime counterculture environmental concerns found a receptive audience among average Seattleites. Ecotope would eventually work with a variety of organizations including the PCC to spread the word about greenhouses, composting toilets, and alternative technology. As Jens Lachmund points out in his essay in this volume, scientists and academics developed the profession of urban ecology in Berlin during the 1970s in part as a response to specific urban conditions. Similarly, in Seattle during the same period, professionals built new institutions and constructed new un-derstandings of nature in the city. During this time, for instance, the Univer-sity of Washington began work on its Center for Urban Horticulture, while the university's landscape architecture program nurtured a professional cul-ture in Seattle that emphasized restoration and a remediation design ethos beginning in the early 1960s. But what distinguished Seattle's urban green ethos by the 1970s was both the grassroots nature of these developments and, more importantly, a grassroots movement that focused, to a signifi-cant degree, on personal consumption and personal solutions, rather than on institutional change as the remedy for environmental problems. Against the backdrop of larger institutional changes in the city and on a national level, therefore, the individual and domestic realm still formed an important center of this movement.

The emerging network of counterculture environmentalists in Seattle provided an alternative meaning of home in which the domestic sphere of private choices had public consequences. These projects set up a new equation for labor and waste in the home, while they held out the possibility of tearing down the walls that isolated the economic choices and productive work of the home from political actions in the community. The personal and the political, private space and public space were, it was hoped, brought closer together in this process. Activists cultivated a new understanding of production, conservation, and consumption of resources—especially food and energy, making these choices within the home seem crucial to the health of the city and nature. Such decentralized experience in urban homes and community made the vision advocated by People's Architecture and Ecotope manifest.

By mid-decade, with the energy crisis settling into the American consciousness, counterculture experiments began to seem less utopian and more practical to the interests of mainstream Americans in hard times. This reassessment of urban strategies emerged against the backdrop of a national recession, which hit Seattle particularly hard as early as 1971, when Boeing Aircraft Company, the largest single employer in the region, began laying off workers. Between January 1970 and December 1971, the company fired or laid off more than sixty-five thousand people, or one-third of its workforce.[22] In this context of recession and energy crisis, the once fringe ideas found in the *WEC* began to appear more creative and sound to "mainstream" Seattleites. Even Seattle policy makers had begun to see the city's future in creating a culturally urbane place close to nature.[23]

Making a Middle City

The Fremont neighborhood in Seattle during the late 1970s, perhaps better than any other district in Seattle, epitomized one version of what counterculture environmentalists thought home in the American middle city could become. As United States energy and economic woes bore down on the city, Fremont citizens took refuge within the boundaries of their little ecotopian neighborhood and in an identity they derived from recycling everything from bottles and cans, to historic buildings and the family home. The logo on Fremont's community newspaper in 1977, the *Fremont Forum*, featured the community motto: "The District That Recycles Itself."[24] In the late 1970s, Fremont found in recycling a resonant metaphor and identity for a neighborhood (and a city) in the midst of a transformation. If suburban sprawl had helped to desiccate Seattle and other cities over the preceding decades, Fremont's recycling ethic would serve as a model for how to consume the old landscape anew. In important ways, Fremont modeled the future of Seattle. At the same time, Fremont's story reveals the transformation of counterculture ideas from the fringe to the mainstream.

In the early 1960s, Fremont was a federal Model Cities neighborhood, but by the mid-1970s it was well into the Block Grant era and in the early stages of gentrification on its way to becoming a bohemian, arts capital of Seattle. Fremont showed how a confluence of federal and city government influence and neighborhood activism combined with the momentum of newly urgent environmental politics in the late 1970s to reshape urbanism. The "district that recycles itself" made waste, conservation, and recycling second nature for Seattleites. Like the *WEC*, Ecotope, and the PCC, the colorful activists in Fremont brought public attention to the flow of wastes and energies, and implications for domestic consumption into a comprehensive picture of urban public citizenship.

In the early 1900s, Fremont was a small logging village northwest of downtown Seattle. One of the farthest stops on the interurban rail line, the village comprised working-class neighborhoods of single-family dwellings situated on the hills around a small town center. By the mid-1960s, the deteriorating area had became so run-down and its population so poor that it was deemed eligible for designation as a Model City in Lyndon Johnson's War on Poverty program. On the urban planning maps in Model Cities publications for Seattle, black lines indicated the "blighted" designation of the Fremont neighborhood. The Model Cities program created the North Community Service Center to coordinate the neighborhood-building efforts for which the program was famous. The service center improved housing, provided access to jobs and food for people in the neighborhood, and helped organize citizens to ensure their "participation" and "advice" at "all levels of decision and policy" in the program.[25] As in other American cities, the Model Cities program stimulated new forms of political organizing. When the program was canceled under Nixon's new federalism, the Seattle Model Cities program in Fremont ceased.[26] But in Fremont, the residual influence of the program subsequently fostered a unique community organization in the mid-1970s called the Fremont Public Association (FPA): "a non-profit community organization providing a variety of social services to meet basic needs of people:

a job, a place to live, food and clothing."[27] By 1977, the FPA had rebounded from the demise of the Model Cities program and had grown "from a few people involved several years ago in the Model Cities program" to become a "'a going concern' with a budget of $200,000."[28] Fremont was still a low-rent neighborhood and remained in a state of "blight," but its small business and cultural life began to pick up in the 1970s as increasing numbers of artists, bohemians, and counterculture community builders arrived in search of the middle city.

Many middle-city neighborhoods like Fremont almost barricaded themselves in their sense of the neighborhood as a self-determining community. Fremont even joked in the *Forum* that it should secede from the city and "open a duty-free port for international trade."[29] "Fremontians" saw the old neighborhood infrastructure as laying the groundwork for a distinctive neighborhood within Seattle. The goal, according to the *Forum*, was to "bring Fremont back to its former glory as a self-sufficient, independent, feisty District that saves treasures of the past from the bulldozer and has a soft heart for people in trouble or transient."[30] Like Portland to the south, Seattle saw a rise in this kind of neighborhood-based, grassroots activism in the 1970s.[31] A revitalized small-community and alternative-press culture accompanied the middle-city renaissance. Newspapers like the *Forum*, the *Outlook*, and the *Seattle Sun* ("a weekly newspaper for the Capitol Hill, University District, Eastlake, Montlake, and Cascade Communities"—all middle-city locales) gave a voice and definition to neighborhood concerns that usually revolved around land-use and urban environmental issues. In the aftermath of antifreeway battles in the late 1960s and early 1970s and efforts to preserve neighborhood character from the developers and the wrecking ball, middle-city communities dedicated themselves to rebuilding neighborhoods from the ground up—with a mixture of dwindling federal funds and entrepreneurial efforts. The Fremont neighborhood's community newspaper expressed the emerging sentiment during the 1970s: "It has become increasingly apparent that we are going to have to assume responsibility for our future as a community, both economically and esthetically, and stop waiting for the 'government' or someone else to do it for us. Self-actualization is the key."[32]

Seattle's middle-city neighborhoods expressed a fierce localism that rivaled that of the emerging anti-tax and anti-urban sentiments of the region's postwar suburbanites. Downtown and the suburbs were villains in their eyes. And yet the localism of urban neighborhoods, the desire for self-sufficiency, required the city's help, and the city government responded.

Wes Uhlman, Seattle's mayor between 1970 and 1978, and a champion of neighborhood activists, went so far as to employ the counterculture's own language and values in city publications. He made community-building gestures in an eco-friendly brown-paper pamphlet that Housing and Urban Development sponsored and that circulated through the Department of Neighborhood Planning to neighborhood groups and public libraries in 1975. The city's *A Sense of Community: Seven Suggestions for Making Your Home and Neighborhood a Better Place to Live* featured tips on crime prevention, house repair, and weatherization; it even encouraged people to ride bicycles. Using the language of the youth culture, the mayor's office recommended "getting it together" in "your community" by creating "neighborhood co-operatives" for buying food or having "neighborhood sales" to raise money for various community efforts. The pamphlet exemplified the unexpected paths that the counterculture environmental ethos would travel. The city even encouraged neighborhoods to form "community councils," "land use review boards," and "neighborhood corporations"; and it recommended that neighborhood groups plant "street trees," providing appropriate varieties and pruning tips, to create "the ultimate living environment." Similarly, the pamphlet gave tips on how to construct playgrounds made from recycled wood and old tires, and it provided extensive diagrams showing citizens how to reshape their neighborhoods by creating traffic diversion islands at intersections, creating "block parks," and dead-ending streets. Such projects, the city argued, helped "instill a feeling of control over the immediate environment which is sometimes lost in the hustle and bustle."[33] If anger at downtown mounted from increasingly empowered neighborhood groups, downtown and successive mayors responded with more of these neighborhood-empowering ideas. The city government, with federal support, encouraged neighborhoods to take charge of their environments.

As an outgrowth of the Model Cities program, the Fremont neighborhood activists already had a well-developed community agenda that revolved around housing issues and especially "blight," or run-down property. By the 1970s, American urban policy shifted away from large-scale programs and toward more personal "sweat equity" solutions to urban housing shortages and problems during the 1970s. The federal government's Urban Homesteading program (only rhetorically related to Aliesan's DOE grant program) debuted in the mid-1970s and encouraged small-scale and personal solutions while evoking individualist imagery that mixed old-western "pioneering" with new-western ideas about reclaiming the middle city.[34] According to one observer of the program, the Urban Homesteading program represented "the shift in federal commitments and trends toward stabilization and conservation rather than renewal."[35]

In Fremont, the LBJ-era focus on poverty had clearly morphed into an environmental agenda that set about recycling and consuming a new kind of urban landscape. An informal poll of Fremont residents in 1977 found that "run-down property" was the prime concern for people in the neighborhood, above crime and unemployment.[36] Eighty-three percent of the residences in Fremont were single-family structures that housed a population of mostly renters (64 percent of the neighborhood's 8,600 people compared with 43 percent in the Seattle area).[37] Addressing these figures, the FPA published articles about obtaining low-interest mortgages, tenants' rights, and information about shelter for people in crisis. Through the *Forum,* the FPA, like Ecotope, encouraged more energy-efficient houses. Reclaiming middle-city neighborhoods required recycling homes and making them more energy-efficient. In successive issues of the *Forum,* editors ran features about the FPA's Block Grant programs for housing counseling, including a new "REHAB program" run by the city. The program encouraged everything from "minor home repairs" and loans for repairs and insulation to "full-scale housing rehabilitation" and homeownership.[38] Counterculture environmental activists in Fremont, like their counterparts in the Bay Area and elsewhere, had long advocated a reclamation of the city through decentralization. By the mid-1970s, the federal government and local government in cities like Seattle had begun to mirror their rhetoric.

As a once-blighted community being reborn as distinct, historical, and recycled, Fremont walked a fine line in the 1970s between an emerging environmental-inspired gentrification and the older urban-crisis poverty agenda. The government walked this line as well. Such programs certainly served the poor, but perhaps as significantly they helped subsidize counterculture environmentalists who shared the "pioneer spirit" of middle-city recyclers.[39]

The pages of the *Forum* provided a picture of this changing community—fewer low-income and more upwardly mobile residents. With still-low rents in Fremont and the recession deepening, Fremont attracted a burgeoning population of university students and artists in search of cheap housing. The *Forum* published news about the Fremont food bank (housed in an old bordello), services for senior citizens, and tenants' rights, but the paper also published profiles of visiting mime troops and artists working in the community, revealing a diverse neighborhood. The *Forum* emphasized that while fixing up homes in the neighborhood was aligned with the earlier antipoverty agenda of the Model Cities program, it also served the middle-city interests of Seattle's counterculture environmentalists and the emerging yuppies, who would gain critical mass in 1980s Seattle.[40] Most of the advertising in the *Forum* reflected the gentrifying side of Fremont. Next to articles about home rehabilitation and news about upcoming tenants' rights seminars appeared advertisements for "The Quiet Man Antiques," which sold "exclusively fine eastern oaks"; "the Antique Company," which called itself "a small shop for the discriminating collector"; and for a store called "General Antiques," which sold "overstuffed furniture." In addition to antiques, local stores like "Stoneway Electric Supply" advertised as co-sponsors of the *Forum*'s housing rehab section, and "Daly's," a store that sold wood-finishing products, told Fremonters: "Refinishing wood work and paneling in an older home, or antique furniture you put in it, requires careful, meticulous work. To do it right, please ask us first."[41] More Seattleites were busy recycling or fixing up homes during the 1970s, and places like Fremont, nearby Wallingford, and other middle-city neighborhoods, with their stock of old bungalows built between 1890 and 1930, fit a more aestheticized version of the middle city for counterculturalists and do-it-yourself urban pioneers.[42] Recycling and refinishing the existing and once neglected urban fabric expressed a commitment to the ecotopian middle-city landscape, and matched the new funding agenda of the federal government blending environmentalist ideas with preservation to justify the early stages of gentrification in Seattle. A reclamation and conservation ethic permeated this sensibility. The emerging middle-city aesthetic supposedly signified a shift away from suburban values and a recommitment to the human-scaled city neighborhood. By recycling houses of the older city and embracing an aesthetic of the historical, organic, wooden, and funky, Fremont citizens demonstrated one aspect of a growing recycling ethos.

By the late 1970s, the community had its own P-Patch community garden, a co-operative grocery store, and many of the other accoutrements of the independent, middle-city, ecotopian neighborhood. But Fremont had broader ambitions to be an "example to the City and to the entire country" and began to reach out to Seattleites in other neighborhoods. To take the idea of recycling to the larger community would require the obsession of one man, Arman Napoleon Stepanian. This bearded evangelist, the "Moses" of the curbside recycling movement in Seattle, was also Fremont's honorary mayor in the 1970s. In the first edition of the *Forum*, Stepanian, a transplant from New York City by way of San Francisco in the late 1960s, reflected on his rise to power: "To the best of my recollection it was an inauspicious February 27th, back in 1973 when I swamped my 35 esteemed opponents (34 human beings and a black Labrador who was clearly the underdog in the race) to begin my reign of terror as Seattle's only unofficial public official."[43] Stepanian brought a sense of humor to his job as a neighborhood booster, but he took community boosterism as seriously as any Rotarian. In the first edition of the *Forum*, he described the changes that he had led in the district that included creating the first Fremont craft fair, the Fremont Public Association, the "Fremont Recycling Station #1," and "creating the world and resting afterward."[44]

The Fremont Recycling Station #1 was the base of operations for the mayor. The station was the point from which the ethos of recycling would spread far and wide, eventually helping to encourage Seattle's citizens and their government to establish a curbside recycling program in the city. But more importantly, Stepanian, his staff of "eco-educators," and the recycling-truck drivers helped to spread awareness of the Seattle consumer's role in the stream of waste and consumption.[45] With recycling, Fremont derived an identity and along the way articulated a vision of "household recycling" that connected home in the community to "virgin stands of timber," Northwest rivers dammed to produce energy for aluminum manufacture, and "dependence on foreign nations." Such sentiments were only beginning to become common in the mid-1970s, so to spread this news to a broad Seattle public required a campaign of some effort to convince "each consumer" that she is "responsible for the problems of waste disposal and [that] each consumer can contribute to a solution."[46] Household recycling, though no "panacea," according to supporters, did bring a connection to nature home to Seattleites who began learning the private and public rituals of recycling.[47]

Beginning in the early 1970s, Fremont hosted an annual arts-and-crafts fair, and it was at this fair during the summer of 1974 that Stepanian's and Fremont's recycling identity was born. Like other street fairs of the time, the Fremont Fair brought together the ubiquitous hand-thrown pottery of the era, jugglers, and street musicians. When the fair began in 1972, there were fifty exhibitors, and by 1977, exhibitors manned more than three hundred booths. According to an article in the *Forum*, recycling started at the fair as "a means of raising a little money to supplement FPA's food and clothing bank." Fairgoers were encouraged to "feed the poor with other people's trash."[48] With the "overwhelming response" at the 1974 fair, Stepanian started the Fremont Recycling Station #1 to serve the Fremont neighborhood. At successive fairs, Fremont increasingly incorporated themes of energy conservation, environmentalism, and waste recycling into the summer celebration. By 1977, the fair advertised "arts, crafts, tasties, energy-saving tips" and filled booths with environmental advocacy groups and representatives of the city government who shared the news about energy conservation.[49]

With a critical mass of organizations like the PCC, Ecotope, and the FPA by the 1970s, Seattle's concerned citizens and counterculture environmental activists began to pressure the city government to expand existing services. The city had been searching for better ways to reduce urban waste for some time, making recycling services available to citizens at the South Seattle transfer station since 1970. But few people in Seattle knew about the city's program, and, for that matter, few had any notion of curbside recycling before Earth Day and before Fremont made it a crusade. In the years after 1974, while Fremont's mayor popularized recycling at the fair, the City of Seattle's Engineering Department struggled with overflowing landfills and new strategies for solid-waste disposal. Throughout the early 1970s, various businesses, environmental groups, and concerned citizens lobbied the mayor's office to expand and simplify recycling in the city.[50] In 1973, Bob Swanson, the Sierra Club's recycling committee head and chairperson of the Committee on the Environmental Crisis for the student section at the university, explained his group's concerns about recycling and the reuse of "a resource as many times as possible before it is returned to the environment where biological processes will break it down." Swanson urged the mayor to consider "our natural resources," the "limited amount of virgin wood fibers" available for paper products, as well as the energy used to manufacture more (the letter was written on recycled paper).[52] The mayor replied to Swanson that "the current energy crisis has probably convinced even the most unaware that we cannot go on forever in our present superconsumer economy. Fuels and material shortages will become the order of the day, and recycling will become imperative." He lauded the Sierra Club's efforts and explained that King County (Seattle's County) was at that very moment involved in a "massive study" of the county's solid-waste system in search of "alternatives," including "recycling and reuse."[53]

The *King County Solid Waste Study*, performed in 1973, suggested various scenarios for dealing with ever-growing urban wastes in the 1970s. Like the PCC counterculture environmentalists composting dinner scraps in their homes, the city imagined similar solutions on a grand scale, including large-scale composting systems that used "sophisticated mechanical digestion" to break down wastes.[54] The authors of the report explored the costs for a citywide recycling system, and ideas about how best to shred paper and use magnets to remove ferrous metals from the process. The city busily measured the market for such recycled products, well aware of the growing crisis. The 1973 waste report concluded, in part, that "for maximum efficiency of a recycle system, there should be home segregation" and that collection of the materials must "concentrate the individual materials to be recycled and bring term to a facility that is most cost effective." Such functions, the report found, were best organized by government, but should be "left to the private sector to operate and manage."[55]

With the county recommending private solutions to the problems of solid waste in Seattle, the city turned to local businesspeople, communities, and individuals in their homes in order to explore the possibility of curbside recycling. Having introduced and popularized the idea of recycling in Fremont, Mayor Stepanian therefore was a natural choice when it came time for the city to try its first run with recycling. As part of a twelve-month study called the Seattle Recycling Project (SRP), Stepanian and his staff at the Fremont Recycling Station #1 applied to perform a study that merged, in one project, the lessons of urban dwelling that Fremont and counterculture environmentalists had been advocating since the late 1960s. The group took the neighborhood-based metaphor of renewal to the public with a Washington State Department of Ecology grant to study the viability of curbside recycling in Seattle between 1 July 1976, and 30 June 1977. The usually flamboyant Fremont group created a rigorous study for the city, written in flawless policy language. According to their report, the objectives were to "maximize citizen participation," "determine the economic feasibility of a solid waste home-based source separation project for the city of Seattle," "design and implement the operation phase of a model home-source separation project," and "evaluate all data collected during the project implementation."[56] The group's final report shows how seriously Fremont's residents took their efforts. A handful of other cities in the United States explored the proposition of bringing recycling into the daily activities of households during the 1970s, but this was the first pilot project in Seattle, and through it Fremont brought its middle-city experiment to a larger public audience.

Over the course of the study, Recycling Station #1 sent out letters to participants in the test neighborhood, a north Seattle residential area called Sacagawea whose average demographics matched those of Seattle. Stepanian was quoted in a North End community newspaper as saying, "Just as Sacajawea led Lewis and Clark to the West coast, the Sacagawea neighborhood shows signs of leading Seattle into a new era of the conservation ethic."[57] As did other counterculturalists, Stepanian drew on stereotypic images of Native Americans as environmentalists. At neighborhood meetings and in news coverage, Stepanian spread the gospel of Fremont recycling: "it is far cheaper to make new out of old than it is to make new out of raw," and "a ton of newspapers save 17 trees."[58] Stepanian and his staff taught the residents of the test neighborhood to place their "ungarbage" of glass, cans, and newspapers in orange Department of Energy bags and place the bags and bundled newspapers on the curb in front of their homes.[59]

On the scheduled days, Stepanian and his group of paid Fremonters, along with a group of work-release laborers, would move through the neighborhood collecting the "urban ore" and then take it back to the Fremont station for processing. The final report and news coverage from the time showed a high rate of participation in the program. Residents reported that they supported the program because it was "establishing patterns within the community" and "recycling habits" that should continue; another resident argued that "it is perhaps a small crumb to throw to the cause of conservation of resources, but also a necessary step both in the minimization of waste and in the higher consciousness of those involved."[60] The Fremont activists helped to raise Seattle's consciousness, tracing the connection between private consumption in the home and the public results of these actions. The City of Seattle would perform several more similar studies in the years to come before finally implementing a curbside recycling program in Seattle in the mid-1980s.

Fremont's experience exemplifies the mixed origins and evolution of Seattle's counterculture environmental movement. The neighborhood and community-centered activism grew from the context of urban poverty programs, the environmental crisis, and the growing power of neighborhood politics in the city. Ultimately, Fremont's emphasis on its unique middle-city identity created the voice it would use to transform the habits of Seattle's consumers. The counterculture environmentalists, opposed to downtown power, were the entrepreneurs and activists to whom the city turned in a time of increasing experimentation with new consumer-based environmentally conscious programs. For a time, Fremont was an ecotopia on a small scale among other middle-city neighborhoods. Such neighborhoods helped create an alternative vision for the city, one that saw urbanites more at home with their city and nature. These connections between domestic design and consumption that Ecotope, Fremont, and other groups made during the 1970s helped to set a tone and style for urban living and environmental activism that would influence the city's postindustrial makeover.

The Changing Western Home

Returning again to the example of the "Urban Homestead" with which I began, we can see both the level of mainstream acceptance of these ideas by the 1980s, but also some of the inherent problems of the new city. Alieson's home was able to combine a decade's worth of environmental ideas and counterculture politics under one roof. Her public work modeled the accumulated insights of the *WEC* and multiple trials and errors of the counterculture. Like many 1960s revolutionaries, Aliesan saw her home as a counter to the landscape of federally subsidized postwar production—the suburban sprawl, freeways, and urban renewal that encouraged mindless consumerism, gender segregation, and environmental destruction. But her example is instructive because, just as the urban homestead or Fremont encouraged more radical ideas of home, community, and sustainability, it also reinforced some of the most traditional American myths about homes and communities. The idea of domestic self-sufficiency, and particularly the idea of the homestead, has deep roots in American history and nationalist myths. Aliesan played on such myths, describing her homestead as "the place" where "you have taken your stand," just as the Fremontians celebrated a break-away ethos.[61]

Aliesan in particular underscored the implications that this domestic sphere had for gender. She embraced this most sacred of American landscapes while criticizing its assumptions. Appearing in the home section of the Sunday paper, her incongruous message served to critique the prevailing assumptions about labor within the home, and the gendered scripts they implied. As a feminist, Aliesan questioned received ideas about the home as a "'domestic' and therefore 'feminine'" space. She saw the homestead, she said, as space that "comprises everybody's free development."[62]

Yet both Aliesan and the homesteaders of Fremont acted within an existing political and economic context that increasingly portrayed houses and personal actions as the remedy to public problems. "Sweat equity" had begun to replace public policy and the large-scale (if often ill-fated) urban spending in the United States. At once the new Seattle middle-city home with its recycling bins and solar greenhouses seemed more connected to its environment and to nature through acts of virtuous self-reliance. In the cases of Fremont and Aliesan, these were always public acts. And yet the ethos of self-sufficiency and liberation also served as a blueprint for retreat from the public realm of the larger city and even, by the 1980s, from national politics. Symbolically, at least, the ideal of the self-sufficient urban home in the middle city could just as easily become a realm separated from the street and in retreat.

Activists like Aliesan were not naïve. They recognized that their focus on the personal was an unstable model. But one reader of Aliesan's columns, who identified himself as a "professional environmentalist," gave voice to the darker aspects of self-sufficiency. He called the homestead a "stereotypical image of wood-burning scavengers wolfing down grapenuts seeking cosmic harmony with Mother Earth." He questioned the homestead's "compatibility . . . with long-range energy goals and environmental quality." "Who the hell cares?" he said about Alieson's project, questioning the individualized approach that she advocated. Another respondent, a visitor to her open house, wrote: "The Open House reflected a certain lifestyle rather than sensible energy conservation, especially for urban dwellers. . . . I suggest you scrap the tour, call yourself the New Age Puritans, and hold church services instead."[63]

These detractors may have been on to something. By the late 1970s, many counterculture ideas had become chic, part of the babyboomers' general quest for the authentic. If the *WEC* expressed the late 1960s zeitgeist, then *Sunset* magazine ("the magazine of western living") had become its late 1970s equivalent. *Sunset* epitomized the evolution and rising acceptance of the ecotopian house and city.[64] By 1977, ideas that had once appeared radical—the off-the-grid independence promised in the *Whole Earth Catalog*—had become increasingly mainstream.

The magazine encouraged individual solutions, but with little reference to the larger community or political context. Many Seattleites and the editors of *Sunset* cultivated an increasingly private and protected landscape. Just as Aliesan, with her "Urban Homestead," had advocated self-reliance and cultivation of urban nature as a means of survival in the 1970s, *Sunset* reiterated this domestic landscape, but emphasized designs that gave "privacy from the street" and ideas that encouraged "privacy from close-in neighbors." In a discussion of one architect-remodeled house in Seattle, "a faded but well-built Seattle bungalow," the magazine described the "subtle relationship of retreat between the house and its developing evergreen [tree] screen." On the one hand, the counterculture's ideas seemed to have had a deep impact on the consciences of middle-class homeowners—causing a positive shift that would lead to significant public programs. But on the other hand, stripped of political content by the 1980s, these ideas became one more fashion, or worse, a rationale for detaching from the public sphere.[65]

At the dawn of the Reagan era, the filtered sunlight of ecotopia shone down on blooming backyards and bags of recycled goods waiting on the curbs in front of Seattle homes. But by the 1980s, the more conservative side of this greener urbanism may have been its tendency to reinforce a trend toward a fractured landscape where people consumed nature as a lifestyle choice rather than continuing to trace the urban environment's impacts on the natural world. Significant, too, is that this urban environment was quickly moving out of the reach of working-class people. Having weathered a turbulent decade, the domestic realm would go on to be the pride, in form and idea, of a growing class of Home Depot do-it-yourselfers. With very different goals, though perhaps no less utopian, the young urban professionals of the 1980s continued a process of change that started with the hard work of activists like Aliesan and the urban homestead of the middle city.

Notes

Material in this essay is from chapter 4 of *Seattle and Roots of Urban Sustainability: Inventing Ecotopia*, by Jeffrey C. Sanders, © 2010. Used by permission of the University of Pittsburgh Press.

1. "Welcome to the Fourth (and Last) Urban Homestead Open House September 20–21, 1980," Jody Aliesan Collection, box 1, University of Washington Library—Special Collections (hereafter UWL-SC), University of Washington Library; Alf Collins, "Recycle, Conserve, Grow, Dry, Chop, Insulate . . .," *Seattle Times*, 13 January 1980, section M. See "'A State of Mind': Columns Urged Self-Reliance," *Seattle Times*, 27 January 1981; Karen Hannegan-Moore to Jody Aliesan, 15 January 1980, Jody Aliesan Collection, "*Times*-Responses," box 1, UWL-SC.

2. Aliesan received at least eight hundred returned postcards from the people who visited her series of open houses and many more letters in response to her weekend *Seattle Times* columns (Jody Aliesan Collection, Post Cards, box 1, UWL-SC). For a discussion of the energy crisis and recession of the 1970s, see Bruce Schulman's *The Seventies: The Great Shift in American Culture, Society, and Politics* (New York, 2001).

3. For the history of postwar suburban expansion in the West and Washington, see Carl Abbott, *Metropolitan Frontier: Cities in the Modern American West* (Tucson, 1993); and Roger Sale, *Seattle: Past to Present: An Interpretation of the History of the Foremost City in the Pacific Northwest* (Seattle, 1976). For links between the history of suburbanization and the rise of environmentalism, see Adam Ward Rome, *Bulldozer in the Countryside: Suburban Sprawl and the Rise of American Environmentalism* (New York, 2001). Activists in Seattle were in part drawn to Seattle's older landscape in reaction to the new suburbs. For a discussion of back-to-the-land communal experiments, see Timothy Miller, "The Sixties Era Communes," in *Imagine Nation: The American Counterculture of the 1960s and '70s*, ed. Peter Braunstein and Michael William Doyle (New York, 2002).

4. My study of the changing idea of home and community in Seattle during the 1970s engages an ongoing discussion among historians about the significance of counterculture environmentalism in the late 1960s and 1970s. In particular, my discussion is informed by the recent work of Andrew Kirk on the counterculture's embrace of alternative technologies and diverse "tools" for creating enduring environmental change in the "whole environment" (see Kirk's "Appropriating Technology: *The Whole Earth Catalog* and Counterculture Environmental Politics," *Environmental History* 6, no. 2 [April 2001]; and his "'Machines of Loving Grace': Alternative Technology, Environment, and the Counterculture," in *Imagine Nation*), and *Counterculture Green: The Whole Earth Catalog and American Environmentalism* (Lawrence, 2008). See Dolores Hayden, *Redesigning the American Dream: The Future*

of *Housing, Work, and Family Life* (New York, 1985), 45–49. For more on gender, environmental history, and environmental activism, see an excellent discussion of lesbian counterculture groups and nature in the 1970s, in Virginia Scharff, ed., *Seeing Nature through Gender* (Lawrence, 2003), xiii–xxii, 3–19. For women and the counterculture, see Gretchen Lemke-Santangelo, *Daughters of Aquarius: Women of the Sixties Counterculture* (Lawrence, 2009). By demonstrating the way activists, and everyday Seattleites, shaped a new notion of the city in nature, I engage the ongoing effort by environmental historians who study American attitudes about nature and urbanism (see William Cronon "Kennecott Journey: The Paths Out of Town," in *Under an Open Sky: Rethinking American Western Past*, ed. Cronon, George Miles, and Jay Gitlin [New York, 1992]; and a similarly inspired work about Seattle, Matt Klingle, *Emerald City: An Environmental History of Seattle* (New Haven, 2007). Although not engaging the environmental movement in any detail in her work, Lizabeth Cohen's definition of "citizen consumer" in *Consumer's Republic: The Politics of Mass Consumption in Postwar America* (New York, 2003), 1–18, is useful to understanding how Seattleites began to see their consumer choices and private decisions as part of civic life. See also Sackman, "Putting Gender on the Table," in *Seeing Nature*, for a discussion elaborating links between nature, gender, and everyday domestic spaces.

5. Ernest Callenbach, *Ecotopia: The Notebooks and Reports of William Weston* (Berkeley, 1975), 1–16.

6. See Roger Sale, *Seattle: Past to Present: An Interpretation of the History of the Foremost City in the Pacific Northwest* (Seattle, 1976), 173–252; and Janet D. Ore, *The Seattle Bungalow: People and Houses, 1900–1940* (Seattle, 2007).

7. Kirk, "Appropriating Technology," 82.

8. This quote comes from the first section of the catalog, in which the editors state the catalog's "function" and "purpose" (*Whole Earth Catalog*, January 1970, 2).

9. Kirk, "Appropriating Technology," 377. For more on counterculture environmentalism, see Robert Gottlieb, *Forcing the Spring: The Transformation of the American Environmental Movement* (Washington, D.C., 1993), 81–114.

10. People's Architecture worked in Berkeley around the time of the People's Park events, and their agenda reflected the blend of concerns that animated many West Coast counterculture environmentalists. People's Park activists argued that "the world of power, politics, and the institutional shape of American society" and the "world of ecology, conservation and the biological shape of our environment . . . are no longer separate or separable issues." These words came from a leaflet advertising a teach-in about the park in which luminaries such as Jane Jacobs and Paul Goodman put their support behind a lineup of speakers that included members of Ecology Action, Todd Gitlin, the Radical Student Union, and city planners ("The Politics of Ecology: A Teach-in to Support People's Park," Sixties Ephemera Collection, Bancroft Library).

11. Garrett De Bell, *The Environmental Handbook: Prepared for the First National Environmental Teach-in* (New York, 1970), 239. In *The Death and Life of Great American Cities* (New York, 1961), Jane Jacobs urged Americans to take another look at "slums" and existing housing structures of the city to find more human-scaled ways for curing the city's problems.

12. De Bell, *The Environmental Handbook*, 240.

13. Ibid., 247.

14. Ibid.

15. *PCC Bulletin*, September 1974; October 1974; Warren J. Belasco, *Appetite for Change: How the Counterculture Took on the Food Industry, 1966–1988* (New York, 1989), 68–108.

16. *PCC Bulletin,* September 1975; Binda Colebrook, *Winter Gardening in the Maritime North-west* (Arlington, Wash., 1977).

17. *PCC Bulletin,* October 1973.

18. "Ecotope Group," circa 1977, Department of Parks and Recreation, series 38, folder 3, Seattle Municipal Archives (hereafter SMA).

19. Ibid.

20. Tim Magee, "A Solar Greenhouse for the Northwest," and Tim Magee, "Ecotope Group's Demonstration Solar Greenhouse," both in Department of Parks and Recreation, series 38, folder 3, SMA.

21. "Ecotope Group," circa 1977, Department of Parks and Recreation, series 38, folder 3, SMA.

22. Sale, *Seattle Magazine,* 232–33.

23. Ibid., 238–52. The voice of neo-progressives, *Seattle Magazine* devoted a special summer issue to the aesthetics and future of Seattle's urban life (see David Brewster, "Is This the Shape of Things to Come?" 16; Ibsen Nelson, "One Way to Revive City Neighborhoods," 21; and "The Good Guys," 14, all in *Seattle Magazine,* June 1969). For a discussion of the increasingly "doomsday" mood of environmentalists and a receptive, if overwhelmed, public during the 1970s, see Kirkpatrick Sale, *The Green Revolution: The American Environmental Movement, 1962–1992* (New York, 1993), 29–45; and Schulman, *The Seventies.*

24. See *Fremont Forum* 1 (March 1977), 1.

25. *Citizen Participation Handbook: Seattle Model City Program* (Executive Department, City of Seattle, 1972), 1, 29.

26. For a local discussion of this experience of shifting from the Model Cities program to Block Grant funding, see "The Housing and Community Development Act of 1974: An Open Letter on the Future of Seattle," a supplement produced by the City of Seattle and circulated in the *Seattle Sun,* 30 October 1974.

27. *Fremont Forum* 1 (March 1977), 1.

28. Ibid.

29. Ibid., 3.

30. Ibid.

31. For a brief history of the "neighborhood revolts" in Portland, see Carl Abbott, *Metropolitan Frontier Cities in the Modern American West* (Tucson, 1993).

32. Carolyn Kelly, "Future," *Fremont Forum* (June 1977), 1.

33. *A Sense of Community: Seven Suggestions for Making Your Home and Neighborhood a Better Place to Live,* pamphlet (City of Seattle, Department of Community Development, Office of Neighborhood Planning, 1975), in the general collection of University of Washington Library. The federal government, through the Federal Extension Service, also published pamphlets that encouraged both community-building organizations and ideas about "environmental quality and conservation" in neighborhoods (see the pamphlets *Community Resource Development: How Cooperative Development Helps* [Federal Extension Service, U.S. Department of Agriculture, GPO, February 1969]; and *People, Cities, and Trees* [Forest Service, U.S. Department of Agriculture, GPO, October 1970, revised March 1974]).

34. The Urban Homesteading program, although using western and pioneering imagery, was a nationwide program with a focus on inner cities in the eastern part of the United States. In Washington State, the program was mostly active in the outlying parts of King County and not in Seattle. In south King County, the county government encouraged would-be homeowners to reclaim "57 HUD-owned vacant properties" ("An Application to the United States Department of Housing and Urban Development for an Urban Homesteading

Demonstration Program," Submitted by King County, Washington in Partnership with the Housing Authority of the County of King [January 1977]). Urban Homesteading encouraged "sweat equity" and "urban conservation," replacing the older ethic of urban renewal (James W. Hughes, *Urban Homesteading* [New Brunswick, N.J., 1975], 1–7).

35. Hughes, *Urban Homesteading*, 1–7.

36. *Fremont Forum* 1 (March 1977), 1.

37. Ibid.

38. "Feature," *Fremont Forum* 1 (August 1977), 2; "Your Home: Before and After," *Fremont Forum* 1 (October 1977), 3; "Rehab Co-op," *Fremont Forum* 1 (December 1977), 3.

39. "Flash," *Fremont Forum* 1 (March 1977), 4.

40. For an excellent definition of "yuppie," see Schulman, *The Seventies*.

41. *Fremont Forum* 1 (October 1977), 2–3.

42. After 1975, the market value of homes moved out of its five-year slump, and older homes (built before 1935) "continued to appreciate faster than middle-aged or more recently constructed homes" (*Real Estate Research Report: For the City of Seattle and Metropolitan Area*, 29, no. 2 [Autumn 1978]: 16, 17). These figures suggest the renewed interest in the middle city and the efforts of rehabilitation of older homes.

43. *Fremont Forum* 1 (October 1977), 3.

44. Ibid.

45. "Proposal to the City of Seattle: Research Project—Solid Waste Source Separation. Request for Grant Assistance, March 31, 1976, Submitted by: Fremont Recycling #1, Armen Stepanian and Dick Nelson," Garbage: Seattle Recycling Project (2) 1976–1977, box 9, folder 6, Legislative Department, SMA.

46. "Household Recycling: What to Recycle/How to Prepare It" (Seattle Recycling Project, 1977).

47. For a discussion of recycling and consumer activism earlier in the twentieth century, see Cohen, *A Consumer's Republic*.

48. "Recycling Is the Mayor's Bag," *Fremont Forum* 2 (May 1978), supplement.

49. Ibid.

50. Bob Swanson, Committee on the Environmental Crisis, to Mayor Uhlman, Department 1973 Recycling, box 78, Mayor's General Files, UWL-SC; Norman C. Jacox, Electric League of the Pacific Northwest, letter and pamphlet (*Outa Sight*) sent to Mayor Uhlman, n.d., Recycling 1972, box 68, Mayor's General Files, UWL-SC.

51. Steven Bender to Mayor Uhlman, n.d., Recycling 1972, box 68, Mayor's General Files, UWL-SC.

52. Swanson to Mayor Uhlman, November 20, 1973, Mayor's General Files, UWL-SC.

53. Mayor Uhlman to Swanson, 20 November 1973, Departmental, Recycling 1973, box 78, Mayor's General Files, UWL-SC.

54. *Summary Interim Report: Solid Waste Management Study* (CH2M Hill, November 1973), Departmental, Recycling 1973, box 78, Mayor's General Files, UWL-SC.

55. Ibid.

56. *Seattle Recycling Project Final Report: A Pilot Study of Voluntary Source Separation Home Collection Recycling, Performed for the City of Seattle, Department of Human Resources by Fremont Public Association*, p. S-1.

57. "Recycling Turnout Is High," *Lake City (Wash.) Journal*, 1 December 1976.

58. "Mining for the Urban Ore," *Lake City (Wash.) Journal*, 6 October 1976.

59. Ibid.

60. Joan Firey to Armen Stepanian, 25 April 1977, "Seattle Recycling," p. AC-2; Helen Pemte

and Gunnar Pemte to Seattle Recycling Project, n.d., "Seattle Recycling," p. AC-8; Victoria Stevens to John Miller, 23 June 1977, "Seattle Recycling," p. AC-3.

61. Jody Aliesan, e-mail to the author, February 2003.

62. Ibid.

63. "Welcome to the Fourth," UWL-SC.

64. "Gray Water Put to Work in Your Garden?" *Sunset*, May 1977, 268–69; "A Revolution in Greenhouses: Going All the Way Solar, Seven Examples," *Sunset*, March 1977, 96–99; "Landscape with Old Railroad Ties (or Even New Ones)," February 1977, 66–69; "Owner Built with Partially Scrounged Wood," *Sunset*, September 1977, 116.

65. "Floor Plan Flip-Flop," *Sunset*, October 1978, 162–63; "This Small City Garden Was Only Recently Just a Concrete Driveway," *Sunset*, July 1974, 56–57; "The Changing Western Home," *Sunset*, November 1977, 108. Certainly aspects of this style and the emphasis on nature—rather than the street—predated the 1970s with the Arts and Crafts movement and as part of the regionally inflected modernism that emerged as early as the 1940s in the Puget Sound area. For examples of early northwestern modernists and the work of the Northwest school of architects, see David E. Miller, *Toward a New Regionalism: Environmental Architecture in the Pacific Northwest* (Seattle, 2005).

The Making of an Urban Ecology

Biological Expertise and Wildlife Preservation in West Berlin

Jens Lachmund

In 1973, a number of institutes and departments of the Technical University in West Berlin merged into a single Institute of Ecology. This was one of various attempts to formally institutionalize the environmental sciences in Germany.[1] Focusing on the complex relations of living beings and their natural environment, ecology seemed ideally suited to tackle the environmental crisis that had become a public concern. It was expected that ecology would provide a more rational basis in particular for practical domains such as nature conservation, environmental planning, and the control of industrial pollution. This practical orientation also characterized much of the research agenda that developed in the Berlin institute. One of the special characteristics of the institute, however, was its relationship to the city. The city of West Berlin was not only the location of the institute, it was also the institute's most prominent research object and practical fieldwork site. This focus on the city was not exclusive to the Berlin institute, nor was urban ecology confined to Berlin. Yet the comprehensiveness and the productivity of Berlin's urban ecology were salient, and set it apart from ecological research in many other locations. Berlin soon became regarded as an important center of the newly emerging field of urban ecology and as the city throughout the world whose ecology was most thoroughly documented.

From the very beginning, Berlin's ecologists actively embroiled themselves in debates on urban planning and the city government's decisions on land-use. They criticized individual construction projects as well as the dominant pattern of urban development for their alleged detrimental effects on wildlife and habitats. By integrating ecological criteria into city planning, they hoped to direct urban development onto a more favorable path. Ecologists have assumed many roles and functions in the shaping of such policies: as stakeholders of their own research interests, as environmental partisans, as expert advisors, and as professional planning consultants. Although the far-reaching wishes of ecologists have rarely been fulfilled, since the late 1970s, ecological problems have been addressed and incorporated in many planning decisions and regulatory practices of West Berlin.

Programmatic concepts such as urban nature, urban ecology, and sustainable cities have come to abound in the planning discourse of many cities around the globe.[2] The relatively early emergence of urban ecology and the outstanding role it played in West Berlin, however, resulted in many ways from its specific situation as the Cold War "frontier city." In 1948, Berlin was politically divided into East Berlin—after 1949, the capital of the German Democratic Republic (GDR)—and West Berlin, which became a de facto exclave of the Federal Republic of Germany (FRG). The construction of the Berlin Wall in 1961 separated West Berlin physically from East Berlin as well as from the surrounding area of the GDR. Green space became a heavily contested issue in that city-island: on the one hand, it was valued as necessary compensation for the lost countryside, which could no longer serve as a recreation ground for the city's citizens; on the other, it was continuously competing with land-use claims made on the scarce remaining ground within the confines of West Berlin. Equally important, field biologists and local naturalists also found themselves locked inside the new city-island. Cut off from their previous research grounds in the neighboring countryside, they tended to seek new fieldwork sites within the West Berlin territory, thereby contributing to the large amount of ecological data that now exists for that city.

West Berlin's urban ecology, however, was not just the direct result of the precarious environmental conditions within the walled city. How people react to their environment, what they consider a problem, and how they search for political solutions are always mediated by the meanings they attribute to their natural surroundings.[3] If we are to understand the extraordinary trajectory of urban ecology in this city, we have to examine the underlying discourses and practices by which nature in the city of West Berlin was framed as a nexus of scientific and political activities. Rather than just providing objective information about the city's flora and fauna, ecologists acted as cultural entrepreneurs who created and promoted new framings of, or ways of conceptualizing, the city, its component parts, its environmental conditions, and the goals of an appropriate urban policy. These new framings were largely based on the practical knowledge-culture that evolved in the collective fieldwork of West Berlin's ecologists. As these framings made their way into institutional politics, they were also shaped by ecologists' interactions with local audiences such as activist groups, public administration personnel, and local policy makers. What eventually came to be acknowledged and tackled as "urban nature" in West Berlin, then, was a socially constructed object that bore the imprint of both ecologists' epistemic practices and the local circumstances under which nature was contested and negotiated.

This essay sheds light on the scientific and political dynamics through which an ecological framing of the city came into being and was institutionalized in West Berlin. It starts by analyzing how ecologists began to study their own city and describes how a new perspective on urban space evolved from this research. The subsequent sections track this ecological construction of urban space as it finds its way into public policy: the establishment of urban nature as a new problem on the urban planning agenda; ecologists' work on a comprehensive Species Protection Program; and, finally, the political struggle for the preservation of urban-wasteland biotopes.

Toward an Ecology of the City

Since the formal beginnings of ecology in the late nineteenth century, its central tenet has been that organisms form interdependent systems that are determined by the specific conditions of their spatial environment. Ecological research, therefore, has largely consisted of fieldwork on the various mechanisms that tie plants and animals to each other, as well as to certain areas of the environment: their so-called "biotopes."[4] Earlier studies by ecologists focused on biotopes such as ponds, lakes, forests, or the sea. Often these studies were related to practical efforts of nature conservation, resource management, or agriculture. If ecological concepts and methods were applied to the city, this was mainly with regard to the interrelationships of humans and their social and physical urban environment. A famous example is the Chicago school of urban sociology, which drew upon ecological concepts such as "natural areas" or "succession" to study the influx of immigrants and the changes of population in different city districts.[5] Likewise, Eugene Odum, in his classic textbook on system ecology, dealt with the city as a system of intensified human relations.[6] In Germany, biologists had also sometimes used ecological terms—often motivated by eugenic aspirations—when dealing with the conditions of life in the modern metropolis.[7] Animal ecologists were the first to argue that the city was also a specific biotope for certain species, notably birds and various sorts of vermin. More typical for ecologists, however, was the view of the city as an environmentally depleting "eco-parasite" or "anthropogenic desert" that was of little potential interest for ecological research.[8] If ecologists attributed any relevance to such research, it was exclusively seen in the practical context of combating vermin, not as means of systematic urban wildlife preservation.[9] It was not until the 1970s that ecologists like those in Berlin began to advocate a more systematic expansion of their research agenda to the city, thereby paving the way for a new planning policy.

The roots of Berlin's urban ecology can be traced back to a tradition of local natural history that had thrived in the city for at least one century. Lists of regional plant and animal species, so-called Floras and Faunas, had been published since the seventeenth century. They focused either on the region of Mark Brandenburg[10] or on the city and its close vicinity.[11] In Berlin as in many other nineteenth-century European cities, natural history had become quite popular among the urban public, notably the educated middle class, or *Bildungsbürgertum*. From this time onward, various associations were formed that were devoted to the study of the local flora and fauna, to physical landscape features or specific elements thereof. These associations organized lectures and excursions, and brought together natural scientists and mostly middle-class amateur naturalists, or "friends of nature" (*Naturfreunde*).[12] With the exception of ornithology, until the end of World War II, these activities focused only rarely on the city proper. This changed in the postwar period, when the large urban rubble areas that had been left by the bombing of the city became populated by new plants and animals.[13] In Berlin, this new focus on the city intensified in 1952, when the GDR refused

Bombed plots in postwar West Berlin, ca. 1960. (Photo by Herbert Sukopp)

West Berlin residents admission to its territory (apart from East Berlin, which, in this period, was still accessible to West Berliners). This was a painful loss for the West Berlin naturalists who, until then, had had their main sampling grounds in the neighboring province of Brandenburg and who had closely cooperated with fellow naturalists in the GDR.

Besides natural-history societies, the local universities provided another base where urban ecology developed. Biological research was conducted at all three universities: the Technical University and the Free University in West Berlin, as well as Humboldt University in East Berlin. Scholars from these institutions were engaged in empirical and theoretical research of zoological ecology and phytosociology, a continental European form of vegetation ecology. Some of these scholars were also active members of natural-history societies and contributed to the study of Berlin's local and regional wildlife.

In the 1970s, the founding of the Institute of Ecology provided an enormous boost to studies of Berlin's urban wildlife and its biotopes. Ecology took shape here as part of a broader reform of the organizational structures and educational programs of the Technical University. In 1970, the former Faculty of Agriculture was dissolved. One of its formal successors became the newly created Department (Fachbereich) of Landscape Development (Landschaftsentwicklung), which comprised a number of environment- and planning-related disciplines. Under this roof, three institutes of the former faculty—the Institutes for Applied Botany, Pedology, and Horticulture—merged into a single Institute of Ecology.[14]

A key role in the ecologists' emerging focus on the city was played by Herbert Sukopp, a botanist who is now often regarded as the founder of urban ecology in Germany. Sukopp, a professor at the Institute of Ecology from 1969 to 1999, formulated a systematic program for an interdisciplinary research field of "urban ecology."[15] Under his supervision, a large number of doctoral theses and expert reports were produced that analyzed the flora, fauna, and ecological conditions of the city or parts thereof. Sukopp also acted as a political protagonist, creating networks between scientists, organizing material and institutional resources, and taking positions on policy and planning issues. Within a few years, Sukopp and a growing number of students and assistants who worked with him became the most renowned representatives of German urban ecology. Although these ecologists later extended their approach to include the study of other cities, Berlin remained their primary research field and object of knowledge.

Regarding the Berlin naturalists, this shift of attention to the city was largely due to ecologists being cut off from potential research sites in the countryside. If the research was part of a student course, a dissertation, or a larger research project, the most pragmatic solution was often to choose fieldwork sites within the political confines of the walled city. As a result, in those years, a considerable amount of urban space in Berlin became the more or less permanent fieldwork sites of urban ecologists. In particular, the various remnants of land that had never been built upon and that existed throughout the city's territory became newly important observation grounds for West Berlin ecologists. Examples are the large woodlands on the edge of the city, a variety of small fens and wetlands, and many pieces of agricultural landscape that had survived the process of urbanization. Such biotopes often existed on small insular patches of land and were under constant threat by a hostile urban environment.

The various wastelands that existed in the city represented another category of fieldwork site. These areas were primarily the rubble areas left from the bombardment during World War II, as well as railway areas that had been abandoned after the war. These sites were of special interest for urban ecology since they allowed the flora and fauna to develop relatively undisturbed.[16] At the same time, these biotopes and their wildlife were completely shaped by the urban condition. According to ecologists, the composition of their flora and fauna—notably the high number of "non-native" plants— was determined by the specificity of the urban soil, climate, and water regime as well as the intensive human and freight traffic that linked the city to virtually the entire world. It was from the observation of these urban wastelands that ecologists derived crucial insights into the basic mechanisms of urban ecosystems.[17]

By the end of the 1970s, West Berlin ecologists had extended their fieldwork over almost the entire city. Parks, railway tracks, street borders, landfills, industrial areas—in all these urban spaces, ecologists had carried out studies, listing and mapping their flora, vegetation, and fauna.

A Political Mission

Ecological fieldwork resulted in both a new discursive framing of the city as well as a related political project of wildlife preservation. Ecologists argued that the cities were not simply devoid of real nature. Sukopp, drawing upon his and other researchers' insights, explicitly rejected the common view that "cities are generally hostile to life."[18] Sukopp conceded that many obstacles to the development of wildlife existed in the city. Yet, he maintained that the studies of urban sites in Berlin and in some other cities revealed that even "totally anthropogenic biotopes can provide a space for characteristic combinations of species."[19] Human influence on the environment, a characteristic of any city, was thus not to be considered simply as a cause of environmental deterioration but rather as a factor that shapes wildlife in its own characteristic way. On the other hand, ecologists also warned that wildlife in the city was endangered by intensifying urban development, and that measures should therefore be taken to integrate nature preservation systematically into the planning process.[20] As Sukopp argued, about 114 species of ferns and flowering plants had already disappeared in Berlin since 1859 due to the changes in the environment. Although this loss was quantitatively compensated for by the introduction of non-native species, ecologists considered it a problem that urgently demanded remedial action.

This ambivalent framing of the relationship between nature and the city would not have been so alarming if it had not been backed up with another claim, which emphasized the value and social utility of inner-urban wildlife. Ecologists argued that nature in the city was not only to be preserved for its own sake, but also for creating better conditions of life for urban citizens.[21] Regular contact with natural environments was considered a mental need of city dwellers and even a prerequisite for the psychologically healthy development of children. Equally important, the preservation of wildlife in the city was represented as a means to strengthen other components of the urban ecosystem, such as the quality of the air, soil, or water supply. The aim of protecting species that sometimes even depended specifically on urban ecosystems linked urban wildlife preservation to the more general issue of protecting biological diversity.[22] Although some of these arguments can also be found in earlier urbanist discourse on urban green space or garden cities, the new discourse on urban nature was couched in distinctly bioecological terms. This discourse called for more than just the existence and accessibility of a sufficient amount of open space for the inhabitants, as traditional green planners would have done.[23] Ecological planners evaluated the quality of any urban environment with respect to different criteria: the presence of certain plant and animal species, the diversity of those species, as well as the overall variety of urban biotope types within a city.

During the 1970s and 1980s, Berlin ecologists were rather successful at getting recognition for their construction of the city both on the public agenda and in the city's policy-making institutions. As already noted, green space and nature were widely perceived as being of critical value in the enclosed city. Since the nineteenth century, it had been a central tenet of Berlin landscape planners that the negative sides of the industrial city (*Industriestadt*) had to be compensated for by providing sufficient green space. After World War II, the so-called "green Berlin"—a term that referred to the city's many parks, gardens, urban forests, and lakes—was also celebrated as a remedy for the psychological depression caused by the destruction of the city, and later, the loss of nature in the countryside of Brandenburg.[24] In the 1960s, however, by their promotion of a more intensive urban development, the West Berlin city government exerted huge pressure on the existing green spaces of the city.[25] In 1965, a comprehensive land-use plan was issued that envisaged a dramatic extension of the built-up area and of traffic infrastructure facilities into the various open spaces that still existed in West Berlin. From the early 1970s onward, citizens fiercely opposed this extension policy. For example, in November 1976, about six thousand people demonstrated against the construction of a new power plant in a large forest at the western fringe of the city.[26] Not only the traditional nature conservation organizations attacked these urban development initiatives. Protest often came from spontaneous citizen-activist groups, so-called *Bürgerinitiativen,* which frequently assembled around contested development projects. In the 1970s and early 1980s, similar positions also found much resonance within the city's political parties.[27] By the late 1970s, increasing pressure from citizens and within the governing parties led to a revision or cancellation of some controversial development projects. Between 1979 and 1983, the West Berlin government—first under a social-liberal coalition and then, from 1981, under a conservative-liberal one—commissioned an ecological working group that published an ambitious Species Protection Program (Artenschutzprogramm) (which itself was part of a larger Landscape Program (Landschaftsprogramm).[28] The actual Species Protection Program that was enacted in 1988 was only a trimmed-down version of that plan, yet it entailed various pro-nature revisions of the former land-use plan (Flächennutzungsplan). Although the actual land-use policy in the 1980s constantly lagged behind these ambitious goals, the issue remained a high priority on the city's public agenda. This was due notably to the flourishing culture of urban protest that existed in West Berlin, as well as the establishment of the Alternative Liste—the Berlin equivalent of the German Green Party—which was elected into the Berlin Parliament in 1981.

Besides these public debates, the increasing political role of Berlin's ecology was also stimulated by a change of federal nature-conservation legislation in West Germany and the subsequent implementation of this law in West Berlin. The new nature-conservation legislation of the 1970s was a result of widespread discontent with the existing Imperial Nature Conservation Act (Reichsnaturschutzgesetz), which itself dated back to 1935 in the Nazi period. This act was primarily intended to foster the preservation of plants, animals, or parts of the landscape that were supposed to either promote emotional attachment to nature and "*Heimat*," or to provide space for physical recreation. Another reason given by the act for designating nature reserves was the respective area's special interest for scientific research. Important features of the act and the executive order that was added to this act were prohibitions on picking plants or hunting animals, the preservation of outstanding natural objects as "nature monuments," and the creation of nature- or landscape reserves.[29] Since the 1960s, critics had maintained that this old nature conservation law was no longer adequate for tackling the more complex problems of landscape and nature that were caused by intensifying land use and development sprawl. It was only in 1976, however, that the German Bundestag endorsed a new Federal Nature Conservation Act (Bundesnaturschutzgesetz).[30] The federal act provided a framework of nature conservation legislation, which left considerable leeway for the states to develop their own nature conservation acts. In West Berlin, such an act was issued in 1979.[31]

One of the main features of the Berlin Nature Conservation Act (Berliner Naturschutzgesetz), as well as of the federal law on which it was based, was a shift from the mere passive preservation of single parts of the landscape toward an active approach of planning the overall shape of the landscape.[32] Accordingly, the law called for actively and comprehensively maintaining the integrity of "nature and landscape." This did not mean that traditional strategies such as the creation of reserves were abolished. However, they were regarded as only one element within a broader set of strategies that were to be guided by comprehensive "landscape- and species-protection programs." Additionally, the so-called "encroachment regulation" (§ 14) provided that any project that was detrimental to nature and landscape had to be avoided or, at least, to be compensated for by renaturalization measures. In contrast to the former law, which applied only to objects and landscape features that were typically located outside of, or at the periphery of, cities, the approach taken by the new act was much broader and therefore, paved the way for planning "nature and landscape" in cities.

Ecologists' views of the city were largely consistent with the goals of critical activists and policy makers. Their expertise and scientific authority also constituted an important resource for the formulation and implementation of the new nature-conservation legislation. Various construction projects that were debated in the 1970s were assessed for their possible environmental impact by Sukopp and/or his collaborators. These included plans for the construction of a new highway adjacent to Berlin's major parkland, the Tiergarten, as well as the power plant at the forest.[33] Since the 1970s, doctoral theses focusing on ecological issues also often explicitly relate their findings to the practical problems of urban planning.[34] Beginning in 1979, Berlin ecologists carried out a comprehensive survey of the West Berlin biotopes that eventually served as the scientific base for the city's Species Protection Program. The boundaries of science and politics were often blurred during these debates, as, on the one hand, ecologists became embroiled in political activism, and, on the other, lay activists and conservation officials drew upon ecological arguments to support their own claims.

Planning the City of Biotopes: The Species Protection Program

One of the most important ways through which ecologists' concerns entered public debate and the policy making of their city was a so-called "biotope-mapping" survey, and the resulting West Berlin Species Protection and Landscape Program. The survey, commissioned by the Senate for Development and Environment, was carried out between 1979 and 1984 by a working group headed by Sukopp at the Institute for Ecology. Although the survey lasted only four years, a considerable amount of data used stemmed from earlier studies that Berlin ecologists had conducted. The final report of the working group was presented in August 1984: a series of maps and plans as well as a two-volume monograph that contained the survey's results, an explanation of its methodology, and proposals for actual species-protection measures.[35]

The enactment of the Species Protection Program was a longer-lasting process of political negotiation that had its own institutional logic and that brought diverse actors and interests to the fore. The department at the Senate Administration for Development and Environment (Senatsverwaltung für Bau, Wohnung und Umwelt) that was responsible for landscape planning elaborated the survey groups' proposals and coordinated them with other planning schemes. Citizens' participation and parliamentary debate constituted further arenas of negotiation. It thus took four years until a reworked program proposal was enacted by the West Berlin City Parliament in October 1988.

The survey and the ensuing Species Protection Program revolved around the representation of the city as a seamless patchwork of biotopes. Using a formalized codification scheme, the entire surface of West Berlin was classified according to fifty-seven predefined biotope types, each of which was considered as an area of homogeneous floristic and faunistic composition.[36] These biotope types served as the basic units in which the results of the survey were arranged, and on which the Species Protection Program centered.

The concept of a biotope type had already been used in the context of earlier surveys that had been carried out in Bavaria by researchers from the University of Munich.[37] In the Berlin survey, however, the concept became more closely linked to the classic urbanist understanding of land use. From the early 1960s, Berlin ecologists were already drawing upon the concept of "hemerobia"[38]—the extent to which an ecosystem is shaped by human influence—to make sense of the peculiar features of nature in the city. Accordingly, in cities, the composition of the flora and fauna was primarily seen as being determined by the intensity and type of human land use.[39] On this conceptual base, different kinds of land use such as open or closed block structures, industrial areas or urban infrastructures such as harbors, railways tracks, streets, filter beds, landfills, and construction sites were reframed as biotope types.[40] Often these categories were further subdivided according to the typical vegetative ecotype to be found on these sites. In a similar way, open spaces such as parks, cemeteries, agricultural areas, waters, and forests were also neatly differentiated according to land-use criteria and their landscape features and ecology.

The result was a representation of the city as a hybrid environment in which spontaneous biological processes and various forms of human influence were closely interwoven. The urban ecosystem was conceived of as being natural and cultural at the same time: an expression of human land use, thus culture, and a specific composition of wildlife, thus nature. The city's biotopes were never purely natural or purely cultural; there was only a continuous gradation between these two poles.[41]

Another important feature of this framing of urban space was that it linked biological knowledge to institutionalized classification practices of urban planning and thereby facilitated communication between academic ecologists and city officials and administrators. Biotopes were defined on the same scale and by similar criteria as the spatial units of urban planning schemes. Evaluations and practical recommendations that focused on these areas could thus be directly transcribed into thematic maps or planning schemes. Moreover, as the authors noted in their report, biotope types were also preferred to more conventional forms of biological mapping—notably the detailed mapping of plant communities—because they could easily be identified by planning officials who did not posses any academic biological training.[42] Although the biotope map integrated a vast amount of esoteric environmental information about urban wildlife and its environmental conditions, it fit very well with the interpretative habits of its recipients in the planning administration.

Biotopes were also the main target of the species-protection measures recommended in the survey. Although the Species Protection Program called for special protection measures for some groups of endangered species,[43] it was based on the assumption that a species could be effectively protected only through preserving the biotope type it required.[44] In many cases, the plan also aimed at the development of the "biotic potential" of biotopes. Biotopes that according to criteria such as biological diversity or the presence of rare species were considered of only minor value were meant to be amended by suitable cultivation measures.

There was hardly any area in the city for which the survey did not offer some practical advice. For biotope types considered relatively "close to nature," management and development measures included, for example, the flooding of dried-up bogs and wetlands or the removal of plant species believed to diminish the character of the biotope. In the built-up areas of the town, the survey called for environmentally friendly gardening practices (no cutting of hedges, no use of herbicides, tolerance of spontaneous vegetation, no removal of fallen leaves), the transformation of lawns into meadows, and the systematic greening of house facades and roofs.

The Species Protection Program also called for the creation of various new nature- and landscape reserves. Many of the proposed reserves represented biotope types on which nature conservation had always focused: bogs, ponds, wetlands, etc. that were typically located at the geographical margins of the city. With respect to biotopes of high recreational importance, the program often suggested turning them into so-called "landscape reserves," a category of area protection that entails less rigid restrictions on land use than those of a nature reserve. One such example was the Tiergarten, a large central park in West Berlin where planners had only recently given up their plans to construct a new highway. The survey also provided protective measures for the city's various wastelands. Whereas hitherto these places were mostly seen as symptoms of urban decay, ecologists elaborated a positive meaning of urban wastelands. They claimed that such areas displayed a complex spontaneous vegetation, that they were a refuge for rare species, and that they ameliorated the city climate. Sites such as a former central marshalling yard (Gleisdreieck), its freight station and adjacent land—the so-called Südgelände in the district of Schöneberg—soon became regarded as emblematic of the potential richness of urban wildlife.

Finally, the Species Protection Program was largely inspired by the concept of biotope networks. Accordingly, the quality of a single biotope hinged not only on its intrinsic qualities but also on its position within a topographically dispersed network of other biotopes. According to the ecologists, such a coherent network was necessary to guarantee a smooth exchange of animals and seeds among the individual biotopes and thereby to sustain the city's biodiversity. Notably, an equal distribution of biotopes throughout the city, the existence of smaller patches (*Trittsteine*) and large connecting linear corridors were considered the basic prerequisites of a viable network of urban biotopes. The proposals of the Species Protection Program aimed at maintaining and increasing the integrity of such a network.[45] On these grounds, for example, the program proposed a large greenbelt from the central Tiergarten to the wasteland areas around Potsdamer Platz to the Südgelände and farther down to the southern fringe of the city.

Although the final version of the Species Protection Program that was enacted by the Berlin Parliament in 1988 was much more modest than the 1984 proposal, it was still one of the most ambitious programs of ecological planning that had ever been created for such a large metropolis. For the first time, a big city had been comprehensively described according to ecological criteria and, on this basis, had become the subject of a highly differentiated ecological master plan. In the long run, however, the actual development of the city did not fulfill the high ambitions of this plan. In terms of its administrative status, the plan was a rather weak instrument. In contrast to conventional urban land-use plans, it was not legally binding but had only a consultative function for the administration. Furthermore, in order to become effective, many of its provisions had to be transposed into the revised West Berlin urban land-use plan (*FNP*) as well as into specific landscape plans of the districts (*Bezirke*), the smaller administrative districts of West Berlin. Since the plan's intentions often conflicted with the various interests of the administration units and the districts, this proved to be a rather long-lasting process in which the content of the plan became further watered down.

A major setback for the Species Protection Program came with the fall of the Berlin Wall in 1989. Both the unification with East Berlin and the subsequent assignment of many central biotope areas according to new development plans for the restored German capital required a major revision of the original Species Protection Program.[46] In 1994, the Berlin Senate issued a new version of the Species Protection Program that also covered former East

Berlin. In accordance with the new political realities of planning Germany's new capital city, many of the existing provisions for nature preservation in the territory of West Berlin were removed from the program.[47]

However, both the 1984 report and the eventual provisions of the plans provided valuable argumentative sources for activists and nature conservation officials and helped them to keep many biotopes free from potentially damaging forms of land use. Thus, although political developments thwarted many of the original goals of the Species Protection Program, it left some important traces on the urban landscape.

Contested Places, Contested Meanings: The Battle for the Wastelands

Wasteland preservation provides a good example of the way in which urban ecology's framing of problems became incorporated into actual urban land-use decision making in West Berlin. No other biotope type encapsulated urban ecologists' ideas about the possible coexistence of city and nature better than did urban wastelands. Shaped by human conditions, yet characterized by great species diversity, wastelands were supposed to represent the "true nature" of the city, as the Berlin ecologist Ingo Kowarik put it.[48] Moreover, ecologists and their advocates linked their calls for wasteland preservation to a new aesthetics of the urban landscape, which emphasized the specific experiential qualities of these sites. Together with activist groups and landscape-planning consultants, they promoted an understanding of these sites as a new form of "wilderness." They maintained that the spontaneous vegetation of wastelands displayed a peculiar beauty and that these areas allowed urban residents more authentic experiences of nature than did the overregulated spaces provided by conventional urban greenery.[49]

These claims for urban-wasteland conservation often focused on the bombed-out areas that remained undeveloped in some parts of West Berlin. Such areas varied in size from single plots to entire former neighborhoods, and they figured as ecologists' most important sampling grounds. Until the early 1980s, notably the northern part of the district Kreuzberg and the adjacent former Diplomatenviertel (diplomat's quarter), still presented the image of a vast landscape of rubble. Ecologists and their advocates also called for the preservation of large wasteland on the abandoned railway facilities, notably the Gleisdreieck and the Südgelände. Although these sites were located in West Berlin, they were under the jurisdiction of the East German railway company. Isolated and fenced off from its adjacent neighborhoods, they had been a no-man's-land that was soon covered with dense, woodsy vegetation.

Calls for wasteland promotion found much resonance with citizen activist groups opposed to the development projects that were planned for these sites. *Bürgerinitiativen* that were formed, for example, at the Südgelände and the Gleisdreieck, launched campaigns, lobbied local politicians, and often initiated lawsuits against administrative public authorities. The public advocacy for wasteland preservation included fanciful forms of protest. For example, activists of the Bürgerinitiative Südgelände were dressed up as plants and animals when they invaded the office of the West Berlin office of planning and construction to voice their concerns about the wildlife that would be lost if the city's plan for a new freight station at that site were realized. In 1988, left-wing activists even squatted in a small wasteland next to the Wall that West Berlin had just purchased from the GDR. The activists established a camp on the site in order to protest the West Berlin government's imminent sacrifice of this allegedly valuable wasteland biotope for the construction of a new highway. The call for wasteland preservation also found many supporters within the West Berlin Parliament. Notably, the Alternative Liste faction in the early 1980s submitted various requests to protect the wastelands of West Berlin's "central area."[50]

As a result of ecologists' lobbying as well as mounting public protest, a number of Berlin's wastelands were designated as protected areas. After 1982, a small grove of black locust trees that had grown at a bombed-out plot in the district of Kreuzberg was developed as a "ruderal vegetation park."[51] Although ecologists could not prevent the construction of a new museum for technology at the fringe of the Gleisdreieck, a considerable part of the adjacent vegetation was turned into a *Naturdenkmal* (nature monument). One of the most successful projects of wasteland preservation, a nature park at the Südgelände, was finished in 2001. The project was the outcome of a long-lasting campaign in which, since around 1980, ecologists and activist groups had successfully opposed other land-use claims that had been made for this site, notably the construction of a new freight station. After unification, Berlin ecologists and activists also extended their claims to include the various wastelands in former East Berlin. At least in one case, that of the former airport in Berlin-Adlershof (Flugplatz Johannisthal), this led to the designation of a large ruderal biotope as a landscape park.

Ecologists, however, were not always so successful. Too often, calls for wasteland conservation clashed with powerful land-use interests, and ecolo-

Urban nature in Berlin:
A meadow in the nature
park Südgelände, 2001.
(Photo by the author)

gists' plans could therefore be only partially realized, or not at all. This became clear in 1986, when a hotel was built at the so-called Dörnbergdreieck,
a rubble area in the Tiergarten that ecologists considered one of their most
important fieldwork sites. Even the joint opposition of academic ecologists,
nature-conservation officials, and neighborhood activists could not keep the
Senate from approving the investor's plan to build the hotel. In the mid-
1980s, most of the wastelands in the northern part of Kreuzberg were sacri-
ficed for housing development. The large, cleared rubble areas in the former
Diplomatenviertel only remained undeveloped because they largely belonged to the extraterritorial former foreign embassies that were destroyed
during the war. After the unification and the subsequent move of the federal
government to Berlin, however, these plots were also quickly developed with
new embassy buildings.

Some of these conflicts lingered long after the fall of the Wall, and were
only settled during the last decade of the twentieth century. Unification and
the subsequent rebuilding of Berlin as Germany's capital made the claims
for ambitious wasteland-protection schemes even less realistic. As with the
Diplomatenviertel, many wastelands of former West Berlin, as well as those
that ecologists had hoped to protect in the East, were eventually developed.
In this sense, the Südgelände and Johannisthal Airport remained the two
outstanding exceptions. Among these "lost" wastelands was the large area
around the Gleisdreieck that, in the 1980s, had even attracted the attention
of ecologists and landscape planners from outside Germany. In the early
1990s, large parts of the area were used as a logistics center for the construc-

tion work at the adjacent Potsdamer Platz. After an intricate debate about financial compensation claims to be given by the developers of Potsdamer Platz, a considerable part of the area is now going being turned into a conventional urban park. With the exception of a small protected grove of black locust trees, however, the vast spontaneous vegetation that once covered this site is gone.

Besides other contingencies of the decision-making process, wasteland preservation has, in the past, often been confronted with two systematic obstacles. The first was the ambivalent public status of ecologists' construction of wastelands as biotopes. Although these constructions were shared by a broad coalition of ecologists, conservationists, and citizen-activist groups, quite different attitudes prevailed among the Berlin citizenry. Many urban residents tended to see wastelands as ugly and uninteresting, as wounds in the urban fabric. Calls for nature protection that were based mainly on ecological parameters such as species diversity or vegetation features had little appeal to those citizens. For example, the author of an article in the local newspaper *Tagesspiegel,* commenting on the plans to construct a magnetic train track on a wasteland (Kemperplatz), showed little understanding for ecologists' claims that this would entail serious damage to nature. As he maintained, the envisioned plantation of neat greenery beside the track would eventually make the site even greener than it was in its present state.[52] It was particularly difficult to create a positive feeling toward the bombed-out areas because many citizens associated them more with death and war than with the experience of nature.

Pleas for urban-wasteland conservation, therefore, were most successful where they coincided with other public concerns. During the Südgelände conflict, for example, citizens' protests were also motivated by a general quest for open space in that neighborhood as well as by residents' fear of nuisances caused by the future freight station. The widespread tendency to design protected wastelands as nature parks with trails or even some aesthetic ornamentation can be seen as an attempt to endow these places with a more appealing public image.[53]

A second obstacle to wasteland preservation was the relatively weak legal standing of ecological claims vis-à-vis other concerns of urban planning. Although the general provisions of the Nature Conservation Act as well the Species Protection Program gave many reasons for the preservation of urban wastelands, decision makers often argued them away by giving priority to "overriding public concerns." The Berlin administration—notably the Senate Department for Urban Development—was also often unwilling to apply the encroachment regulation to the inner-urban area. According to officials in this department, the encroachment regulation applied only to construction projects in the so-called outer area (*Außenbereich*), that is, in undeveloped parts of the city. Nature conservationists, in contrast, argued that the provisions of the Nature Conservation Act applied to the entire territory. On this basis, they often called for an application of the encroachment regulation to prevent construction projects damaging the urban ecology, or at least to provide for significant mitigation or compensation measures. It was only in 1993, when a change in legislation integrated the encroachment regulation into the stipulation of urban-building schemes, that the encroachment regulation was more regularly applied to inner-urban areas.[54] In the heated land-use conflicts of the post-unification period, this rarely helped ecologists to prevent the various building projects envisioned for the new German capital, which were often located on former wastelands. In line with the encroachment regulation, however, plans such as the rebuilding of Potsdamer Platz included at least minor provisions for compensation measures that were meant to mitigate the loss of the former ruderal biotope.[55] At the same time, wasteland preservation could benefit from the need to compensate for encroachments in other urban biotopes. This was the case at the Südgelände, which was legally "upgraded" from a railroad and marshalling yard to a green space in order to compensate for the loss of green space entailed by railway construction in Berlin's "central area." It was in such a limited way that ecologists' construction of the city became inscribed into Berlin's very physical territory.

Conclusion

The division of Berlin created a closed-off urban universe that displayed unique political, social, and cultural features. The development and practice of urban ecology was among the various outstanding peculiarities that characterized the political culture of the walled city. From the 1950s onward, ecologists had turned their city-island into a laboratory for scientific research and ambitious political experiments.

A main force behind this process were the ecologists themselves, who were seeking new research fields after they had lost their former sampling grounds in what had become territory of the GDR. By establishing the city—or urban ecosystems—as a distinguished object of scrutiny, and by organizing themselves as a specialized subfield of "urban ecology," they managed to turn their geopolitical handicap into an asset. West Berlin, in this respect, offered them many opportunities. Not only had Berlin always been a remarkably "green" city, but it was also a city that had been severely damaged by the war and whose marginal economic position hampered the progress of reconstruction of wastelands created by the war.

Besides doing academic research, ecologists also successfully staked out a new institutional role for themselves as political advisors in urban planning affairs, a domain that had hitherto been dominated by urban planning experts and architects. This was achieved through their own local campaigns for the conservation of urban nature, as well as by the new nature-conservation legislation and the ensuing demand for ecological expertise.

The remarkable political success of West Berlin's urban ecology, however, was also due to the favorable circumstances provided by the civil society and the institutional policy context of West Berlin. Ecologists benefited from the prominent place that urban green space had occupied on the policy agenda of the German capital, notably after the division of the city. Although couched in a distinct bio-ecological vocabulary, their vision of a city of biotopes resonated well with the city residents' preoccupation with "Green Berlin." West Berlin was also unusual in its lively culture of urban protest that, in the 1980s, took up some of the ecologists' issues and thereby further fueled the success of that project.

As urban ecology was a product of West Berlin, so also was West Berlin affected by urban ecology and the latter's constructions of urban space. Until about thirty years ago, nothing in that city had ever been defined as an "urban biotope." It was only through the representation of urban biotopes in ecological fieldwork and discourse that such an entity emerged as a scientific, political, and legal phenomenon. In this process, the meaning of the urban and of nature themselves were re-created. In the emerging city of biotopes, the natural and artificial lost their former oppositional meaning. The city became naturalized, and nature became urbanized. By categorizing and delineating urban places according to bio-ecological criteria, urban ecologists made "naturalness" a quality of urban space. Nature and wildlife, on the other hand, were no longer associated with relatively untouched landscapes, or transhistorically stable biological traits. As "urban nature," they became an expression of the complexities and histories of the human activities through which it had been molded.

It is important to note that the place of nature that ecologists have envisioned in Berlin has been a highly selective construct. What distinguishes Berlin's construction of urban nature from various other attempts to "green" cities, some of which are discussed in this volume, is not so much the intrinsic qualities of the Berlin environment but the way in which the latter has been framed within the particular local and historical context of this city. Nature in Berlin has become increasingly conceived of and shaped within the cognitive and moral framework of ecological fieldwork practices. It was debated, contested, regulated, and eventually designed in terms and categories that derived from the research practice of urban ecologists. As a consequence, the spaces that most closely resemble the favorite and most productive fieldwork sites from which ecologists derived their knowledge have come to be considered the most valuable form of nature in the city.

Although the fall of the Wall has reopened the landscapes of the adjacent Brandenburg area for Berlin field ecologists, and although the ambitious urban nature-preservation plans have been trimmed in the rush of capital building, urban ecology is still a lively tradition in Berlin. Berlin ecologists still capitalize on their intimate knowledge of their urban fieldwork sites, their extraordinary treasure of long-term observation data, their institutional networks, and, notably, their reputation as a center of urban ecology. The recent establishment of a graduate program in urban ecology at the Technical University has added a new institutional layer to this local knowledge culture.

In contrast, environmental planning finds itself now largely in a defensive position vis-à-vis more conventional land-use priorities. It is mainly due to the inertia of organizational practices and legal regulations—such as the encroachment regulation—that issues of urban nature conservation have not completely disappeared from the political agenda. The time for pioneering model projects seems to have passed. Small and large preserved urban biotopes like Südgelände remain as today's testimonies to the making of urban ecology and its impact on city politics in Berlin.

Notes

1. Whereas ecology before had been a rather marginal field of biology, this period witnessed an increasing institutionalization of the environmental sciences (see Günter Küppers, Peter Lundgreen, and Peter Weingart, eds., *Umweltforschung—die gesteuerte Wissenschaft?* [Frankfurt, 1977]).

2. See, for example, Timothy Beatley, *Green Urbanism: Learning from European Cities* (Washington, D.C., 2000); Herbert Girardet, *Cities, People, Planet: Liveable Cities for a Sustainable World* (Chichester, 2004); and David Satterthwaite, *The Earthscan Reader in Sustainable Cities* (London, 1999).

3. This has been amply demonstrated by constructivist studies in environmental history and sociology; see, for example, John Hannigan, *Environmental Sociology* (London, 1995); John

Urry and Phil Macnaghten, *Contested Natures* (London, 1998); and Alan Irwin, *Sociology and the Environment* (Cambridge, U.K., 2001).

4. Ecologist have often distinguished the "biocoenesis" (the community of animal and plant species) from the "habitat." Both together are defined as an "ecosystem." The term "biotope"—which is roughly equivalent to the English term "habitat"—was introduced by the German animal ecologist Friedrich Dahl in 1908. On the history of ecological thinking, see Donald Worster, *Nature's Economy: A History of Ecological Ideas* (Cambridge, U.K., 1968); and Ludwig Trepl, *Geschichte der Ökologie* (Frankfurt a.M., 1987).

5. Robert Ezra Park, Ernest W. Burgess, and Roderick McKenzie, eds., *The City* (Chicago, 1925)

6. Eugene Odum, *Fundamentals of Ecology* (Philadelphia: Saunders, 1953). On the specific development in Germany, see Küppers, Lundgreen, and Weingart, *Umweltforschung;* Eugene Citadino, *Nature as the Laboratory: Darwinian Plant Ecology in the German Empire, 1880–1900* (Cambridge, Mass., 1990); and Sarah Jansen: *Schädlinge: Zur Geschichte eines wissenschaftlichen und politischen Konstrukts* (Frankfurt a.M., 2003).

7. B. de Rudder and F. Linke, *Biologie der Großstadt* (Dresden/Leipzig, 1940); H. Peters, *Biologie einer Großstadt* (Heidelberg, 1954).

8. W. Kühnelt, "Zur ökologischen Kennzeichnung der Großstadt," *Natur und Landschaft* 36 (1961): 84–88.

9. Peters, *Biologie;* H. Peters, "Aufgaben der Kommunal-Biologie während Krieg, Zerstörung und Wiederaufbau," in Verband Deutscher Biologen, *Festschrift zur Jahreshauptversammlung Hamburg* (Stuttgart, 1956).

10. Johann Sigismund Essholtz, *Flora marchia, sive catalogus plantarum quae partim in Hortis Electoralibus Marchiae Brandenburgicae primaries, Berolenensi, Aurangiburgico & Potsdamensi excoluntur: Partm sua sponte passim proveniununt* (Berlin: 1663); Johann Gottlieb Gleditsch, "Verzeichnis der Gewächse, die sich in der Mark Brandenburg befinden," in *Historische Beschreibung der Chur- und Mark Brandenburg,* ed. Johann Christ Beckmann (Berlin: 1751); Johan Heinrich Schulz, *Fauna marchica* (Berlin: 1845); Paul Ascherson, "Die verwilderten Pflanzen in der Mark Brandenburg," *Zeitschrift für ges. Naturwissenschaft* 3 (1854): 435–63.

11. C. W. Willdenow, *Flora Berolinensis Prodromus* (Berlin: 1787); K. S. Kunth, *Flora Berolinensis sive enumeration plantarum circa Berolinum sponte crescentium* (Berlin: 1813); Paul Ascherson, *Verzeichnis der Phanerogamen und Gefäßkryptogamen, welche im Umkreise von sieben Meilen um Berlin vorkommen* (Berlin, 1859).

12. On the emergence and the activities of natural history associations in German cities, see Lynn K. Nyhard, "Civic and Economic Zoology in Nineteenth-Century Germany: The 'Living Communities' of Karl Möbius," *Isis,* 89 (1998): 605–30; and Denise Phillipps, "Friends of Nature: Urban Sociability and Regional Natural History on Dresden, 1800–1850," in "Science and the City," ed. Sven Dierig, Jens Lachmund, and Andrew Mendelsohn, special issue, *Osiris* 18 (2003): 43–59.

13. On the history of the rubble areas as a fieldwork site of German plant ecology, see Jens Lachmund, "Exploring the City of Rubble: Botanical Fieldwork in Bombed Cities in Germany after World War II", in "Science and the City," ed. Dierig, Lachmund, and Mendelsohn, 234–54.

14. The Institute of Ecology was divided into four departments, each of which was each directed by a professor: pedeology, botany, horticulture, and ecosystems theory and vegetation science (since 1974). In 1976, two new sections were added: bioclimatology and limnology.

15. For the earliest outline of an ecology of the city, see Herbert Sukopp, "Die Großstadt als Gegenstand ökologischer Forschung," *Schriften zur Verbreitung naturwissenschaftlicher Kenntnisse* 113 (1973): 90–140. Later Sukopp co-edited a textbook on urban ecology: Sukopp and Rüdiger Wittig, eds., *Stadtökologie* (Stuttgart, 1993).

16. For a more detailed analysis of this botanical research in rubble areas of Berlin and other German cities, see Jens Lachmund, "Exploring the City of Rubble."

17. Alexander Kohler and Herbert Sukopp, "Über die Gehölzentwicklung auf Berliner Trümmerstandorten," *Berichte der Deutschen Botanischen Gesellschaft* 76 (1964): 389–406; Herbert Sukopp, "Beiträge zur Ökologie von Chenopodium botrys L.," *Verhandlungen des Botanischen Vereins der Provinz Brandenburg* 108 (1971): 3–74.

18. Sukopp, "Die Großstadt," 91.

19. Ibid.

20. Ibid., 135.

21. Axel Auhagen and Herbert Sukopp, "Ziel, Begründungen und Methoden des Naturschutzes und der Stadtentwicklungspolitik von Berlin," *Natur und Landschaft* 58 (1983): 9–15.

22. Arbeitsgruppe Artenschutzprogramm, *Grundlagen für das Artenschutzprogramm Berlin,* vols. 1–3, Schriftenreihe des Fachbereichs Landschaftsentwicklung der TU Berlin Nr. 23 (Berlin, 1984), 21.

23. From the time of the Weimar Republic, the conceptualization of green spaces was based mostly on the so-called "*Freiflächentheorie*" (open space theory), formulated by Martin Wagner, "Das Sanitäre Grün der Städte: Ein Beitrag zur Freiflächentheorie" (Ph.D. diss., TU Berlin, 1915). On the practical development of green-space planning in Berlin, see Rainer Stürmer, *Freiflächenpolitik in Berlin in der Weimarer Republik* (Berlin, 1991).

24. For the romanticizing of the nature that was left within "Green Berlin," see, for example, the collection of photographs by Gerda Wirth, *Berliner Landschaft* (Berlin, 1964).

25. On this phase of urban development, see Harald Bodenschatz, *Platz frei für das Neue Berlin! Geschichte der Stadterneuerung seit 1871* (Berlin: 1987), 171–76.

26. See H. J. Mielcke and Heinrich Weiß, "Kraftwerksbau im Landschaftsschutzgebiet Spandauer Forst," *Berliner Naturschutzblätter* 3 (1976): 219–24.

27. For example, both the liberal FDP—the coalition partner of the governing SPD—and the opposition CDU proved to be very critical of the project and welcomed the 1977 court decision to stop the envisioned clearing of the forest (see "Grundsatz: 'Energie ist gut, Natur ist besser,'" *Der Tagesspiegel*, 3 May 1977, 13).

28. Arbeitsgruppe Artenschutzprogramm, *Grundlagen*.

29. On the development of the *Reichsnaturschutzgesetz* and its particular approach, see Michael Wettengel, "Staat und Naturschutz 1906–1945: Zur Geschichte der Staatlichen Stelle für Naturdenkmalpflege," *Historische Zeitschrift* 257 (1993): 356–99; and Thomas M. Lekan, *Imagining the Nation in Nature: Landscape Preservation and German Identity, 1885–1945* (Cambridge, Mass., 2004).

30. BNatSchG (Bundesnaturschutzgesetz), *Bundesgesetzblatt* 1 (1976): 2849–59.

31. NatSchGBln (Gesetz über Naturschutz und Landschaftspflege von Berlin, Berliner Naturschutzgesetz), *Gesetzes- und Verordnungsblatt Berlin* (1979): 183.

32. This "active" approach goes back to the idea of a comprehensive *Landespflege* as it had already been developed in the Weimar Republic (see Lekan, *Imagining the Nation*). The increasing influence of this approach in discussions of nature conservation and the related critique of the traditional Nature Conservation Act in the FRG has been analyzed by Sandra

Chaney, "For Nation and Prosperity, Health and Green Environment: Protecting Nature in West Germany, 1945–1970," in *Nature in German History*, ed. Christof Mauch (New York, 2004), 93–118.

33. Sukopp et al., *Ökologisches Gutachten über die Auswirkungen von Bau und Betrieb der BAB Berlin (West) auf den Großen Tiergarten* (Berlin, 1979); Sukopp, "Zur ökologischen Beurteilung von Standorten für ein Kraftwerk in Berlin-Spandau," *Berliner Naturschutzblätter* 20 (1976): 166–70.

34. Wolfram Kunick, "Veränderungen der Flora und Fauna einer Großstadt, dargestellt am Beispiel von Berlin (West)" (Ph.D. diss., Technical University Berlin, 1974).

35. Arbeitsgruppe Artenschutzprogramm, *Grundlagen*.

36. Ibid., 1: 85–57.

37. Giselher Kaule, Jörg Schaller, and Hans-Michel Schober, *Schutzwürdige Biotope in Bayern: Auswertung der Kartierung: Außeralpine Naturräume* (Munich, 1979).

38. The concept was introduced by J. Jalas, "Hemerobe und hemerochore Pflanzenarten: Ein terminologischer Reformversuch," *Acta Soc. Flora Fauna Fenn* 72 (1955): 1–15. See also Sukopp's early studies on "human influence" on the vegetation: (Sukopp, "Der Einfluß des Menschen auf die Vegetation und zur Terminologie anthropogener Vegetationstypen," in *Pflanzensoziologie und Landschaftsökologie: Bericht über das 7. Internationale Symposium in Stolzenau/Weser 1963 der Vereinigung für Vegetationskunde*, ed. Reinhold Tüxen [The Hague, 1986], 65–74).

39. Kunick, "Veränderungen."

40. Arbeitsgruppe Artenschutzprogramm, *Grundlagen*, 1: 85–57.

41. On the rise of biotope mapping surveys and their implications for the nature-culture relationship, see also Jens Lachmund, "Mapping Urban Nature: Bio-Ecological Expertise and Urban Planning," in *Experts in Science and Society*, ed. Elke Kurz-Milcke and Gerd Gigerenzer (New York, 2004), 231–48.

42. Arbeitsgruppe Artenschutzprogramm, *Grundlagen*, 1: 333.

43. Ibid., 2: 726–831.

44. Ibid., 1: 49–50.

45. Ibid., 1: 60–61.

46. On the planning of the new capital and its wider impact on Berlin's urban space, see Elizabeth Strom, *Building the New Berlin: The Politics of Urban Development in Germany's Capital City* (Lanham, Md., 2001).

47. Senator für Stadtentwicklung und Umweltschutz, *Landschaftsprogramm/Artenschutzprogram Berlin* (Berlin, 1994).

48. Ingo Kowarik, "Stadtnatur—Annäherungen an die 'wahre' Nature der Stadt," in *Ansprüche an Freiflächen im urbanen Raum*, ed. Jürgen Gill (Mainz, 1993).

49. Such an aesthetic can be found in various publications of the proponents of wasteland conservation. For example, the Bürgerinitiative Südgelände (1975) published a leaflet with descriptions and pictures of the Südgelände titled *Das verborgene Grün von Schöneberg* (The Hidden Green of Schöneberg). The new aesthetic of spontaneous vegetation and wastelands was not restricted to West Berlin (see, for example, the essays in Michael Andritzky and Klaus Spitzner, eds., *Grün in der Stadt: Von oben, von selbst, für alle, von allen* [Reinbek, 1981]).

50. "Anträge der AL-Fraktion zu Grün- und Verkehrsmaßnahmen im 'Zentralen Bereich' Berlin (West)", *Drucksachen Berliner Abgeordnetenhaus* 9/1783–1800 (9.5.84); "Antrag der AL-Fraktion zu Sofortmaßnahmen zum Naturschutz. Brachflächen," *Drucksachen Berliner Ab-*

geordnetenhaus 9/1847 (8.6.84); "Anträege der AL zu Grün- und Verkehrsmaßnahmen im 'Zentralen Bereich,'" *Drucksachen Berliner Abgeordnetenhaus* 10/123–10/135 (18.6.85).

51. Martin Schaumann, "Erschließung eines Ruderalbiotops in Kreuzberg," *Das Gartenamt* 33 (1984): 160–61.

52. See "Magnetbahnbau von OVG in allen Punkten bestätigt," *Der Tagesspiegel*, 18 January 1977.

53. Again, the Südgelände provides a good example. There, a group of metal artists designed a fancy track system with various metal sculptures attached to it. This so-called "walkable sculpture" allowed visitors to move through the ecologically sensitive areas of the nature park without damaging its flora and fauna (see "Die Gruppe Odius: Kunst mit Zugkraft," in *Zehn Jahre Allianz Umweltstiftung*, ed. Lutz Spandau [Munich, 2000]).

54. In 1993, the Investionserleichterungs- und Wohnbaulandgesetz (Federal Investment Facilitating and Land for Residential Building Act) (InvErlWobauldG) provided that encroachments should be evaluated and compensated for in every new urban-area planning scheme (*Bebauungsplan*). This law was primarily an attempt of the conservative Kohl government to "de-bureaucratize" planning procedures in order to facilitate the development of infrastructure in East Germany. It was also intended to reduce public participation in the planning procedures. The encroachment regulation was to be applied exclusively at the level of development plans so that extensive conflicts or even lawsuits around single building projects could be prevented. At the same time, however, the new act made clear that the encroachment regulation as such also applied to the urban environment. For the InvErlWobauldG, see *Bundesgesetzblatt*, April, pt. 1, 466.

55. The development plan provided for the greening of roofs and the creation of a park at Potsdamer Platz as well as a program for "ecological enhancement" in adjacent districts. The developers also had to provide financial support for a new park to be created at the Gleisdreieck, a former wasteland that has been severely devastated by its use as a logistic center. Moreover, in order to prevent negative impact on the adjacent vegetation of the Tiergarten, the actual construction work had to be carried out in such a way that the ground-water level in the adjacent area was kept stable.

Contributors

Dorothee Brantz is an Assistant Professor of Urban History and Director of the Center for Metropolitan Studies at the Technical University of Berlin. She has been a postdoctoral fellow at the German Historical Institute in Washington, D.C. Her research and publications focus on urban environmental history, human-animal relations, and the environmental history of warfare.

Peter Clark is a Professor of European Urban History at the University of Helsinki and was previously director of the Centre for Urban History at the University of Leicester. His recent publications include *European Cities and Towns 400–2000* (2009); and the edited collections *The European City and Green Space* (2006) and, with M. Niemi and J. Niemelä, *Green Space, Sport and Recreation in the European City* (2009). He is currently preparing the multiauthored "Oxford Handbook on Cities in History."

Lawrence Culver is an Associate Professor in the Department of History at Utah State University. His areas of research and teaching include the United States–Mexico borderlands, the American West, and U.S. cultural, environmental, and urban history. His dissertation received the 2005 Rachel Carson Prize for Best Dissertation in Environmental History. His first book, based on that dissertation, is *The Frontier of Leisure: Southern California and the Shaping of Modern America* (2010).

Konstanze Sylva Domhardt is a Research Associate at the Institute of History and Theory of Architecture at the Swiss Federal Institute of Technology (ETH) in Zurich and a consultant for urban planning and building conservation. Her primary research field deals with the CIAM discourse on urbanism and the preservation of the city in the twentieth century. She has taught at the Universidad de Navarra and the ETH, and conducted extensive research on the transatlantic exchange of planning theories in the 1930s and 1940s as a Visiting Scholar at Harvard University.

Sonja Dümpelmann is an Assistant Professor of Landscape Architecture at the University of Maryland. She is the author of a book on the landscape architect Maria Teresa Parpagliolo Shephard (2004). Her other published work includes articles on the transnational transfer of design ideas and on landscapes and garden culture during the era of Italian fascism. She was a postdoctoral fellow at the German Historical Institute in Washington, D.C., in 2004–5.

Zachary J. S. Falck has taught history at Carnegie Mellon University, Washington University in St. Louis, and Point Park University. He is the author of *Weeds: An Environmental History of Metropolitan America* (2011).

Stefanie Hennecke is an Assistant Professor of the History and Theory of Landscape Architecture at the Technical University of Munich. She has been an Assistant for Teaching and Research in the Department of Garden Culture and Open Space Development at Berlin University of the Arts (UdK). Her dissertation (2010) examines the politics of urban development in Berlin between 1990 and 1999. She has organized several interdisciplinary conferences at the UdK and, together with Gert Gröning, has edited two conference volumes: *Hwa Gye und Da Guan Yuan* (2009), on Korean and Chinese garden culture; and *Kunst—Garten—Kultur* (2010) on recent research projects in garden history and design.

Sonia Hirt is an Associate Professor of Urban Affairs and Planning at the College of Architecture and Urban Studies at Virginia Polytechnic Institute and State University. Her primary research areas include eastern European urbanism, comparative planning models, and planning theory and history. She is the author, with Kiril Stanilov, of *Twenty Years of Transition: The Evolution of Urban Planning in Eastern Europe and the Former Soviet Union, 1989–2009*. She has also published articles in numerous urban planning, design, and geography journals.

Salla Jokela is a Ph.D. candidate in the Department of Geography at the University of Helsinki. Her dissertation examines the evolution of tourism imagery in Finland. Her work is part of a larger research project, "Land-scape, Icons, and Images," funded by the Academy of Finland. Her research interests include tourism geography, identity politics, visual methodologies, cartography, and landscape studies. She has worked as a research assistant in the project "Green Space and Sport since the First World War" at the University of Helsinki Department of History.

JENS LACHMUND is a Lecturer at Maastricht University, the Netherlands. He has published widely on the sociohistory of modern medicine, including *Der abgehorchte Körper: Zur historischen Soziologie der medizinischen Untersuchung* (1997). His current research interest is the relationship between science and urban planning. He is completing a monograph on the history of urban ecology in Berlin, and is the coeditor of a collection of essays entitled *Science and the City* (2003).

GARY MCDONOGH, an urban anthropologist, is a Professor in the Growth and Structure of Cities Department at Bryn Mawr College. He has worked in Barcelona for more than three decades and is the author of *Good Families of Barcelona* (1986) and *Iberian Worlds* (2008), among other works based in that city. He has also conducted fieldwork in the American South (*Black and Catholic in Savannah*, 1993) and Hong Kong (*Global Hong Kong*, with Cindy Hing-Yuk Wong, 2005). He is currently engaged in a study of global China-towns.

JARMO SAARIKIVI is a Ph.D. candidate in the Department of Environmental Sciences at the University of Helsinki. His research focuses on urban ecology and biodiversity. He is especially interested in the animal species assemblages of urban green space, including sports sites such as golf courses.

JEFFREY CRAIG SANDERS is an Assistant Professor of Environmental and U.S. West History at Washington State University. He studies the linked histories of the post-1950s environmental movement and the development of the metropolitan West. His most recent book is entitled *Seattle and Roots of Urban Sustainability: Inventing Ecotopia* (2010). He is currently researching the environmental history of childhood.

ALFONSO VALENZUELA AGUILERA is a Professor of Urban Planning at the State University of Morelos, Mexico. He was a postdoctoral fellow at the French Institute of Urbanism in Paris, a Fulbright Scholar at the Massachusetts Institute of Technology, and he held the Alfonso Reyes Chair at the University of Paris-Sorbonne. He was awarded a 2008 John Simon Guggenheim grant for Latin America. Valenzuela is currently a Visiting Scholar at the Institute of Urban and Regional Development, University of California, Berkeley.

INDEX

Italicized page numbers refer to illustrations.

hood unit, 141–47; on organicism, 139–40; postwar urban-planning theory, 134, 135–36, 141; recentralization as goal of, 137; seventh congress (1949), 137; sports areas as concern of, 11; toward a gradual layout of the city, 142–47, 150; on zoning, 49–50. See also *Heart of the City, The: Towards the Humanisation of Urban Life* (Tyrwhitt, Sert, and Rogers)

Científicos, 37, 38

cities: as biotopes, 12, 206, 222; changing views of nature's relationship to, 1–7, 12; "city" in "urban constellation," 144; distinct way of life associated with, 2; dual-scripting of, 19; eastern European, 31; ecology and the urban environment, 157–227; as ecosystems, 6–7; function of nature in, 113–56; German ideologies of nature and, 75–94; green space and public space in CIAM debates (1942–52), 133–56; increasing density of inner, 5; industrial, 17, 18–19, 76, 170, 211; inequities between suburbs and, 22; lack of nature as defining, 17–18; livability of, 2; nature and urban identity, 55–111; nineteenth-century, 17, 23; as organisms, 2; sport and nature in the European city, 115–32; urban focus of environmental activism, 182. See also city planning; urban ecology; urban sprawl; *and specific cities by name*

City Beautiful movement: city planning develops during, 4; "comprehensive planning" concept of, 136; Los Angeles fails to adopt plan of, 97; monumental city movement in, 19; on parks as places of repose, 96

city centers, 143–48

city planning: on balance of individual freedom and social cohesion, 140; CIAM's postwar theory, 134, 135–36, 141; compactness versus dispersal in conflict in, 30–31; "comprehensive planning" concept, 136, 138, 141, 150, 151; decentralization emphasized during and after World War II, 6; dispersal idea in, 20–21, 23; ecology in, 204–5, 222; emergence in nineteenth century, 17; landscape architects as pioneers

of, 4; in Los Angeles, 97–99; in Mexico City, 37–54; natural features in, 9; overview of international planning ideas, 18–22; parks and parkways included in plans, 3; regional thinking in, 21–22; reunion of city and nature as goal of, 19; reurbanization becomes goal of, 22; scientific, 48; in Sofia, 17–36; sports grounds as component of, 115, 122; transnational dimension of, 4; urban ecology in, 204–5, 222; wasteland preservation and, 220–21. See also City Beautiful movement; garden city movement; zoning

"city-region" concept, 139

civic garden campaigns, 5

Clark, Peter, 11

Cleveland, Horace William Shaler, 3

"Cluster City: A New Shape for the Community" (Smithson and Smithson), 150

Colonia Balbuena (Mexico City), 49

Colonia Ferrocarrilera (Orizaba), 41

Colonia Güell (Spain), 61

Columbus (Ohio), 162

Comas, Joan, 65

Committee for the Protection of Wild Birds (Mexico), 44–45

community centers, 142–43, 146

community garden movement, 5, 185

"comprehensive planning" concept, 136, 138, 141, 150, 151

Comstock, Anna, 164

Congrès Internationaux d'Architecture Moderne. See CIAM (Congrès Internationaux d'Architecture Moderne)

Contreras, Carlos, 46–52; in Díaz circle, 37; European ideas influence, 10, 52; at International Planning Conference (1925), 54n36; master plan for Mexico City, 50–52, *51*; National Association of Planners of the Mexican Republic, 48–49; *Planificación*, 47, 48; "La Planificación de la República Mexicana," 47–48; *Plano Regulador del Valle de Mexico*, 48–50; as preeminent Mexican urban planner, 47

Cooley, Charles Horton, 142

Corbusier. See Le Corbusier

cores, hierarchy of, 144, 147, 149, 150, 151